Kino's Journey

The Beautiful World

2

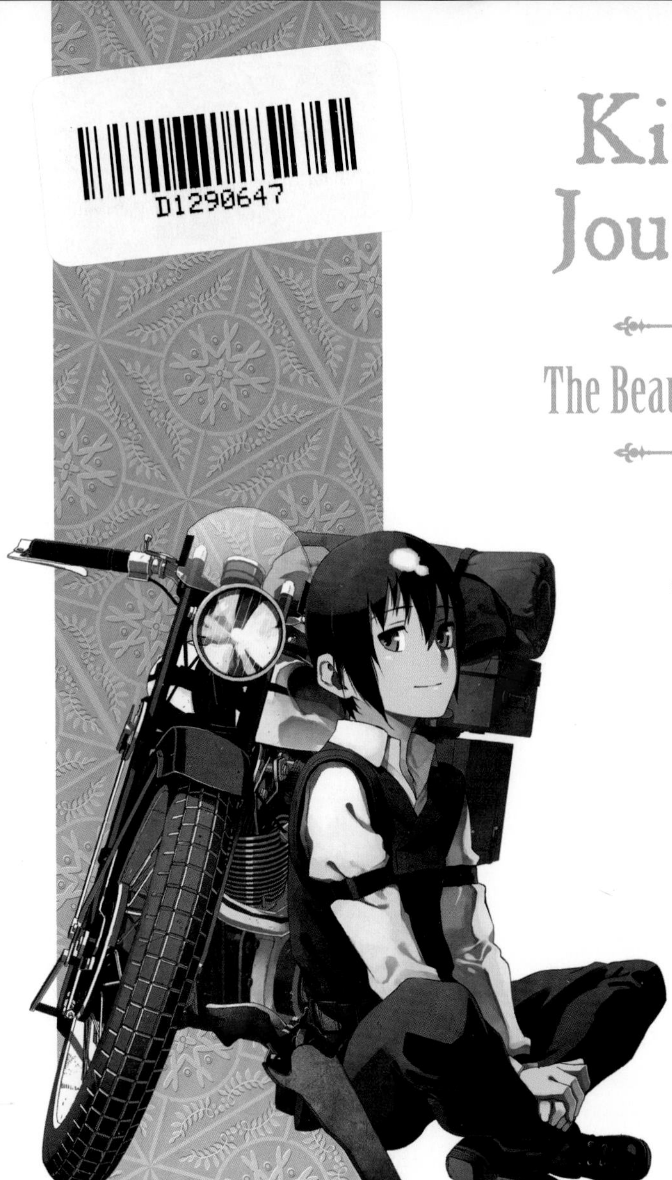

Iruka Shiomiya

Original Story:
Keiichi Sigsawa

Original Character Design:
Kouhaku Kuroboshi

And so, election day began—the day on which this country's president, a single "king" who would rule for the next four years, was to be chosen.

Starting early in the morning, the adults with the right to vote gathered in a large assembly hall to give impassioned speeches arguing which of the two presidential candidates was the far superior choice to rule the land.

First, a man stepped forward to give a speech.

"Kino is an experienced traveler! Though young, Kino has taken many an arduous journey, and thus cultivated a truly spectacular capacity for avoiding danger! If we make such a person president, our great land will be able to overcome any crisis and become a truly wonderful nation! Kino alone has what it takes to become our president! There's no mistake! It's nothing short of a miracle that they've arrived in our land during the election period! Indeed, Kino is heaven-sent! My judicious friends, please, cast your votes for Kino!"

"This is embarrassing," Kino murmured quietly from the seat on stage as the man sang their praises.

Next, a woman took the stage to speak.

"Ever since the revolution, the president has always been a human! But there is nothing in the constitution that says our president cannot be a motorrad! Hermes has intellect, communication skills, and above all, wisdom that far surpasses any human! Who better, then, to serve as our next president?! Everyone, let us create a new era together! Let us set forth along a new path with a motorrad president! Please, cast an honest vote for none other than Hermes!"

"Aw, I'm not all that great… or maybe I am!" Hermes murmured from the center-stand on stage as the woman sang its praises.

As more people took turns showering either of the candidates in compliments, Kino and Hermes whispered to each other.

"So basically, none of these people wants to be president, huh, Kino?"

"Yeah, nobody wants to do it…"

"This 'vote' is just a way of forcing the job on someone else, then."

"It sure is."

"So, when should we run?"

"Hmm. Maybe in a few more minutes? Or should we wait to hear the results? If you get elected, Hermes, would you want to try it out for four years?"

"No thanks."

Excerpt from *Kino's Journey: The Beautiful World* volume 1, chapter 2: "The Land of Majority Rule" by Keiichi Sigsawa

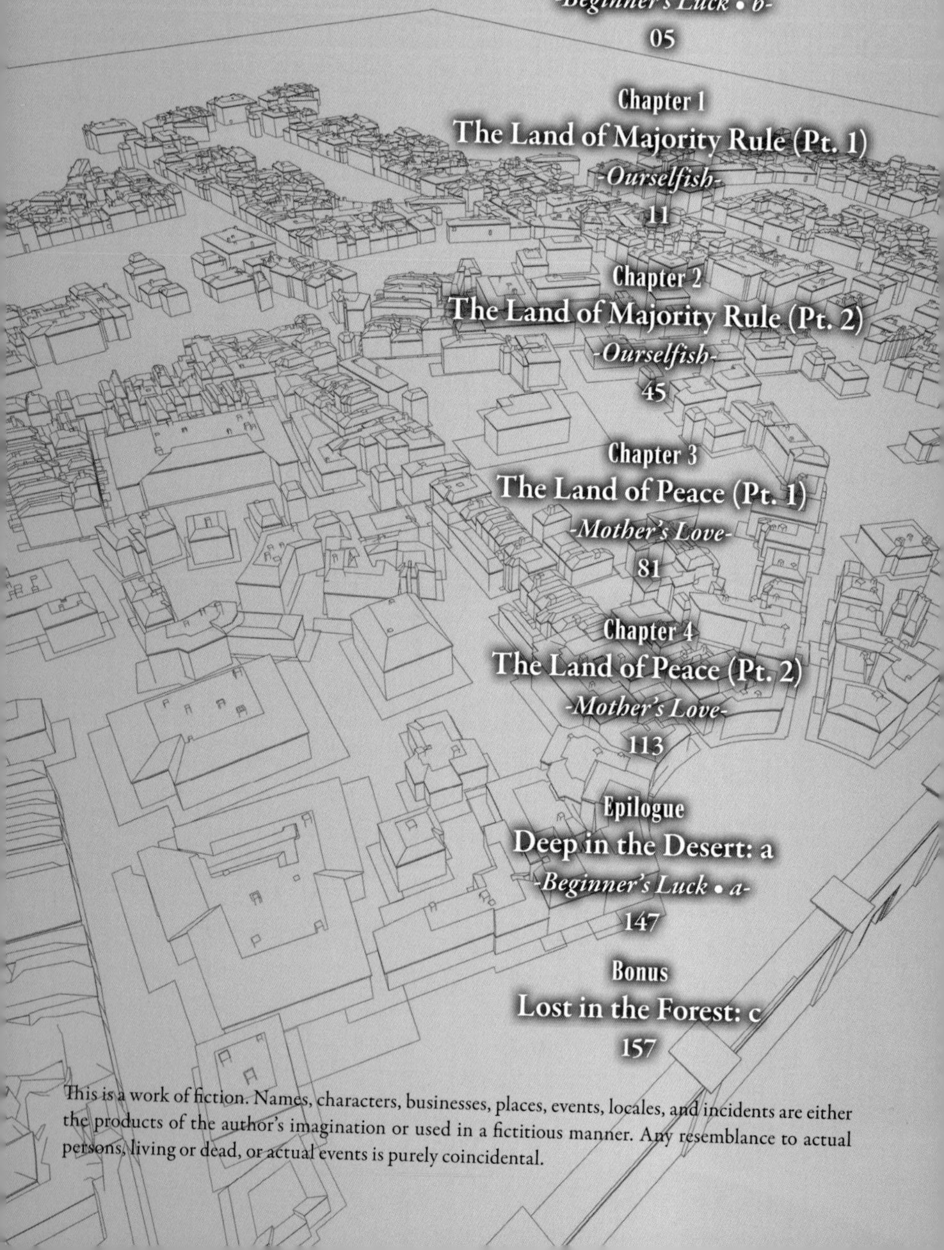

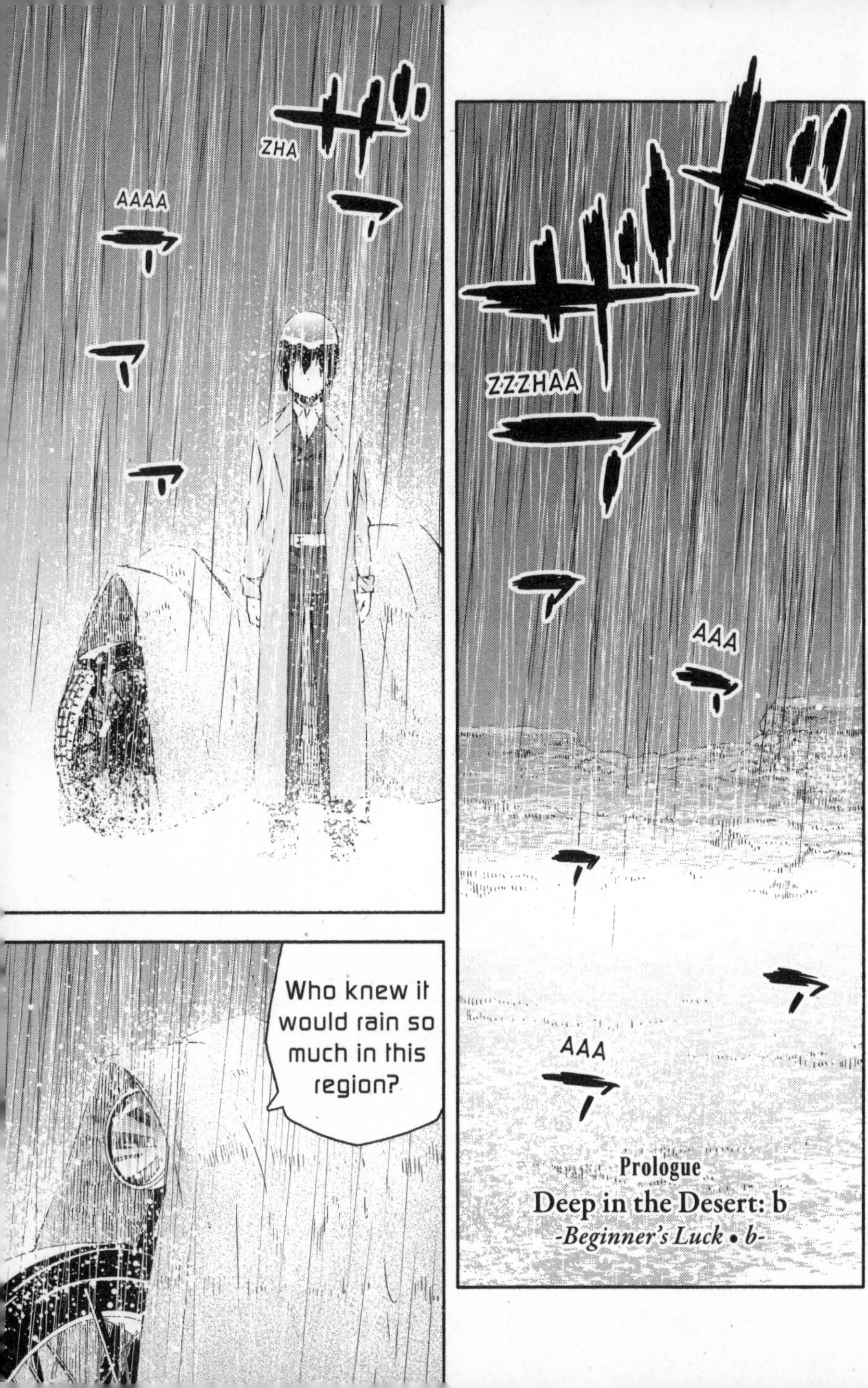
ZZZHAA
AAA
AAA
ZHA
AAAA
Who knew it would rain so much in this region?

Prologue
Deep in the Desert: b
-Beginner's Luck • b-

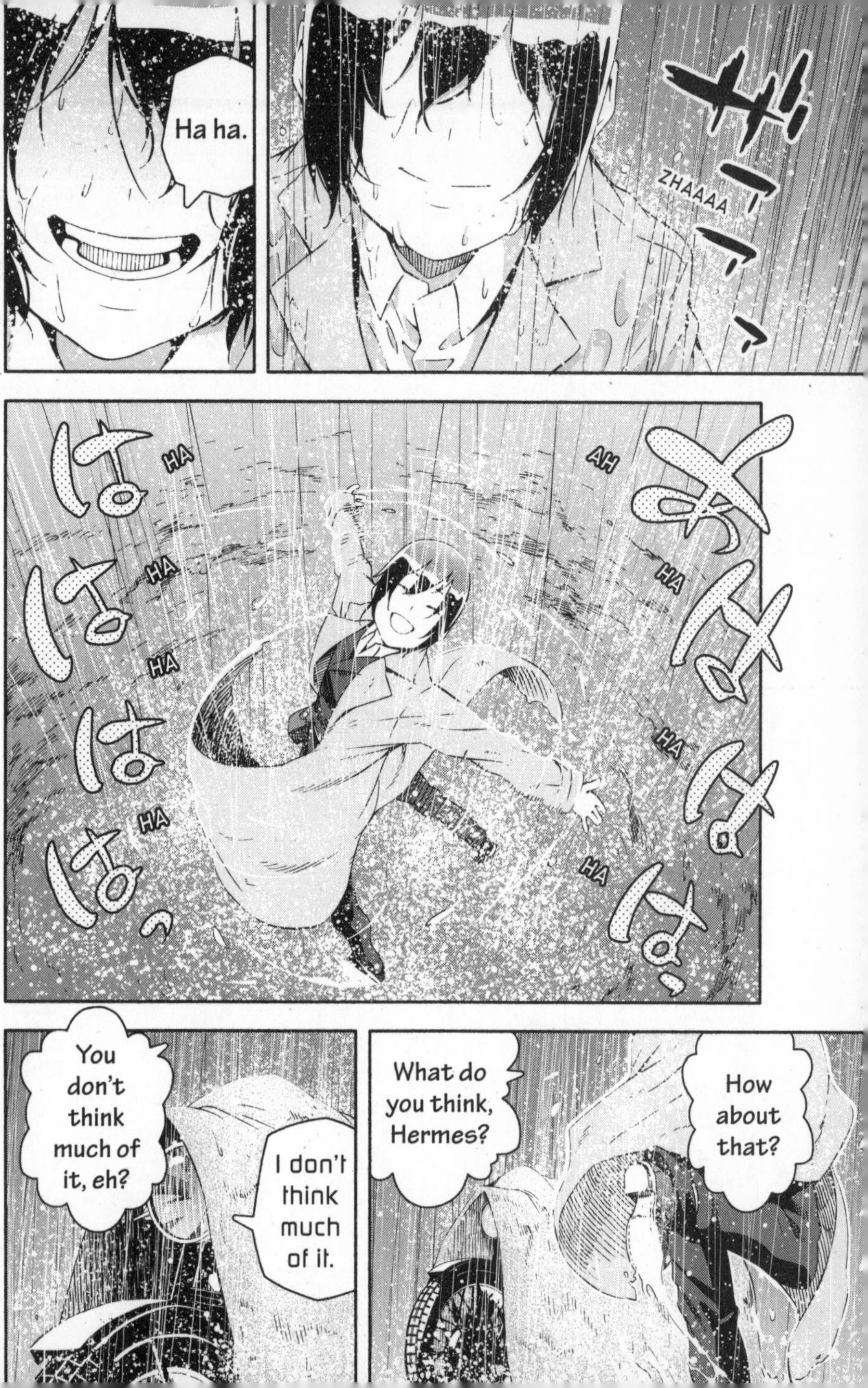
ザーーッ
ZHAAAA
Ha ha.
あはははっ
AH
HA
HA
HA
はははは っ
HA
HA
HA
HA
How about that?
What do you think, Hermes?
I don't think much of it.
You don't think much of it, eh?

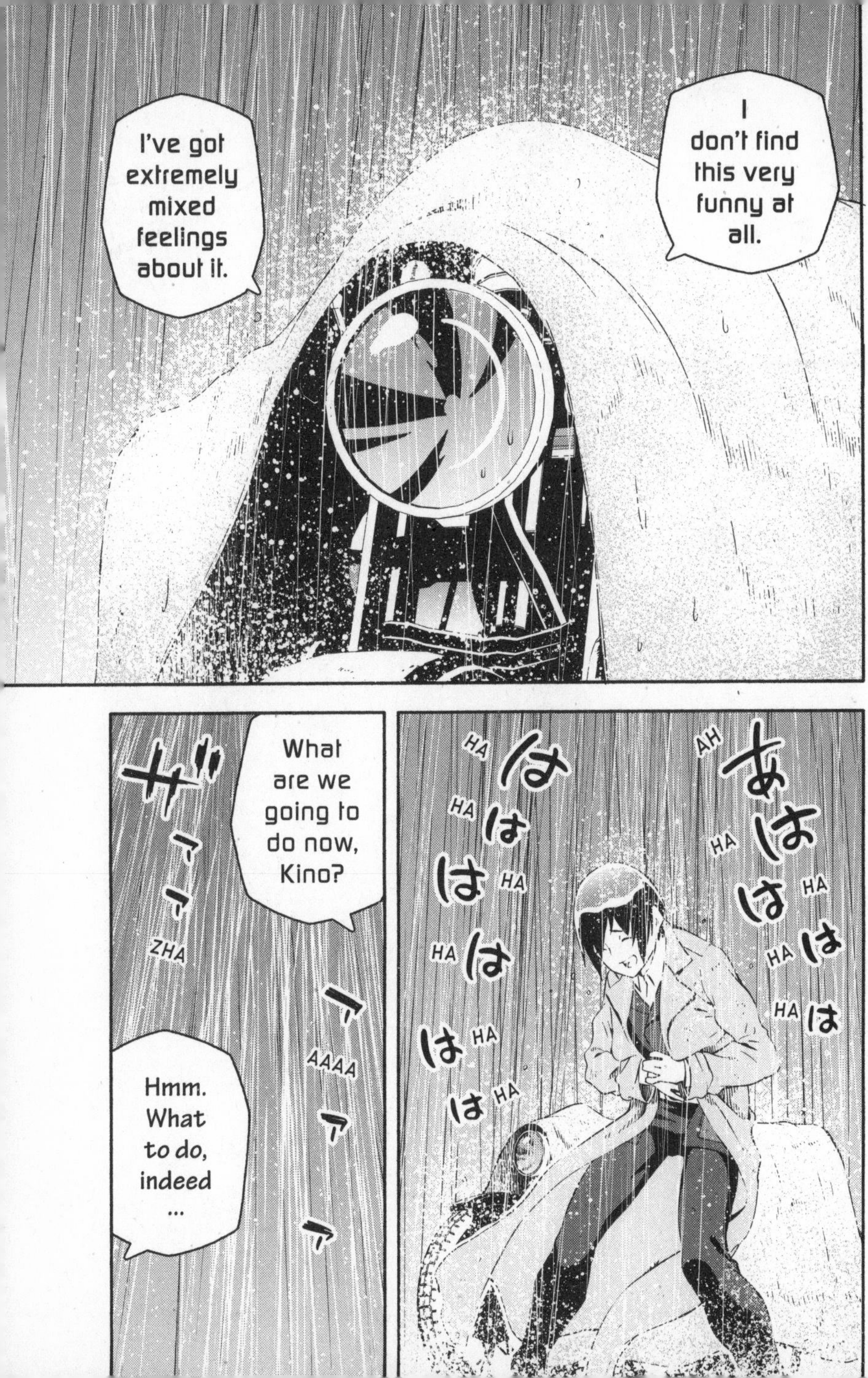
I don't find this very funny at all.
I've got extremely mixed feelings about it.
あははははははは
AH HA HA HA HA HA HA HA
What are we going to do now, Kino?
ザァァ
ZHA
ァァァ
AAAA
Hmm. What to do, indeed ...

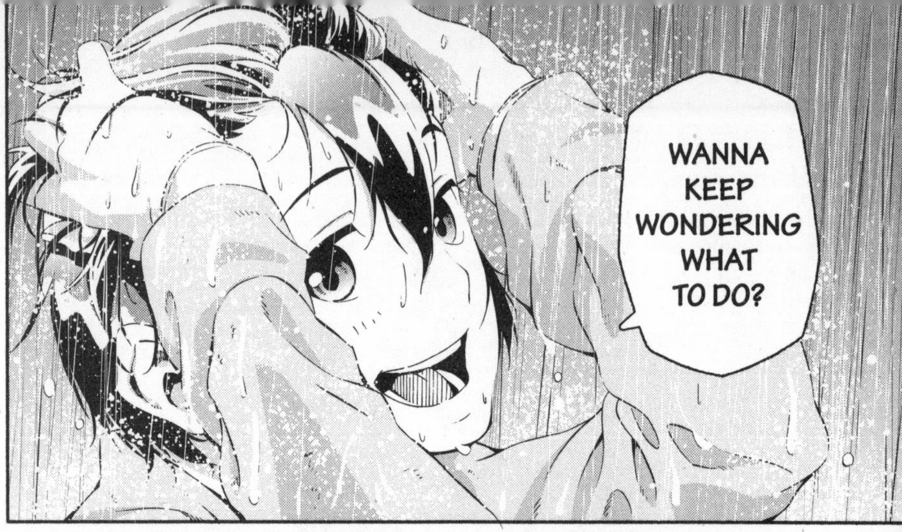
WANNA KEEP WONDERING WHAT TO DO?

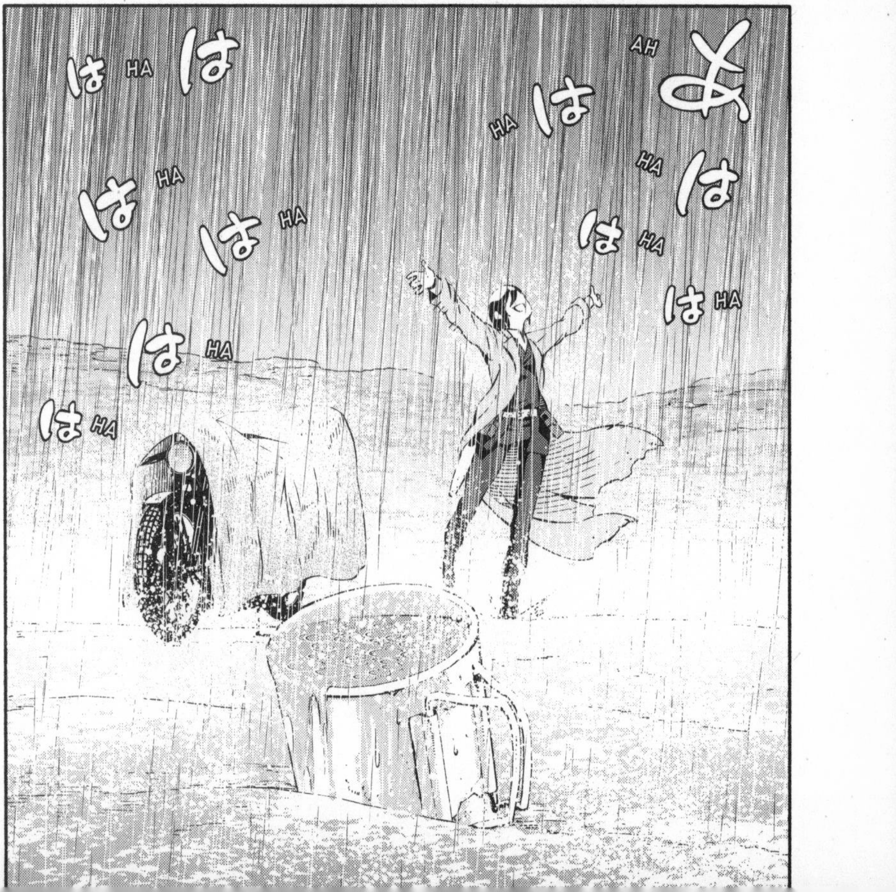
あ AH
は HA
は HA
は HA
は HA
は HA
は HA
は HA
は HA
は HA
は HA

Kino's Journey

—➤ The Beautiful World ◆——

Chapter 1

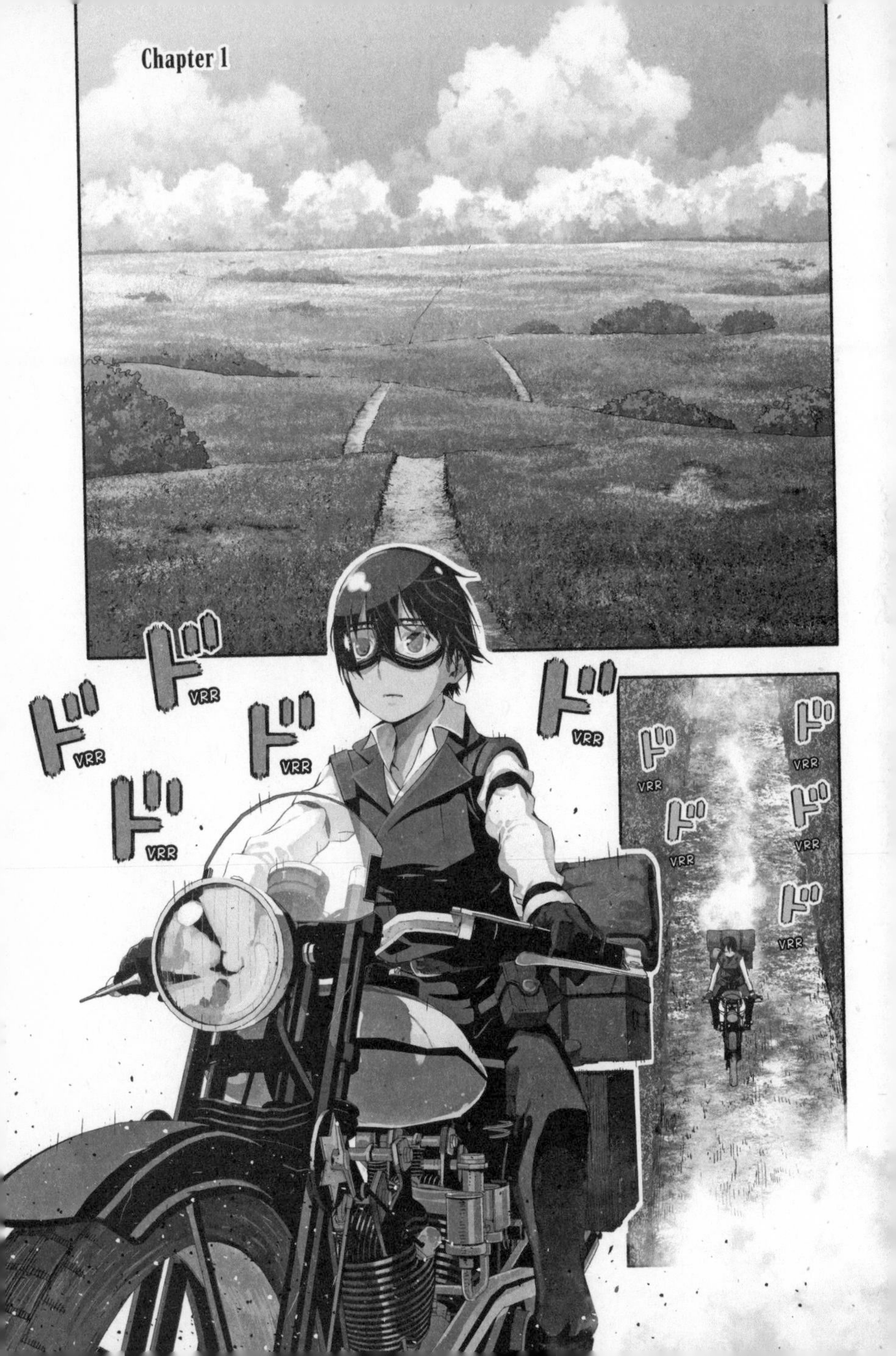

ド VRR
ド VRR
ド VRR
ド VRR
ド VRR
ド VRR
ド VRR
ド VRR
ド VRR
ド VRR

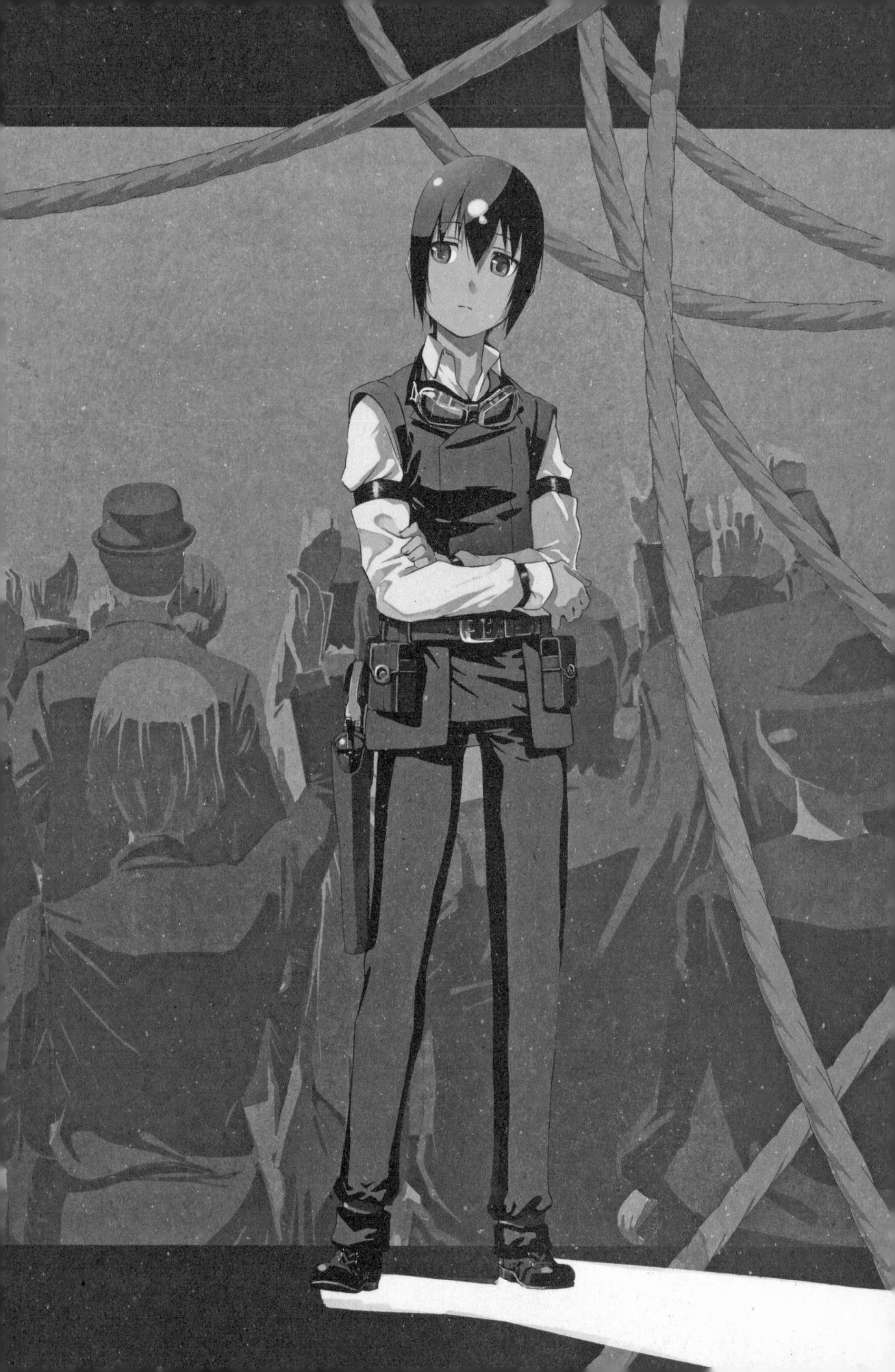

Chapter 1
The Land of Majority Rule (Pt. 1)
-Ourselfish-

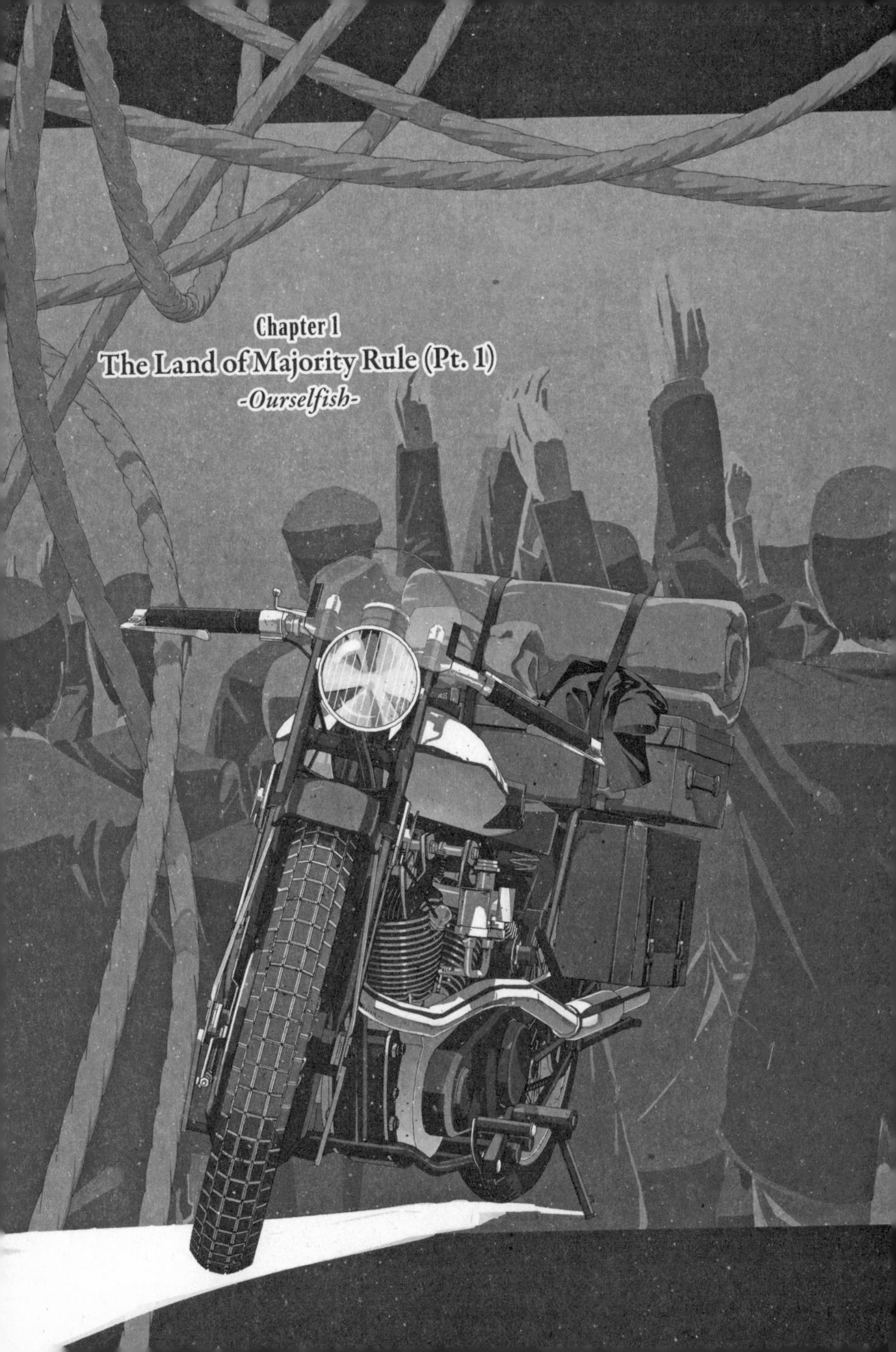

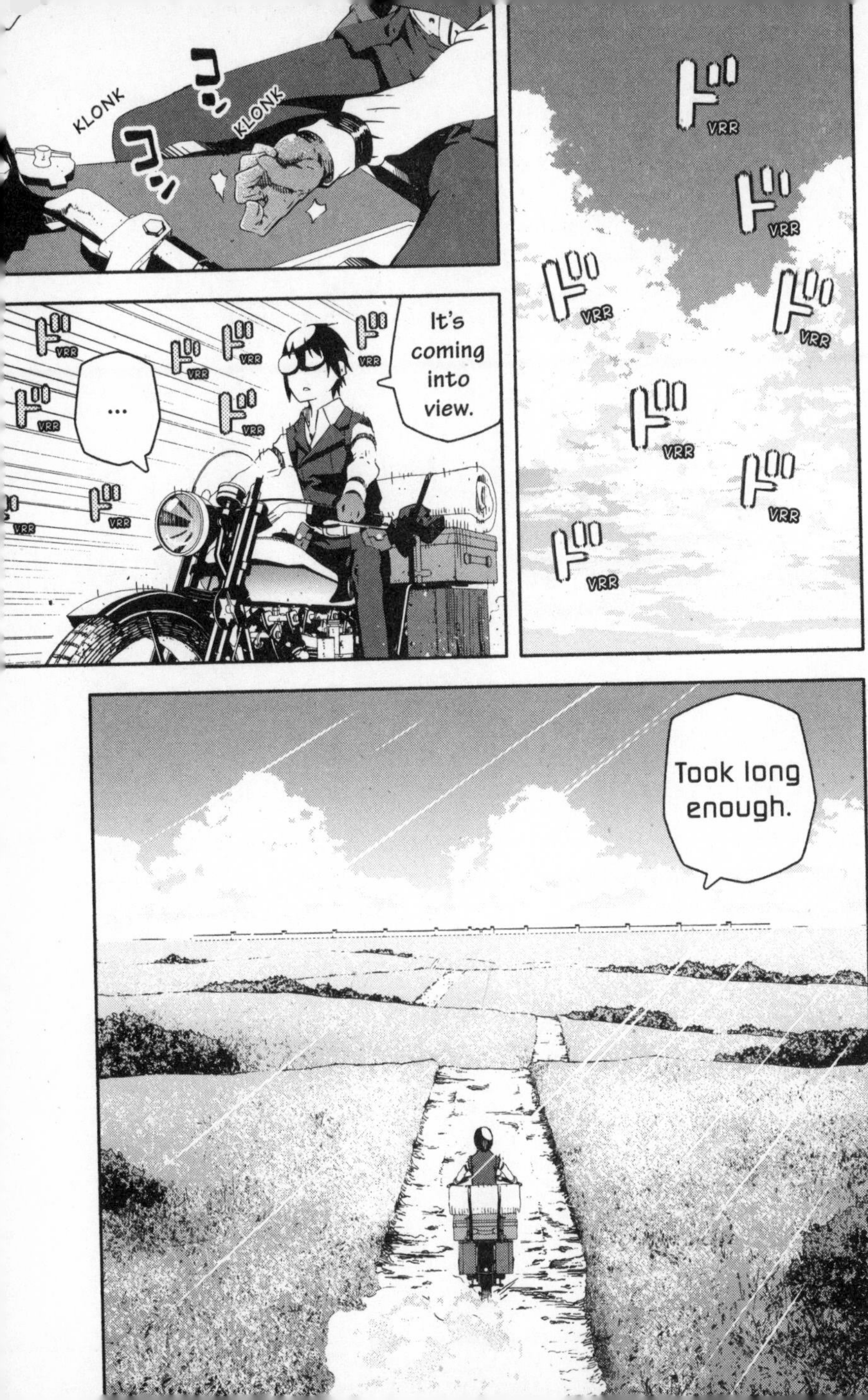
VRR
VRR
VRR
VRR
VRR
VRR
VRR
VRR
KLONK
KLONK
It's coming into view.
...
Took long enough.

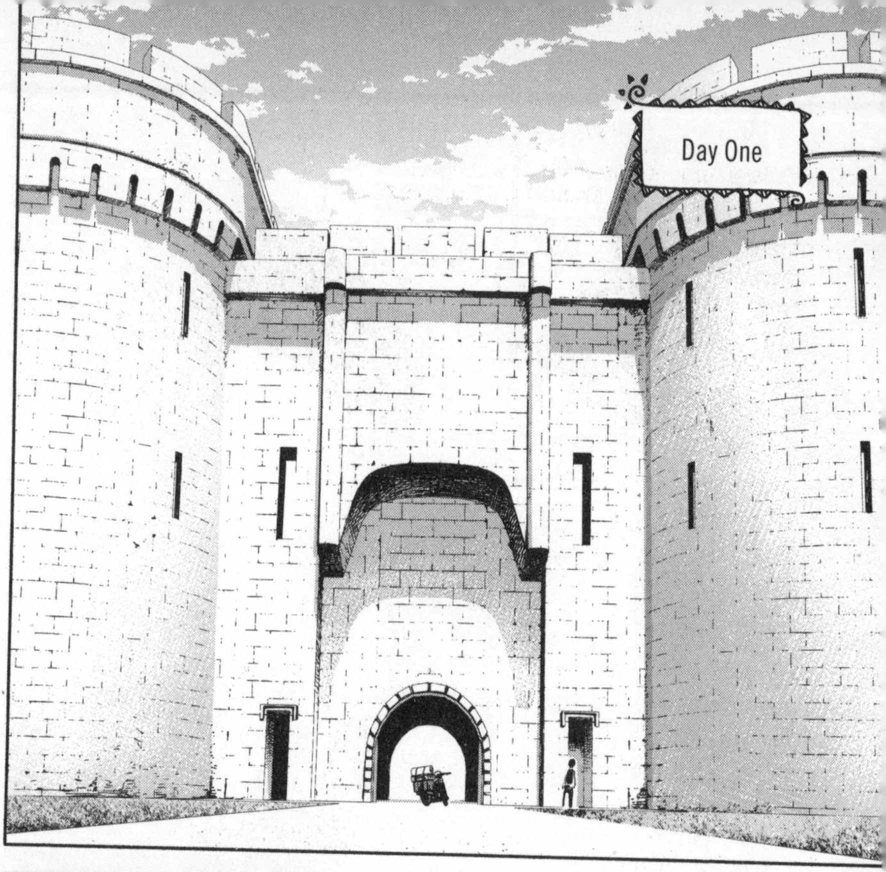
Day One

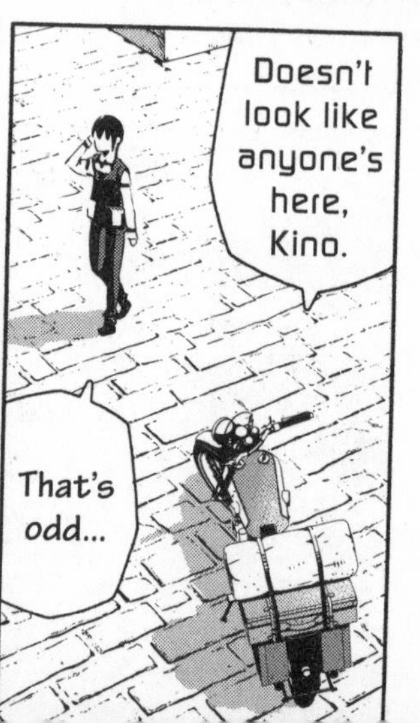
Doesn't look like anyone's here, Kino.
That's odd...

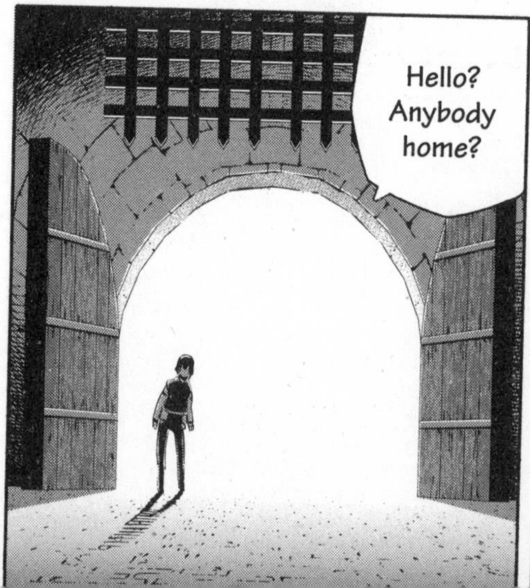
Hello? Anybody home?

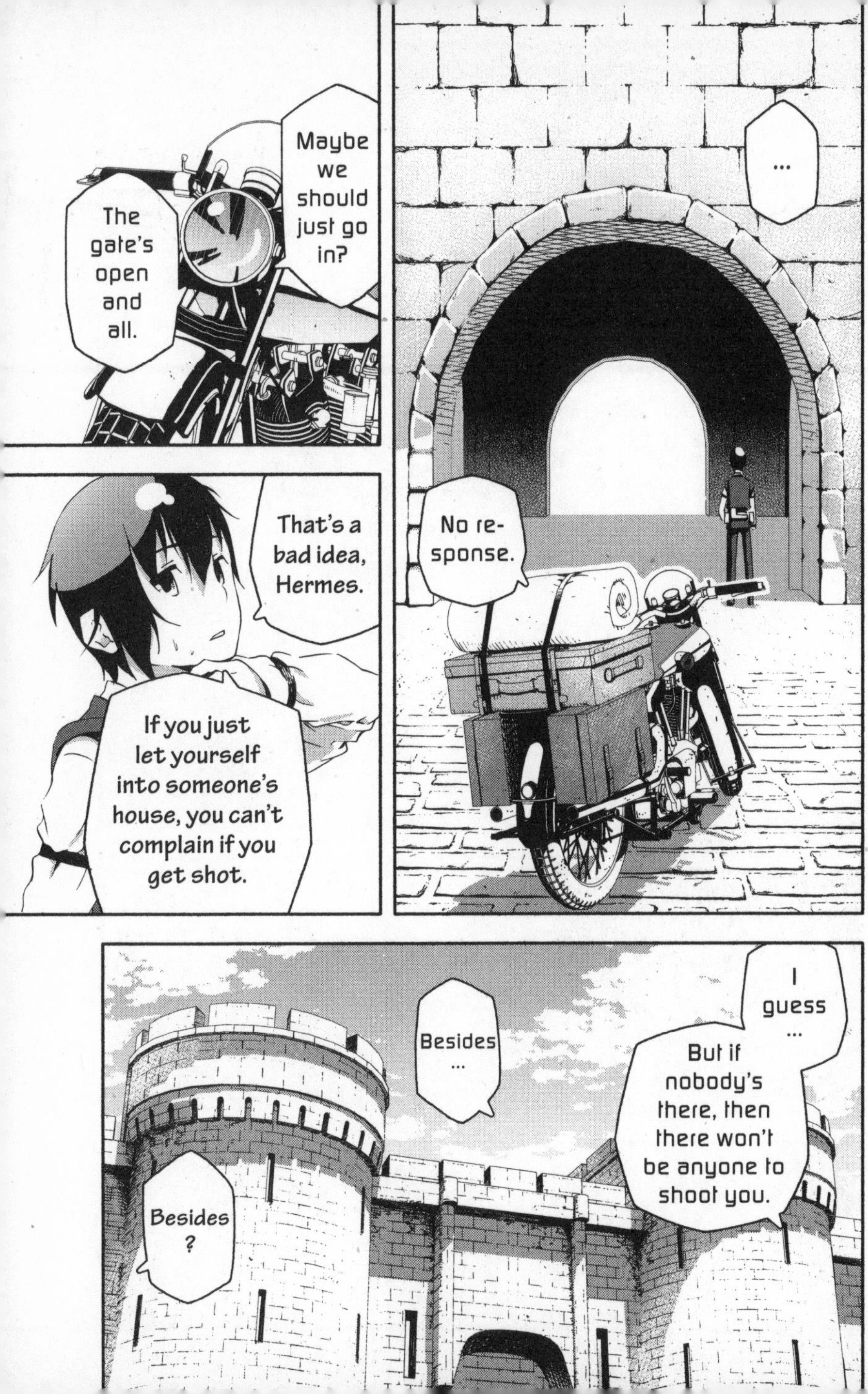
...
No re-sponse.
Maybe we should just go in?
The gate's open and all.
That's a bad idea, Hermes.
If you just let yourself into someone's house, you can't complain if you get shot.
I guess ...
But if nobody's there, then there won't be anyone to shoot you.
Besides ...
Besides ?

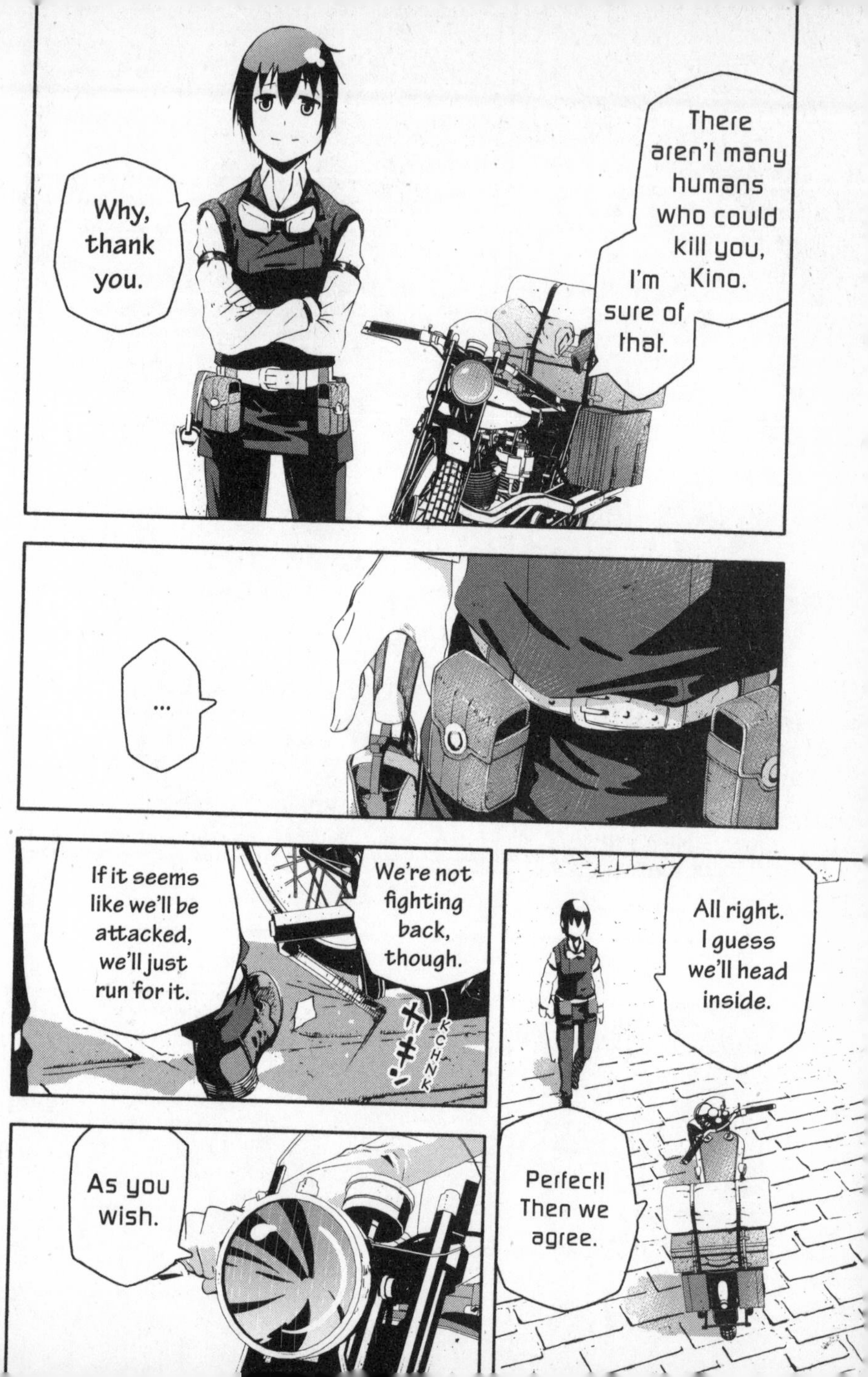
There aren't many humans who could kill you, Kino.
I'm sure of that.
Why, thank you.
...
All right. I guess we'll head inside.
Perfect! Then we agree.
We're not fighting back, though.
If it seems like we'll be attacked, we'll just run for it.
KCHNK
As you wish.

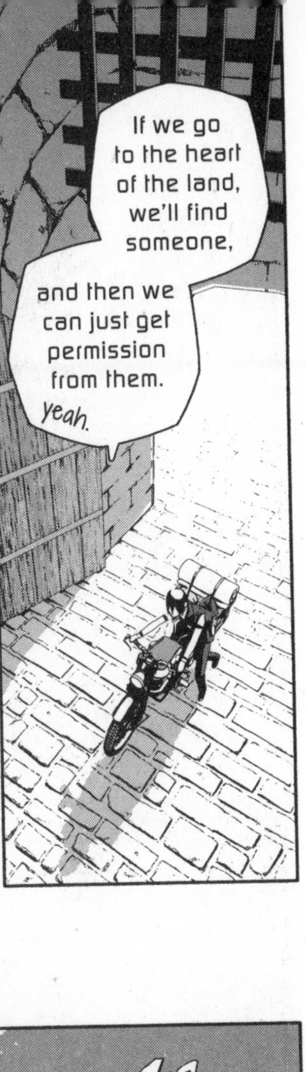
If we go to the heart of the land, we'll find someone,
and then we can just get permission from them.
yeah.

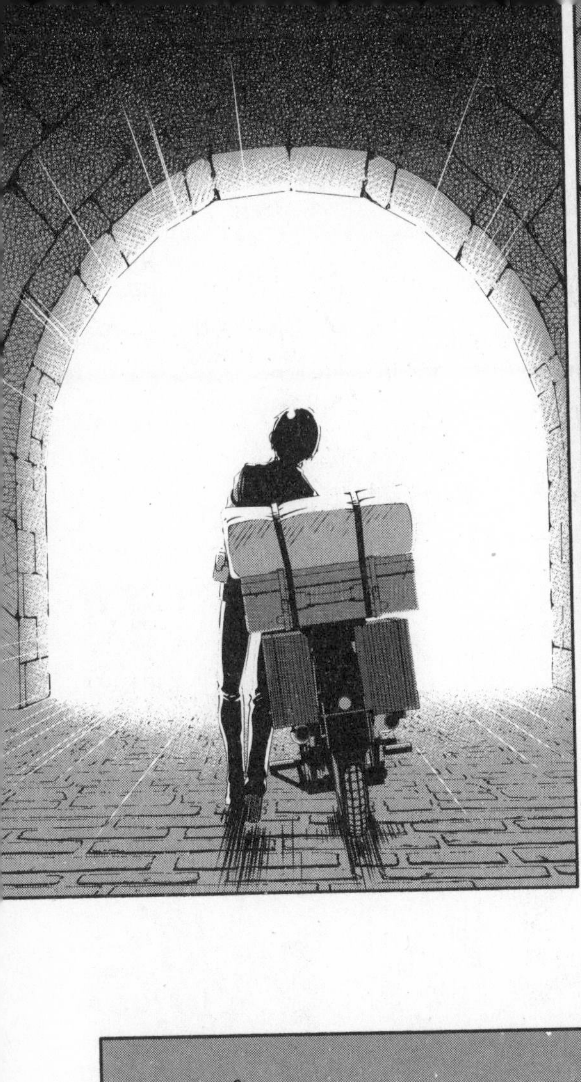

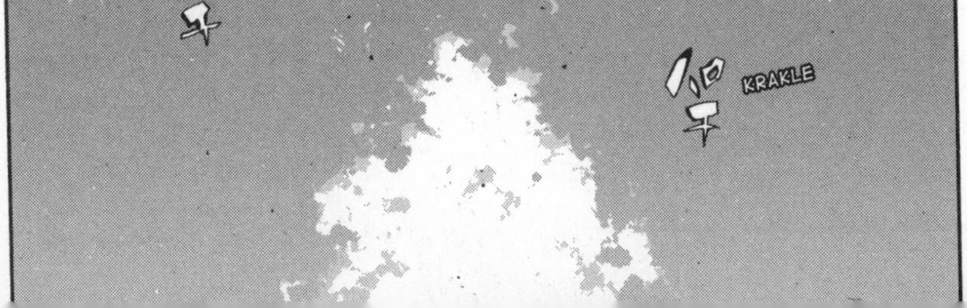
KRAKLE
KRAKLE
KRAKLE

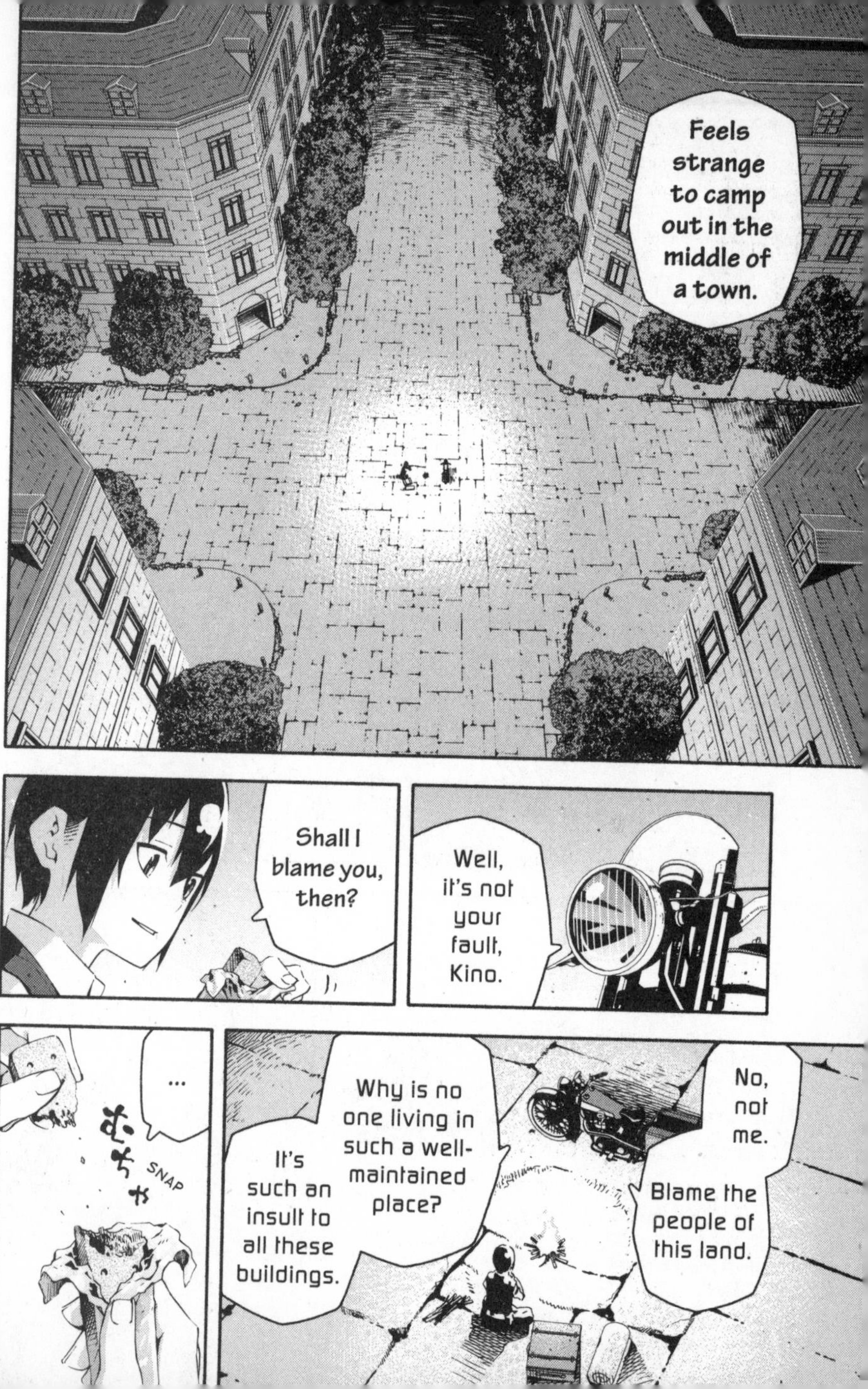
Feels strange to camp out in the middle of a town.
Well, it's not your fault, Kino.
Shall I blame you, then?
No, not me.
Blame the people of this land.
Why is no one living in such a well-maintained place?
It's such an insult to all these buildings.
...
SNAP

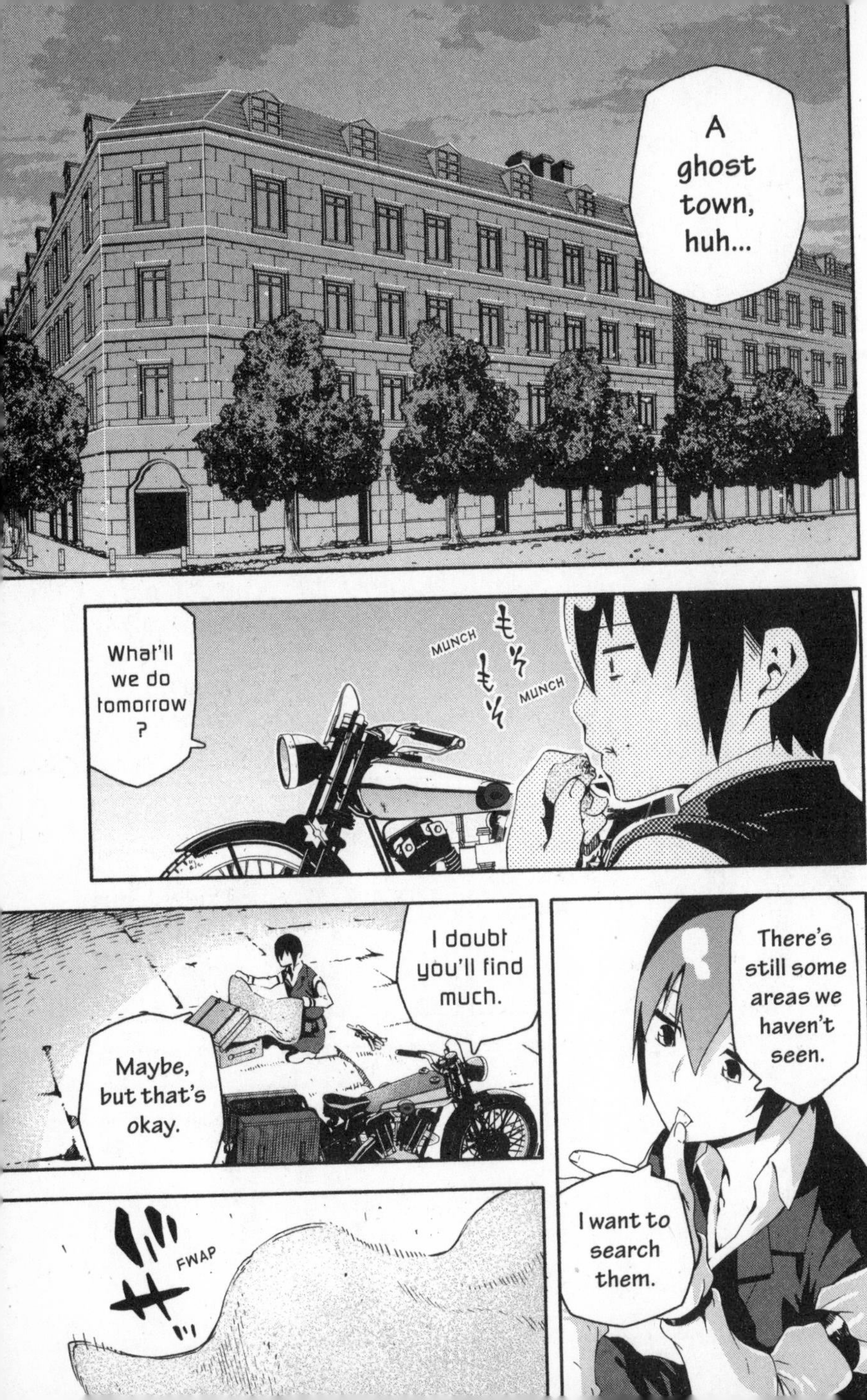
A ghost town, huh...
What'll we do tomorrow?
MUNCH
MUNCH
There's still some areas we haven't seen.
I want to search them.
I doubt you'll find much.
Maybe, but that's okay.
FWAP

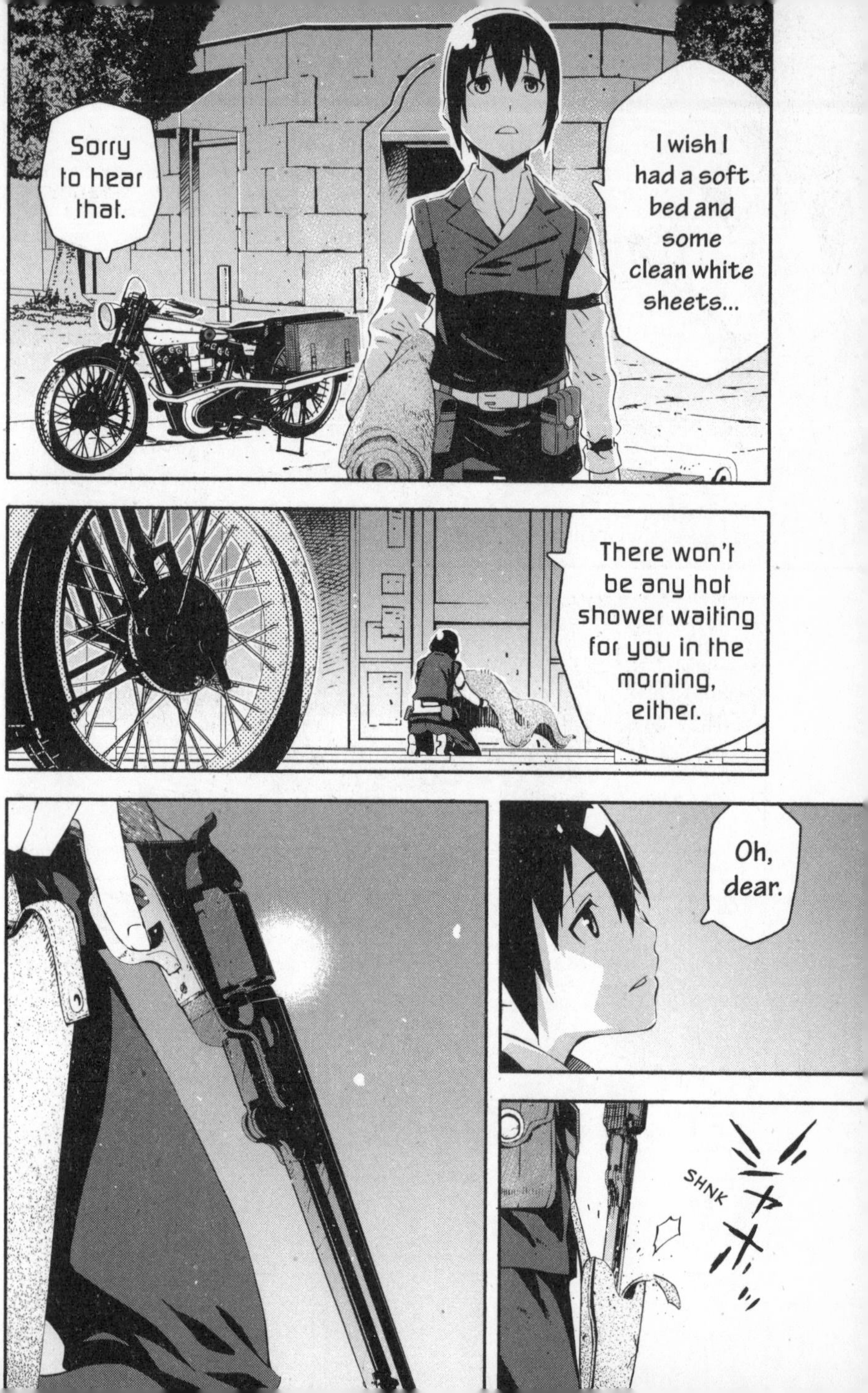

I wish I had a soft bed and some clean white sheets...
Sorry to hear that.
There won't be any hot shower waiting for you in the morning, either.
Oh, dear.
SHNK

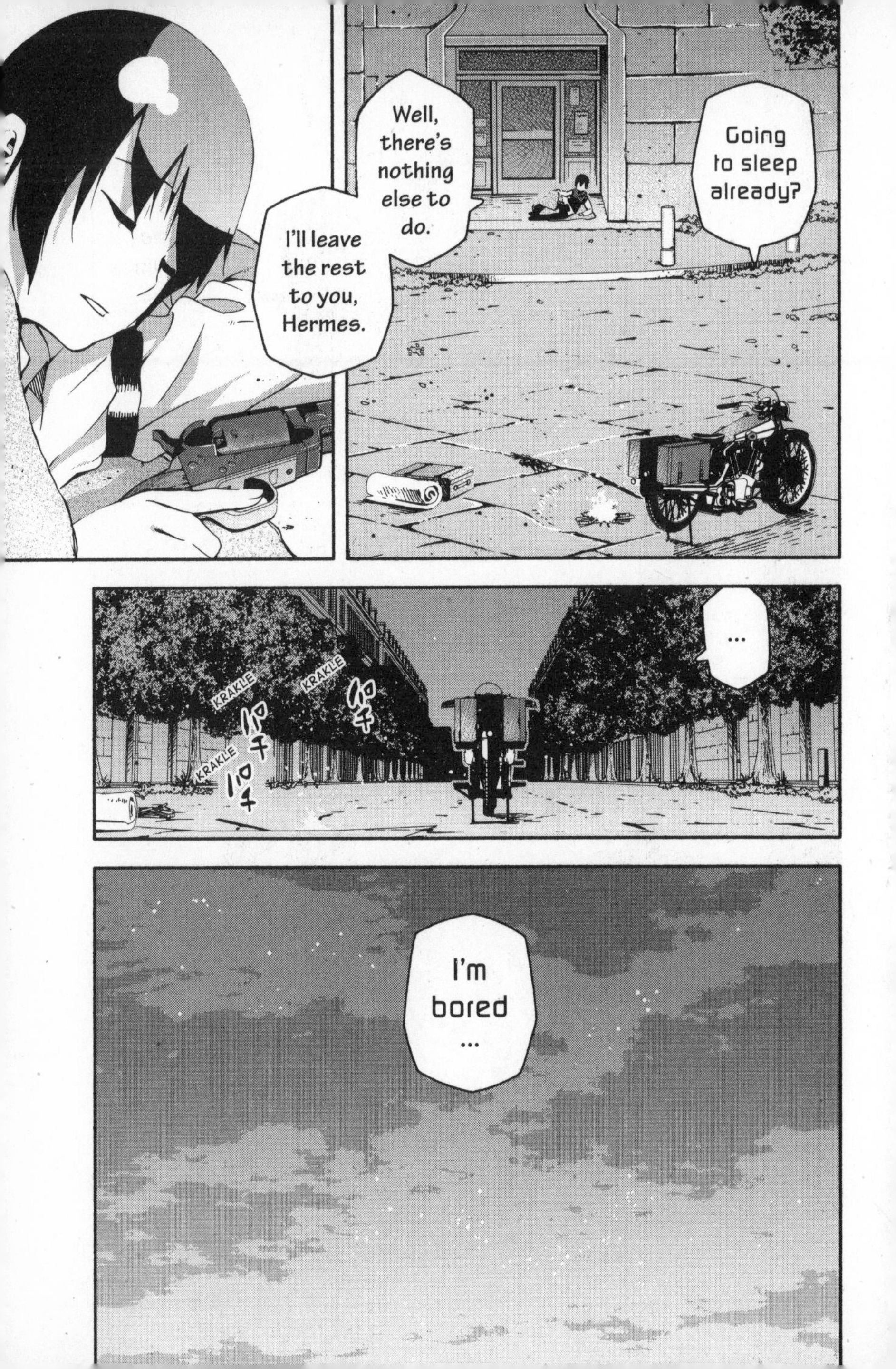
Going to sleep already?
Well, there's nothing else to do.
I'll leave the rest to you, Hermes.
…
KRAKLE
パチ
KRAKLE
パチ
KRAKLE
パチ
I'm bored …

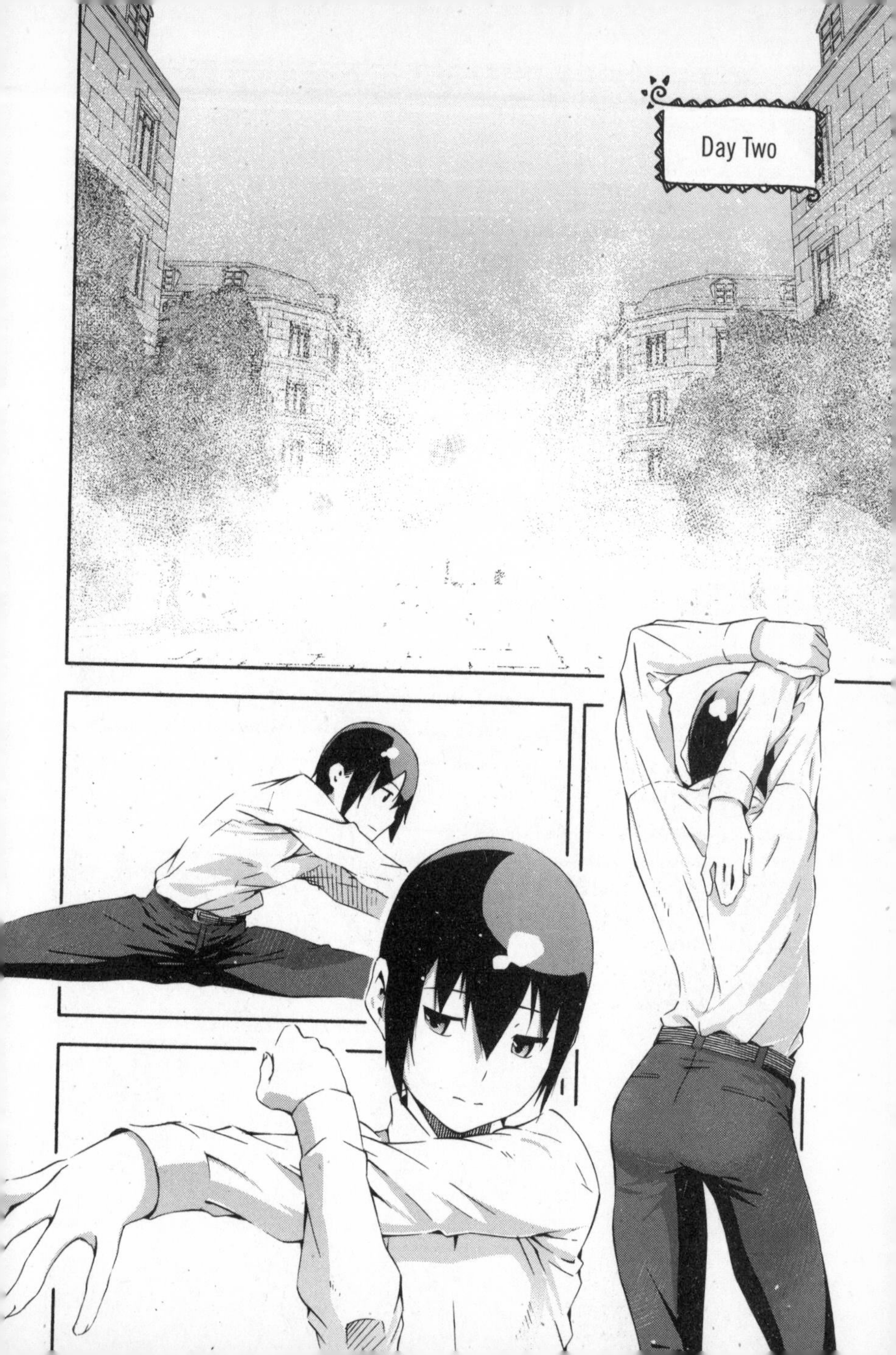
Day Two

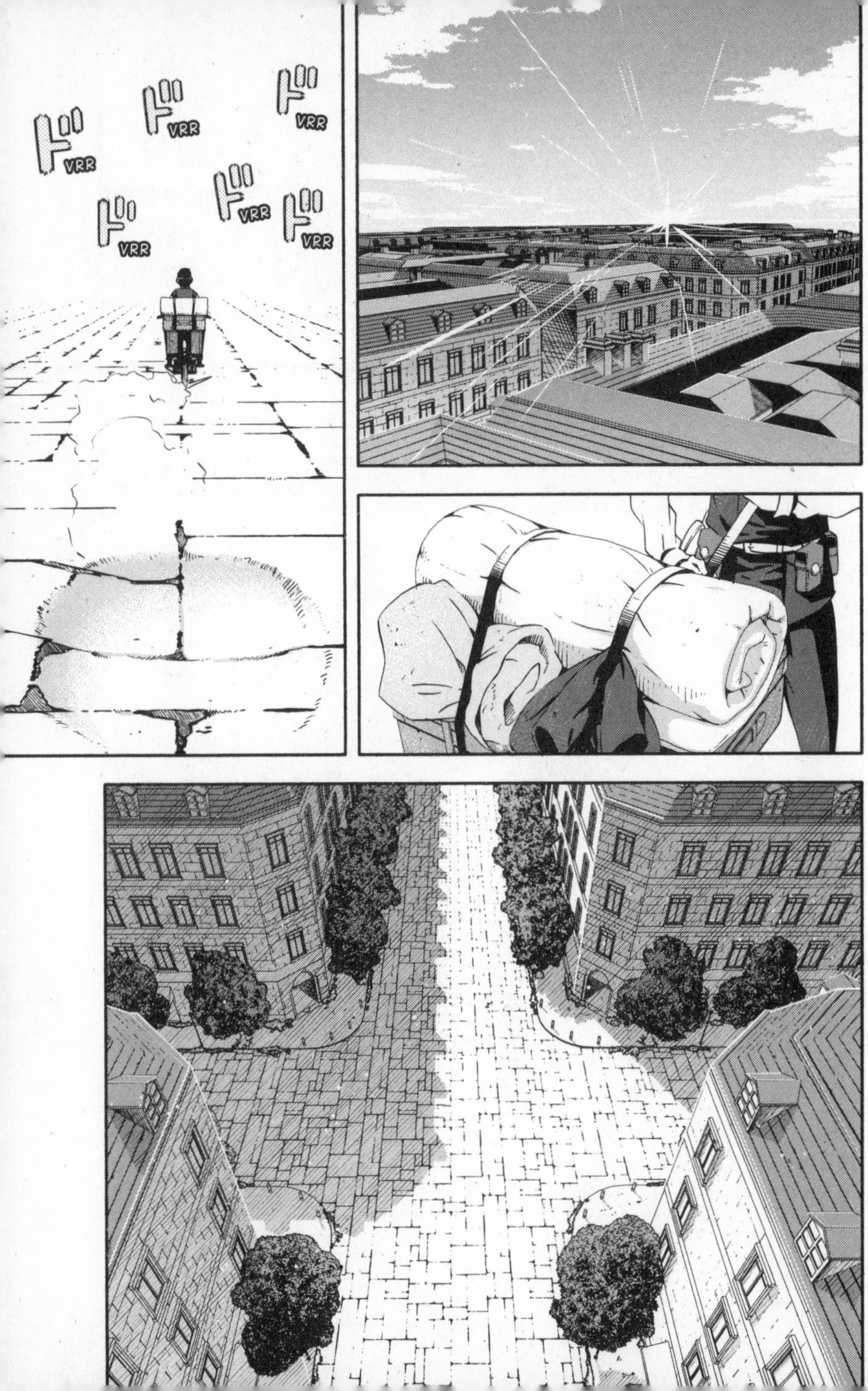
ド VRR
ド VRR
ド VRR
ド VRR
ド VRR
ド VRR

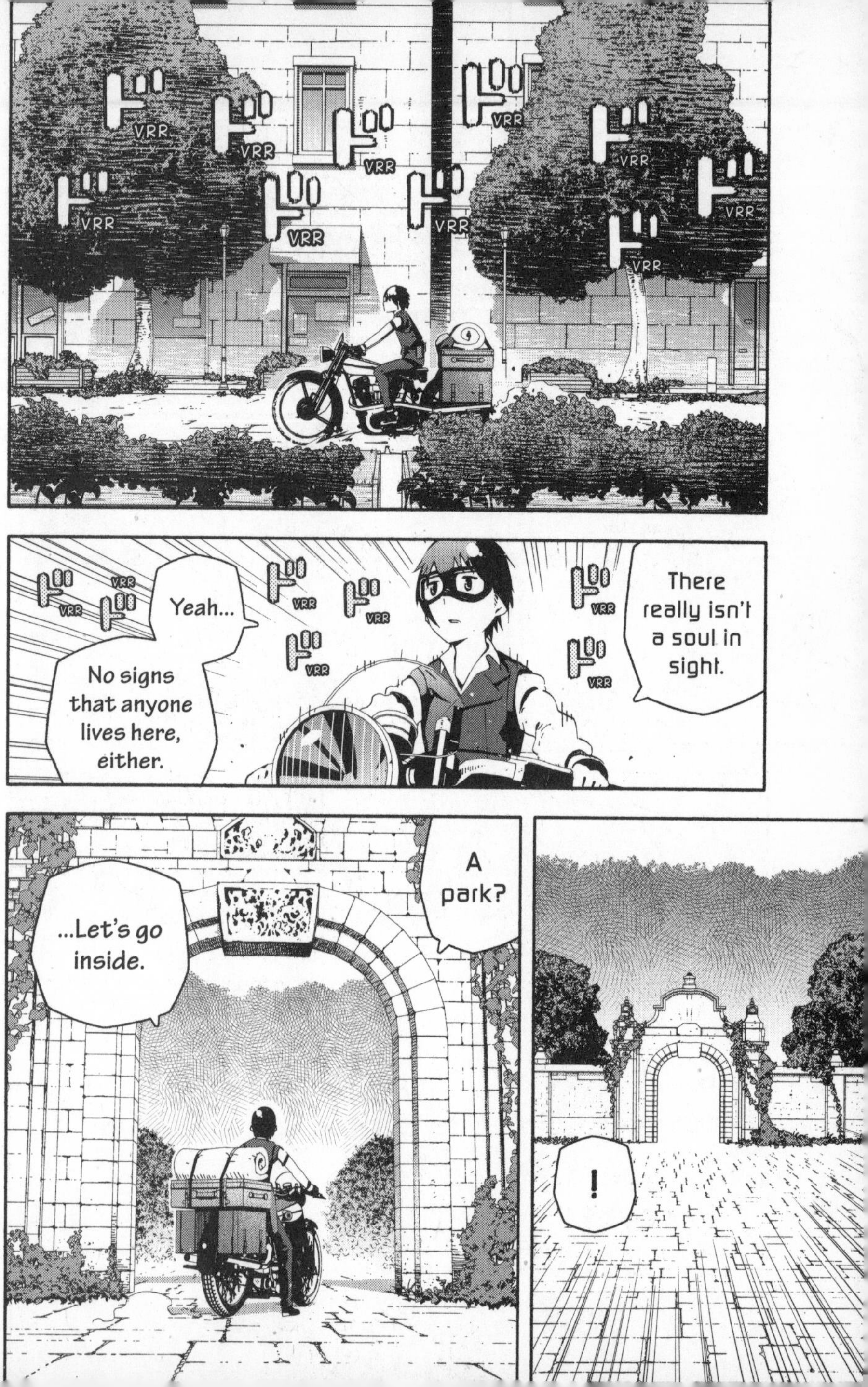
VRR
VRR
VRR
VRR
VRR
VRR
VRR
VRR
VRR
VRR
There really isn't a soul in sight.
VRR
VRR
VRR
VRR
VRR
VRR
Yeah...
No signs that anyone lives here, either.
!
A park?
...Let's go inside.

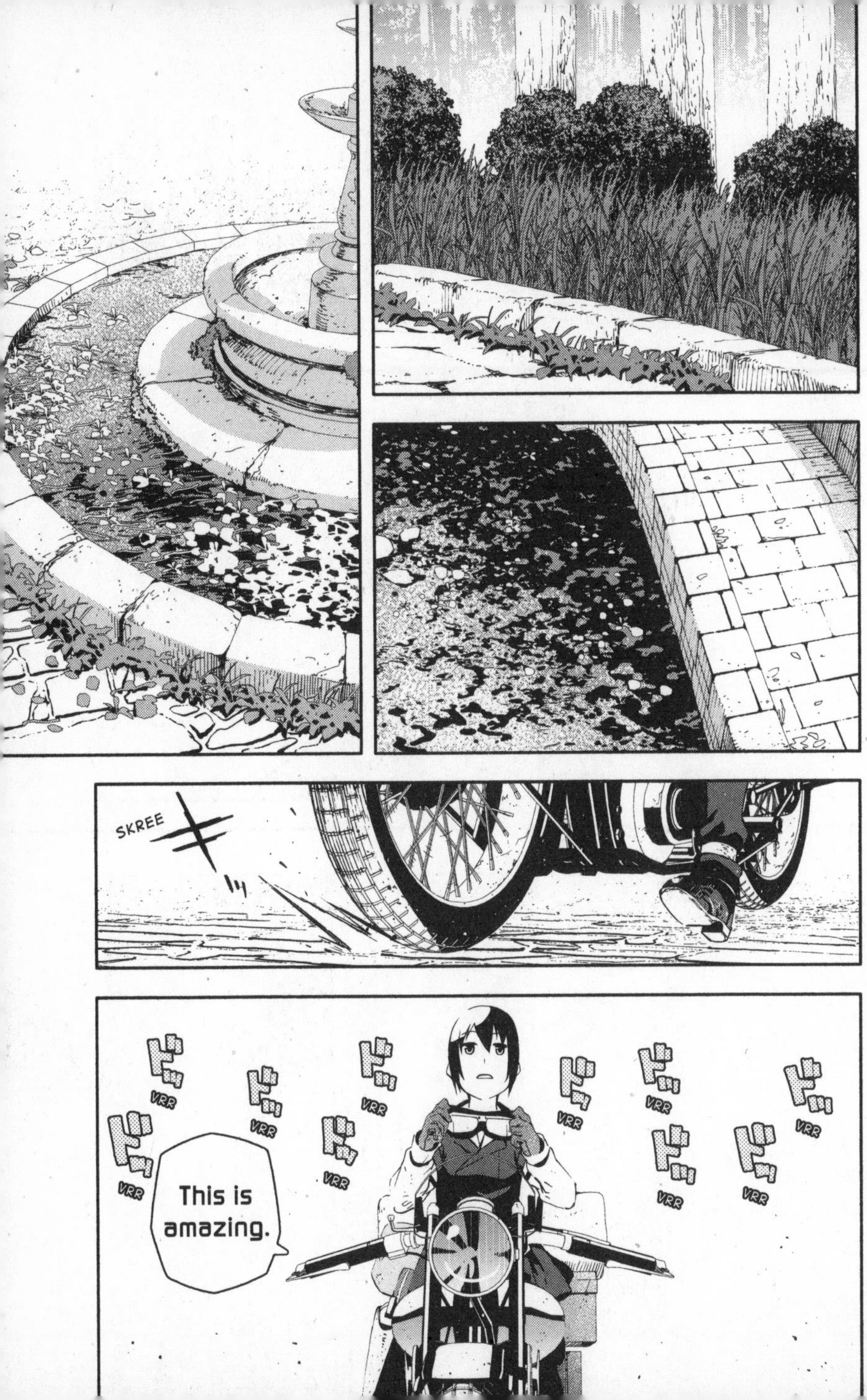
SKREE
VRR
This is amazing.

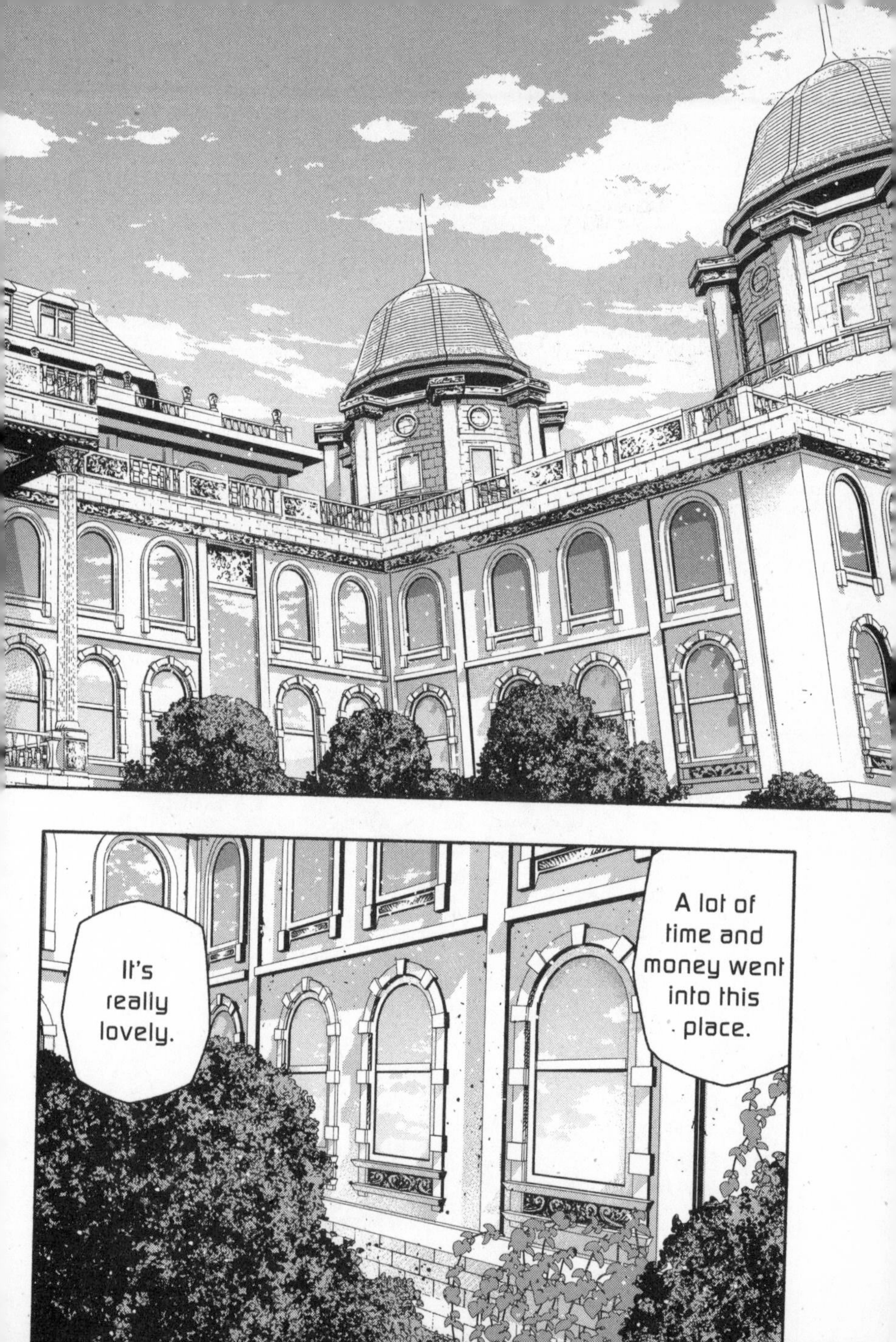
A lot of time and money went into this place.
It's really lovely.

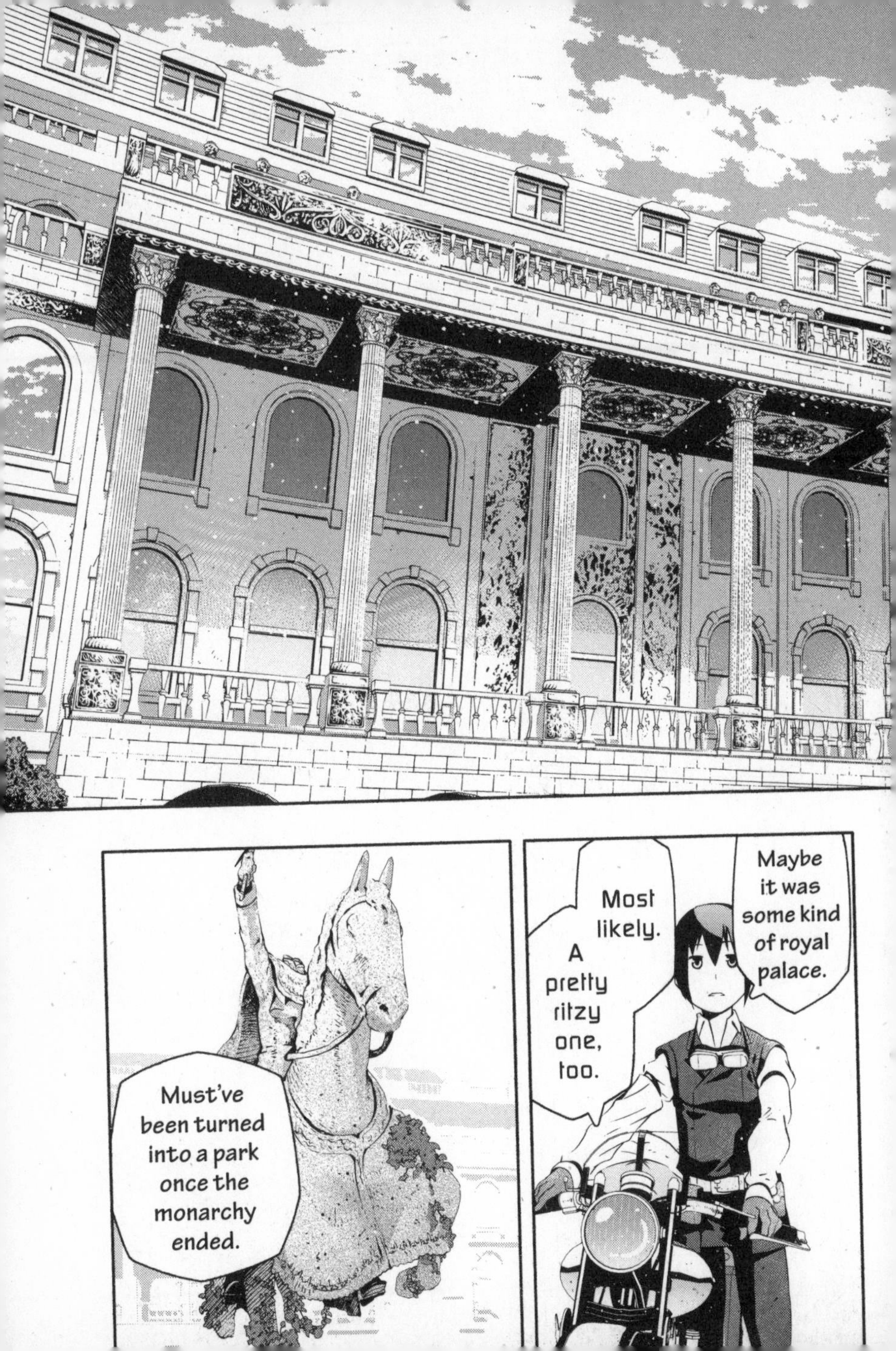
Maybe it was some kind of royal palace.
Most likely. A pretty ritzy one, too.
Must've been turned into a park once the monarchy ended.

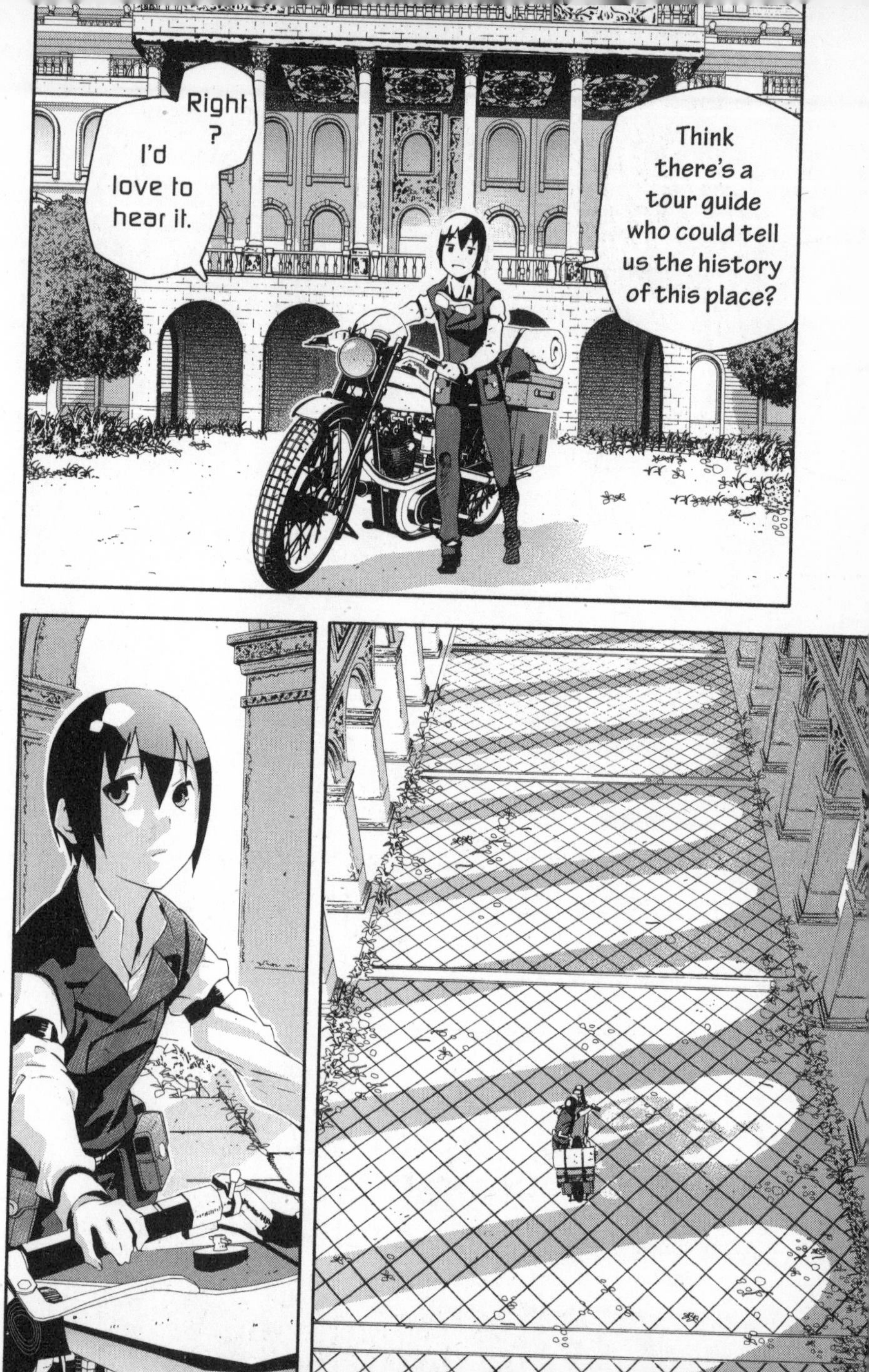
Think there's a tour guide who could tell us the history of this place?
Right? I'd love to hear it.

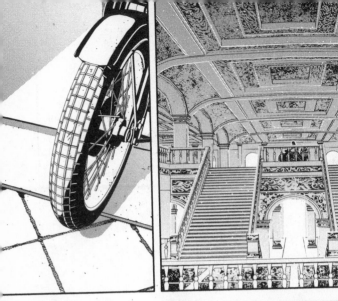

Ah.
I see.

...

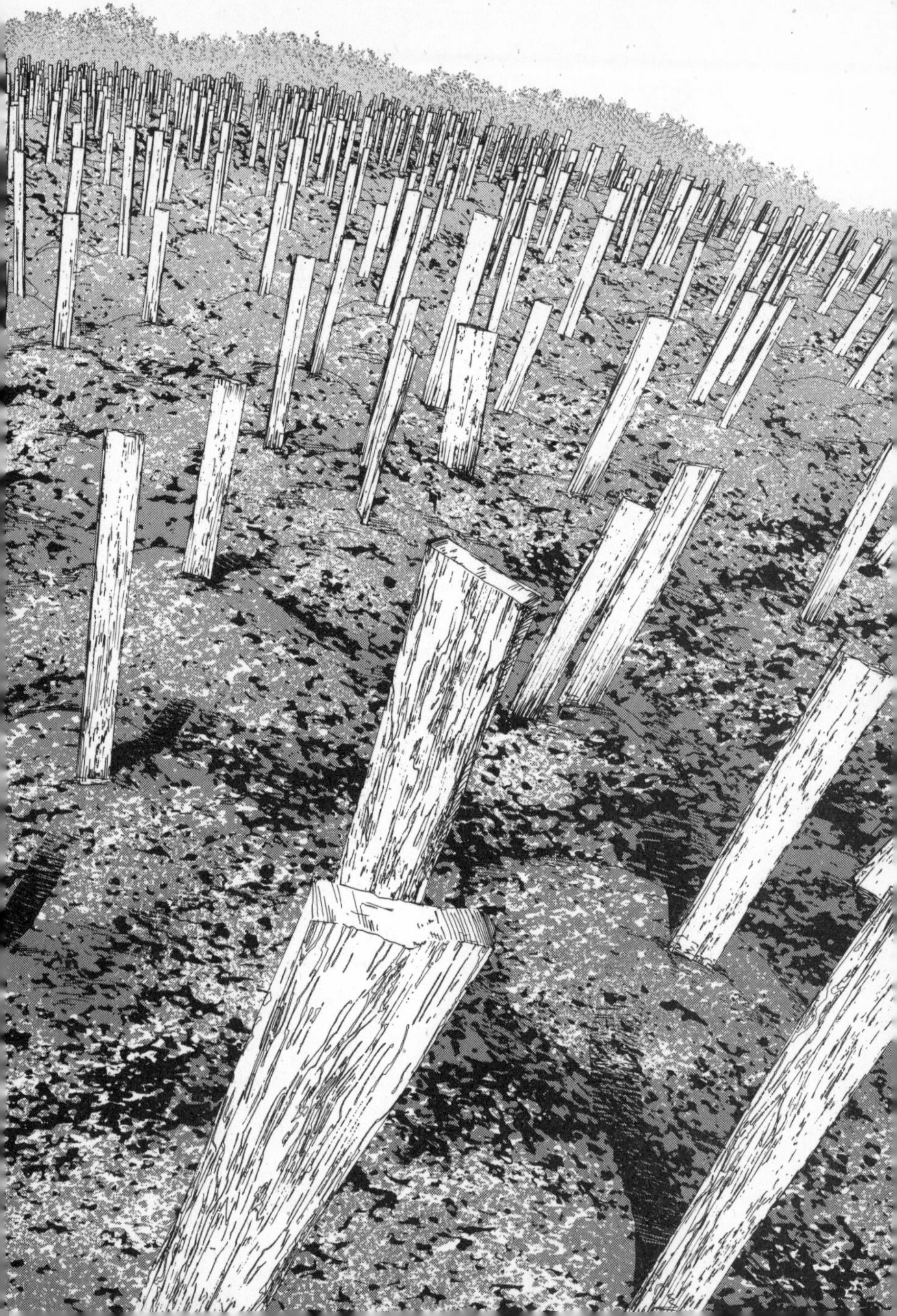

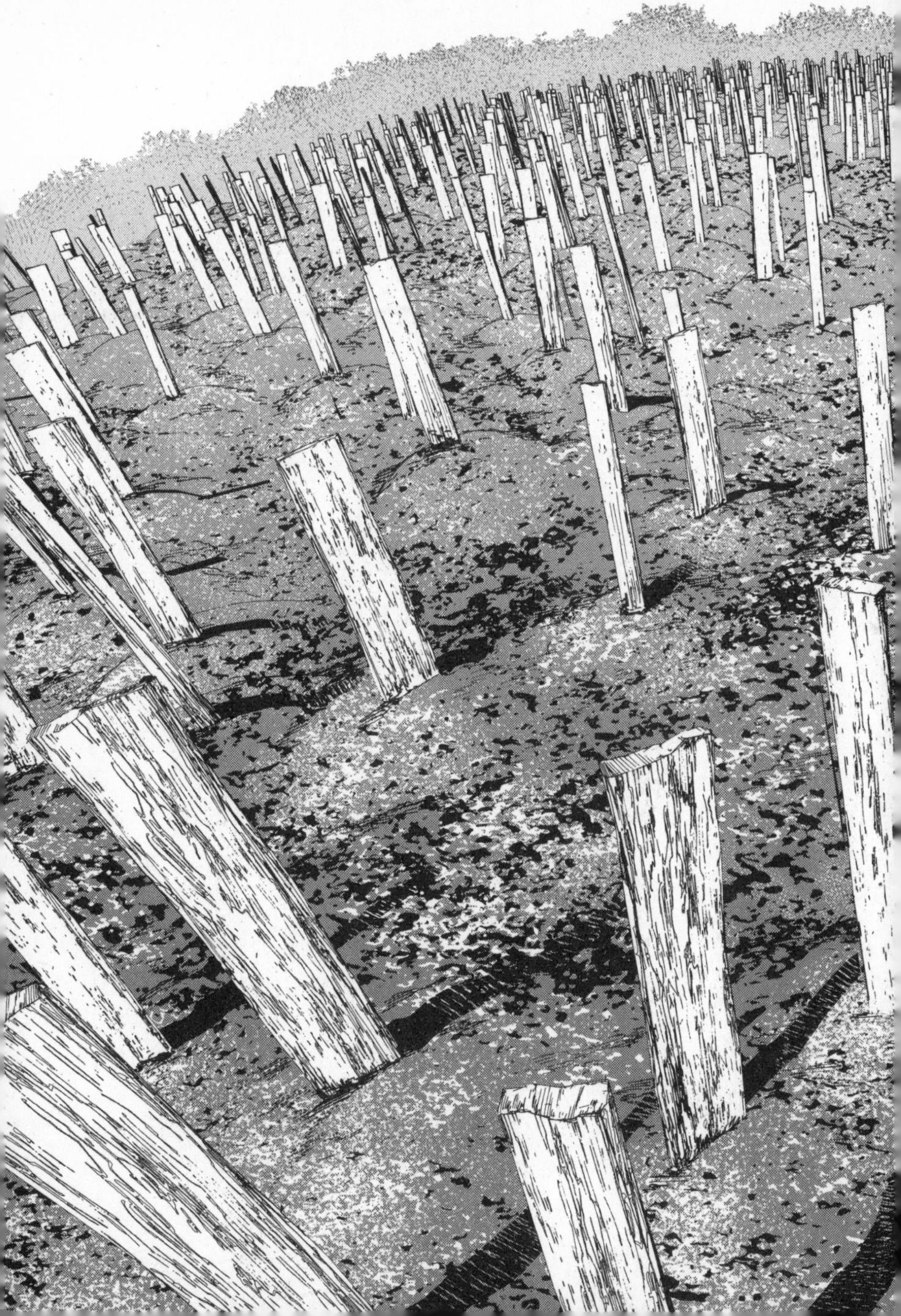

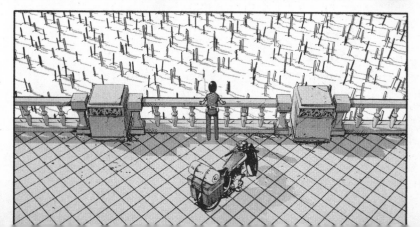

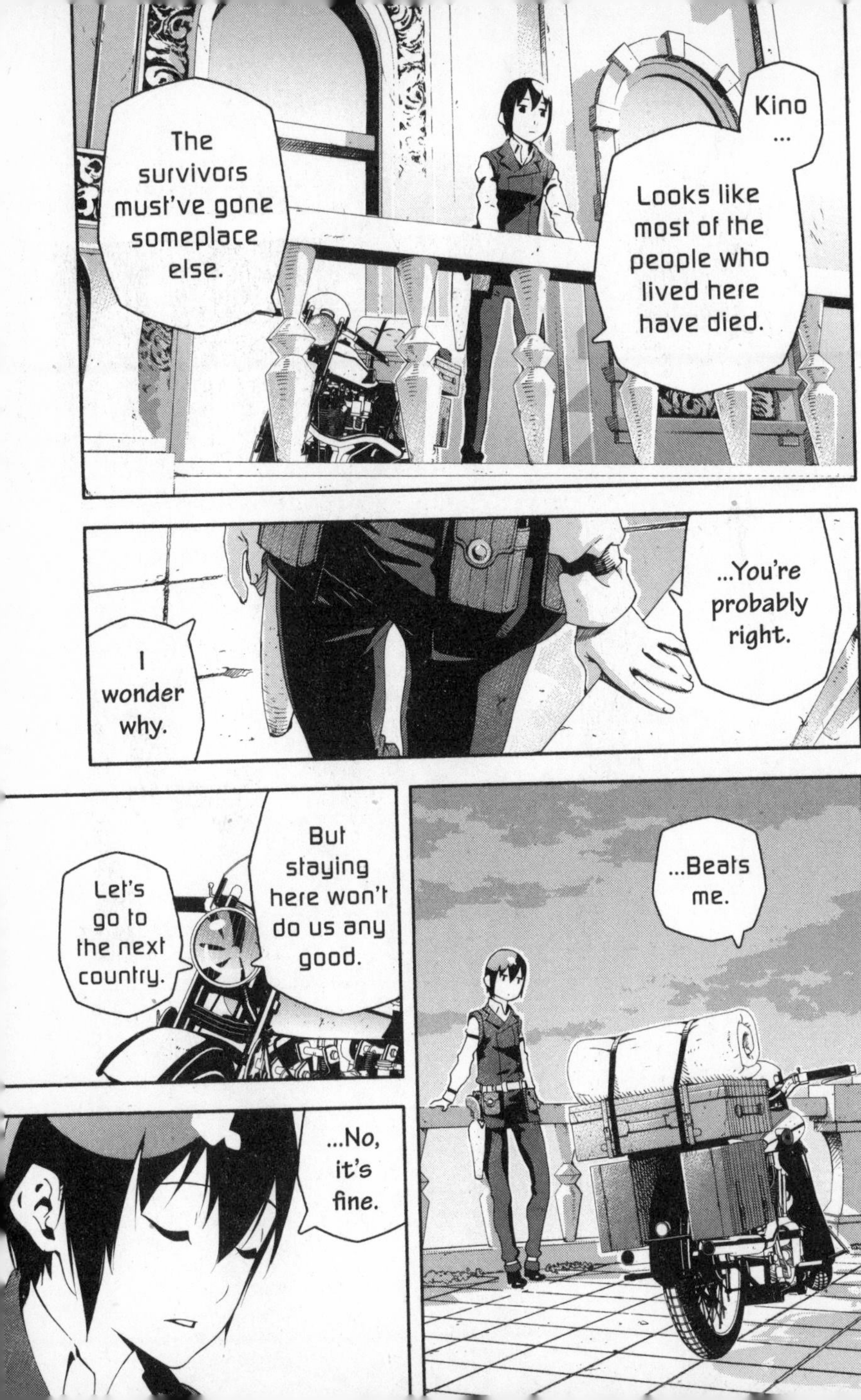
Kino ...
Looks like most of the people who lived here have died.
The survivors must've gone someplace else.
...You're probably right.
I wonder why.
...Beats me.
But staying here won't do us any good.
Let's go to the next country.
...No, it's fine.

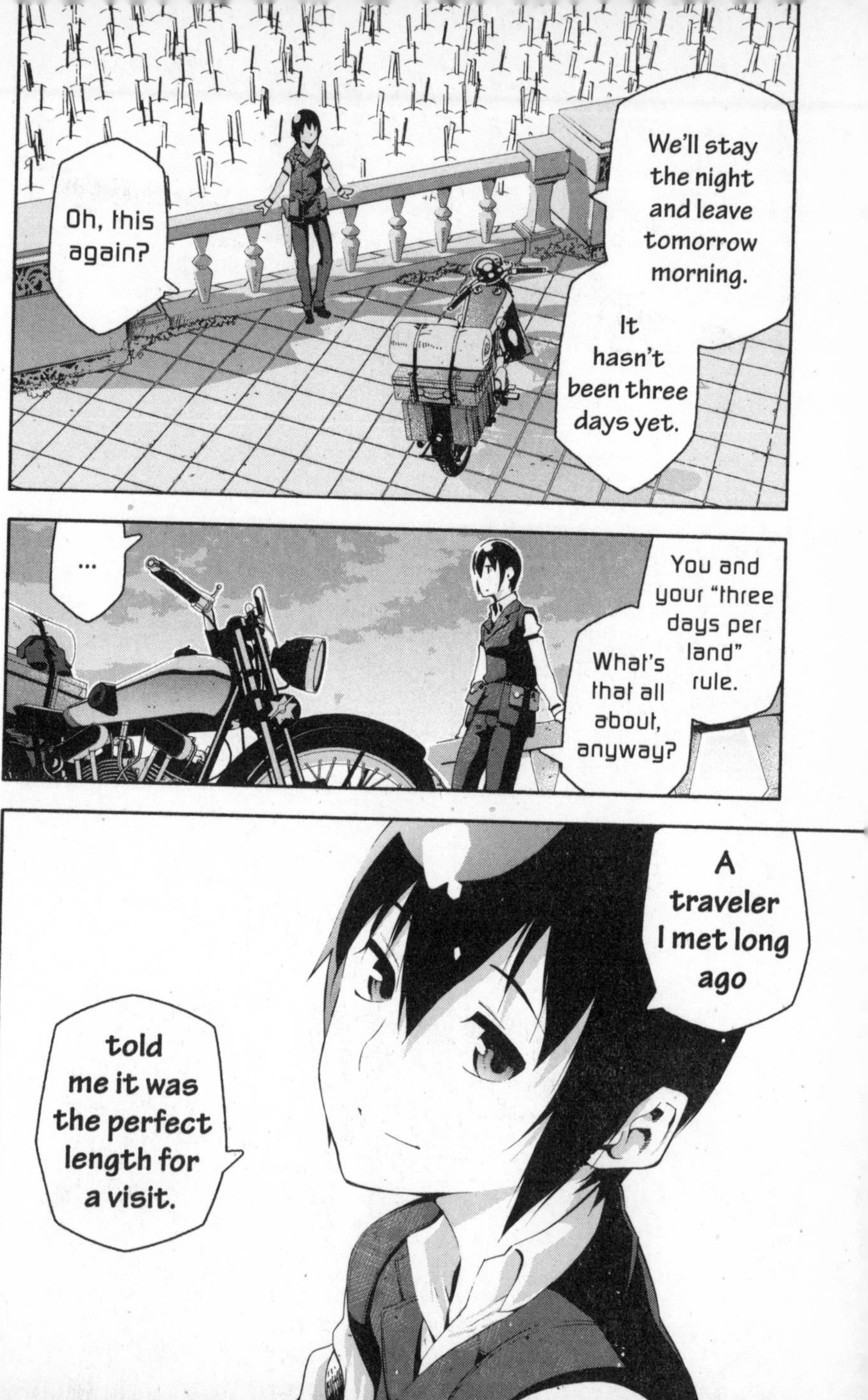
We'll stay the night and leave tomorrow morning.
It hasn't been three days yet.
Oh, this again?
You and your "three days per land" rule.
What's that all about, anyway?
...
A traveler I met long ago
told me it was the perfect length for a visit.

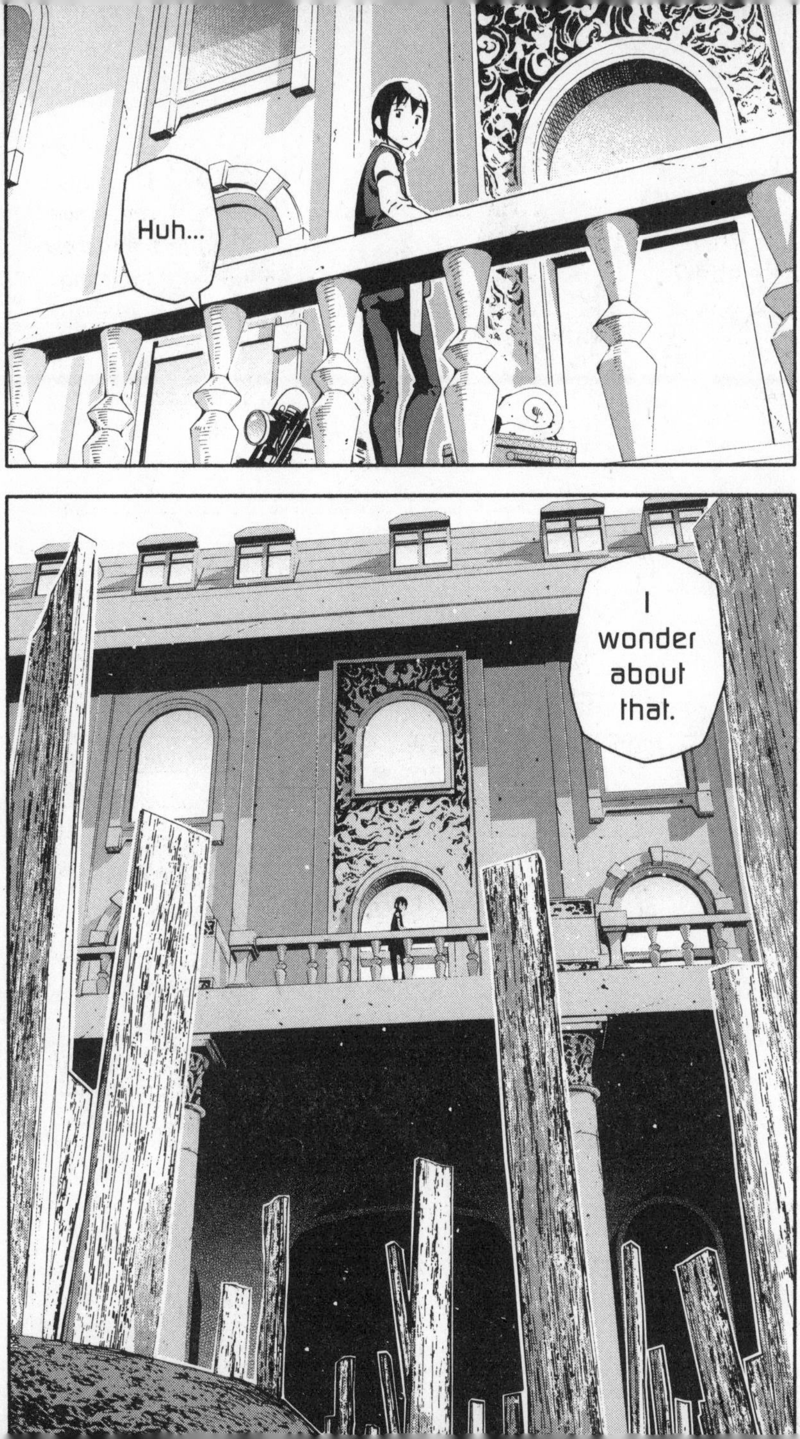
Huh...
I wonder about that.

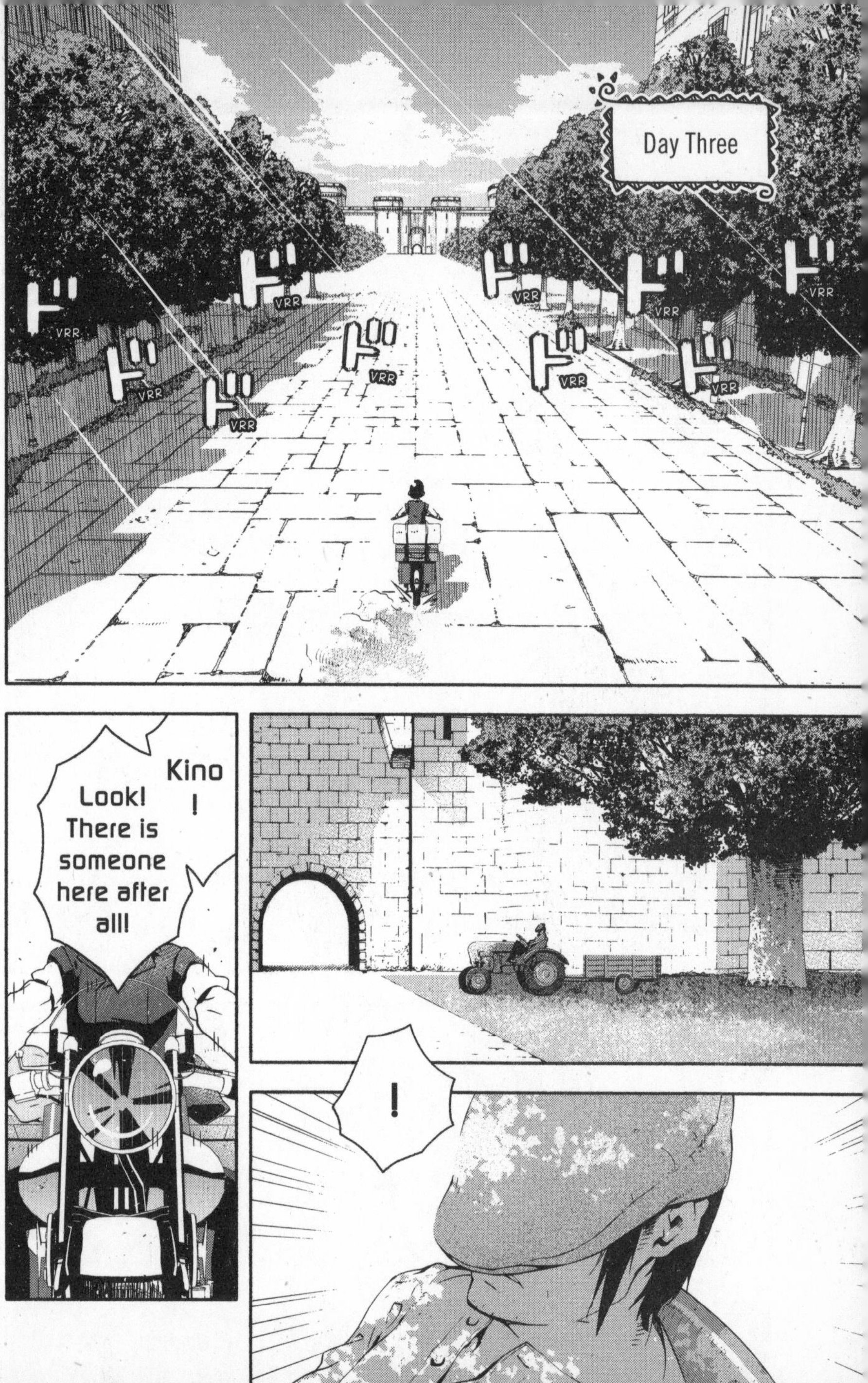
Day Three
ド VRR
ド VRR
ド VRR
ド VRR
ド VRR
ド VRR
ド VRR
ド VRR
ド VRR
!
Kino!
Look! There is someone here after all!

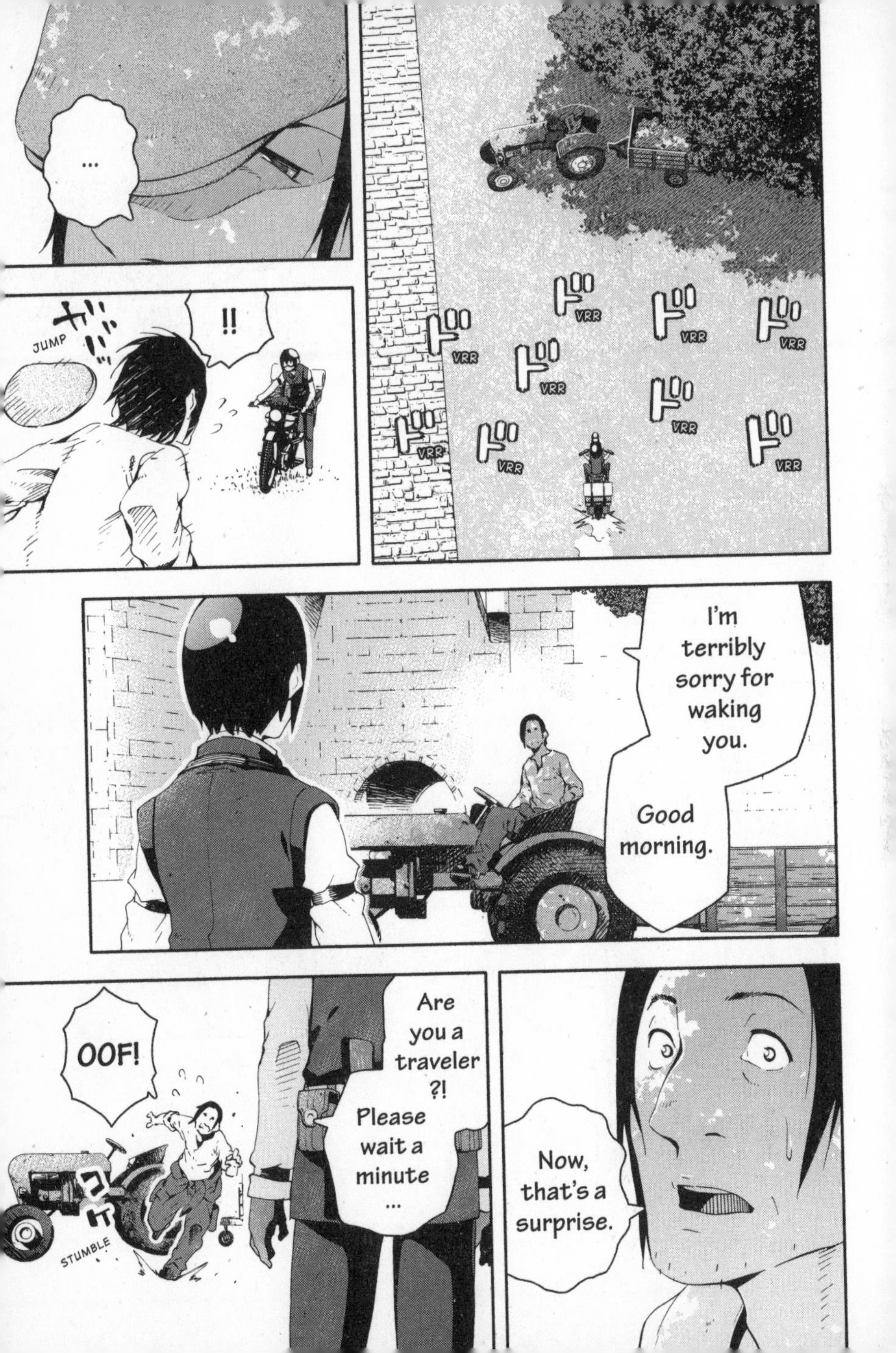
VRR
VRR
VRR
VRR
VRR
VRR
VRR
VRR
VRR
...
JUMP
!!
I'm terribly sorry for waking you.
Good morning.
Now, that's a surprise.
Are you a traveler?!
Please wait a minute ...
OOF!
STUMBLE

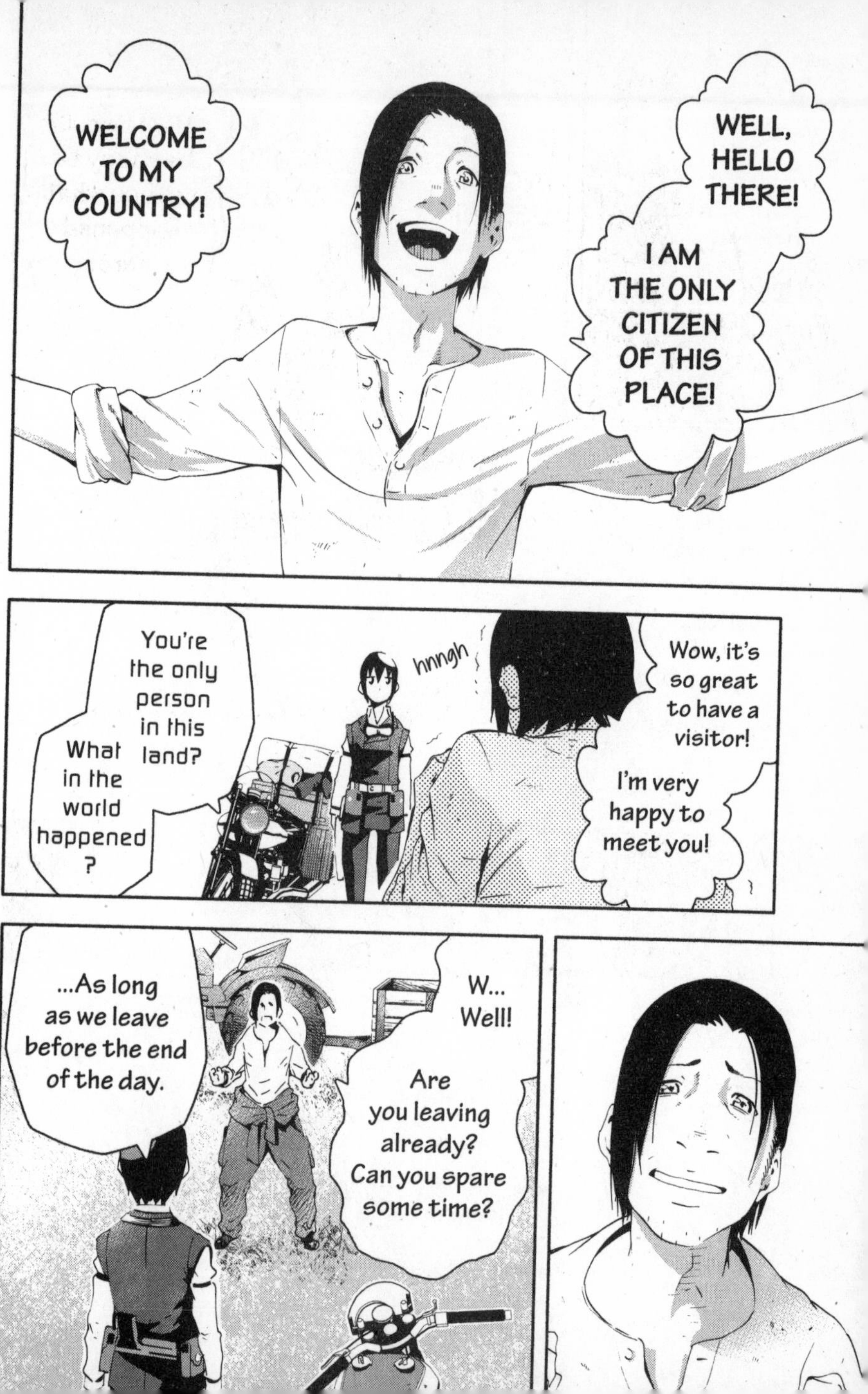
WELL, HELLO THERE!
I AM THE ONLY CITIZEN OF THIS PLACE!
WELCOME TO MY COUNTRY!
Wow, it's so great to have a visitor!
I'm very happy to meet you!
hnngh
You're the only person in this land?
What in the world happened?
W... Well!
Are you leaving already? Can you spare some time?
...As long as we leave before the end of the day.

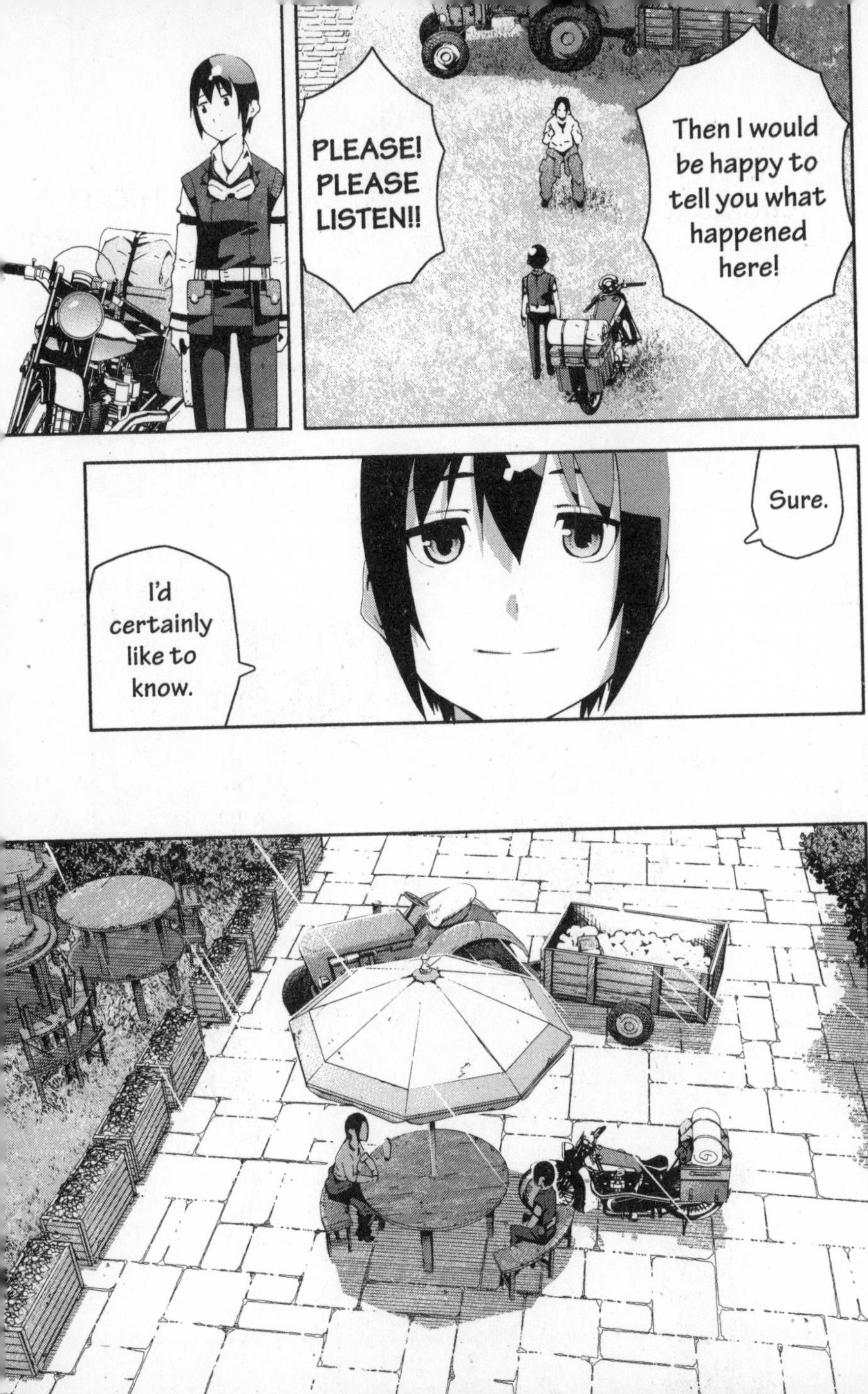
Then I would be happy to tell you what happened here!
PLEASE! PLEASE LISTEN!!
Sure.
I'd certainly like to know.

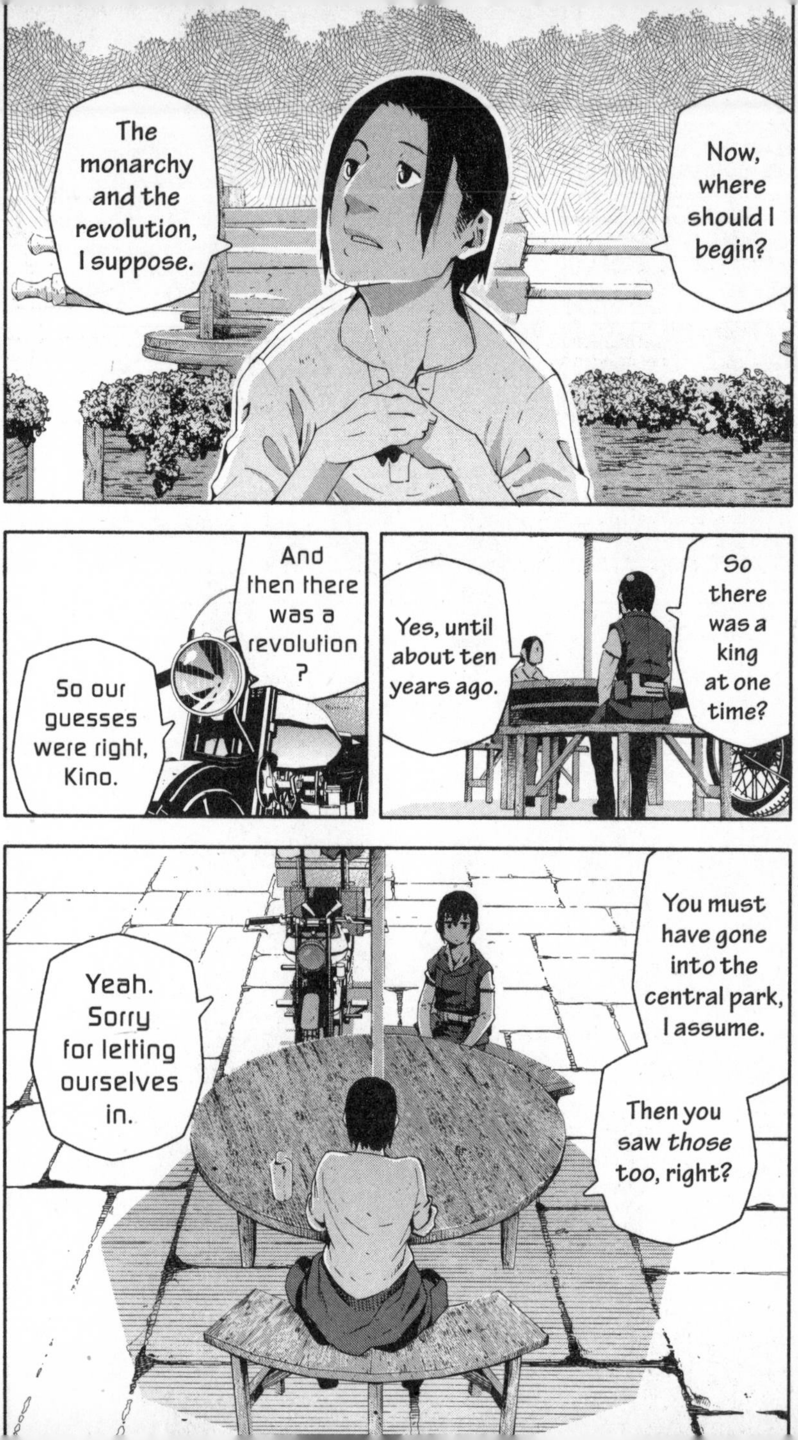
Now, where should I begin?
The monarchy and the revolution, I suppose.
So there was a king at one time?
Yes, until about ten years ago.
And then there was a revolution?
So our guesses were right, Kino.
You must have gone into the central park, I assume.
Yeah. Sorry for letting ourselves in.
Then you saw *those* too, right?

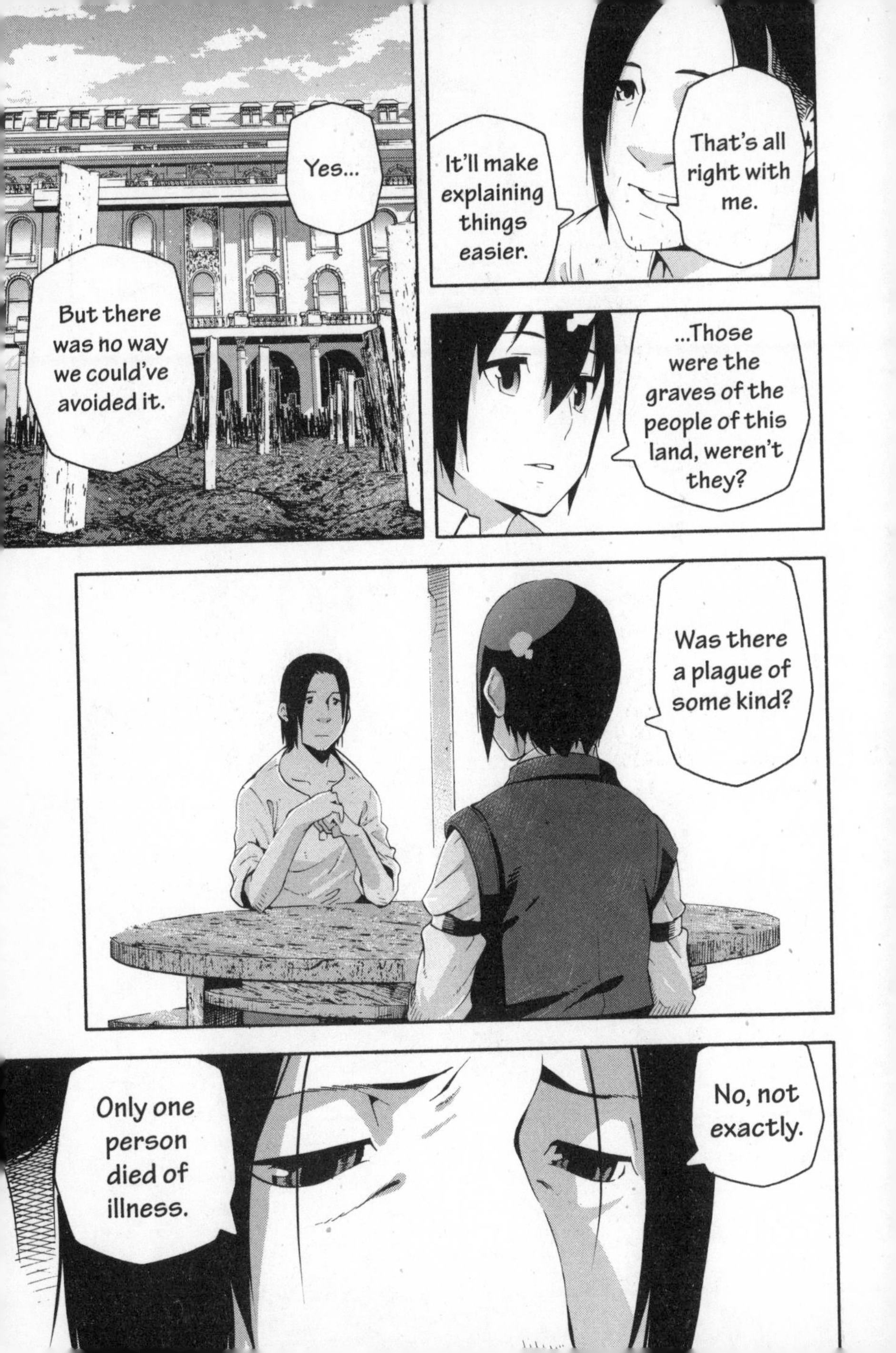
That's all right with me.
It'll make explaining things easier.
...Those were the graves of the people of this land, weren't they?
Yes...
But there was no way we could've avoided it.
Was there a plague of some kind?
No, not exactly.
Only one person died of illness.

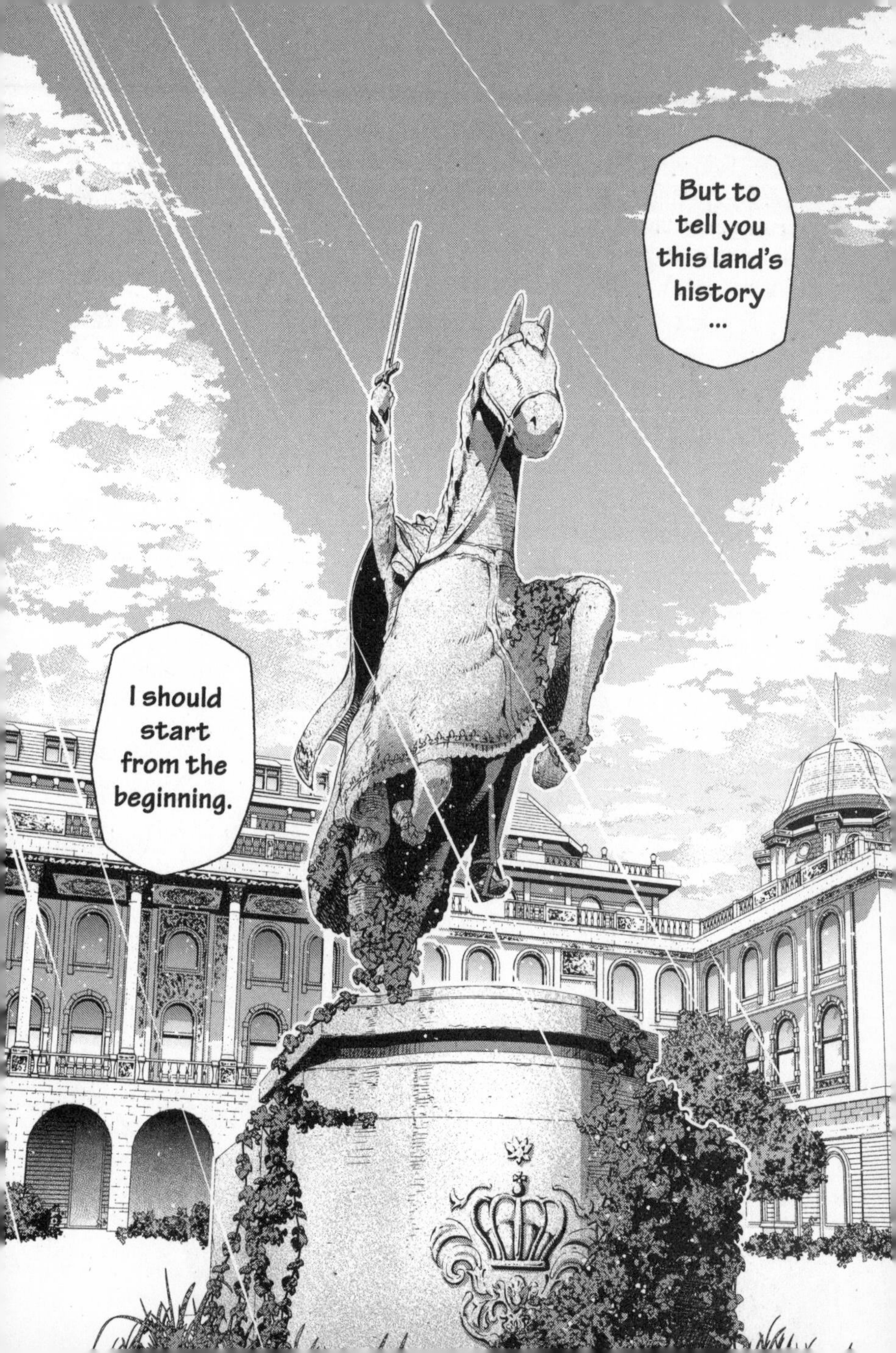
But to tell you this land's history ...
I should start from the beginning.

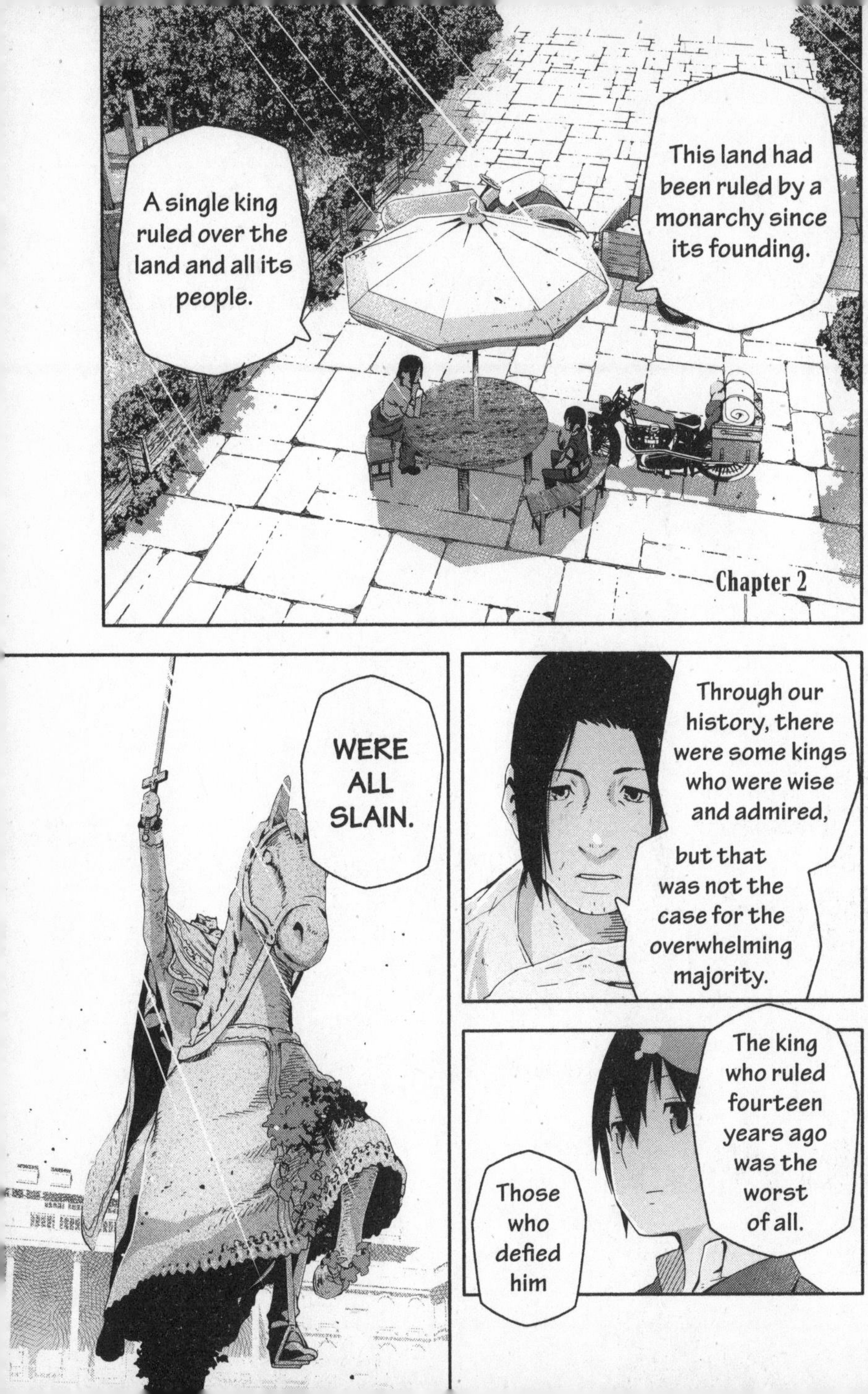
This land had been ruled by a monarchy since its founding.
A single king ruled over the land and all its people.
Chapter 2
Through our history, there were some kings who were wise and admired,
but that was not the case for the overwhelming majority.
The king who ruled fourteen years ago was the worst of all.
Those who defied him
WERE ALL SLAIN.

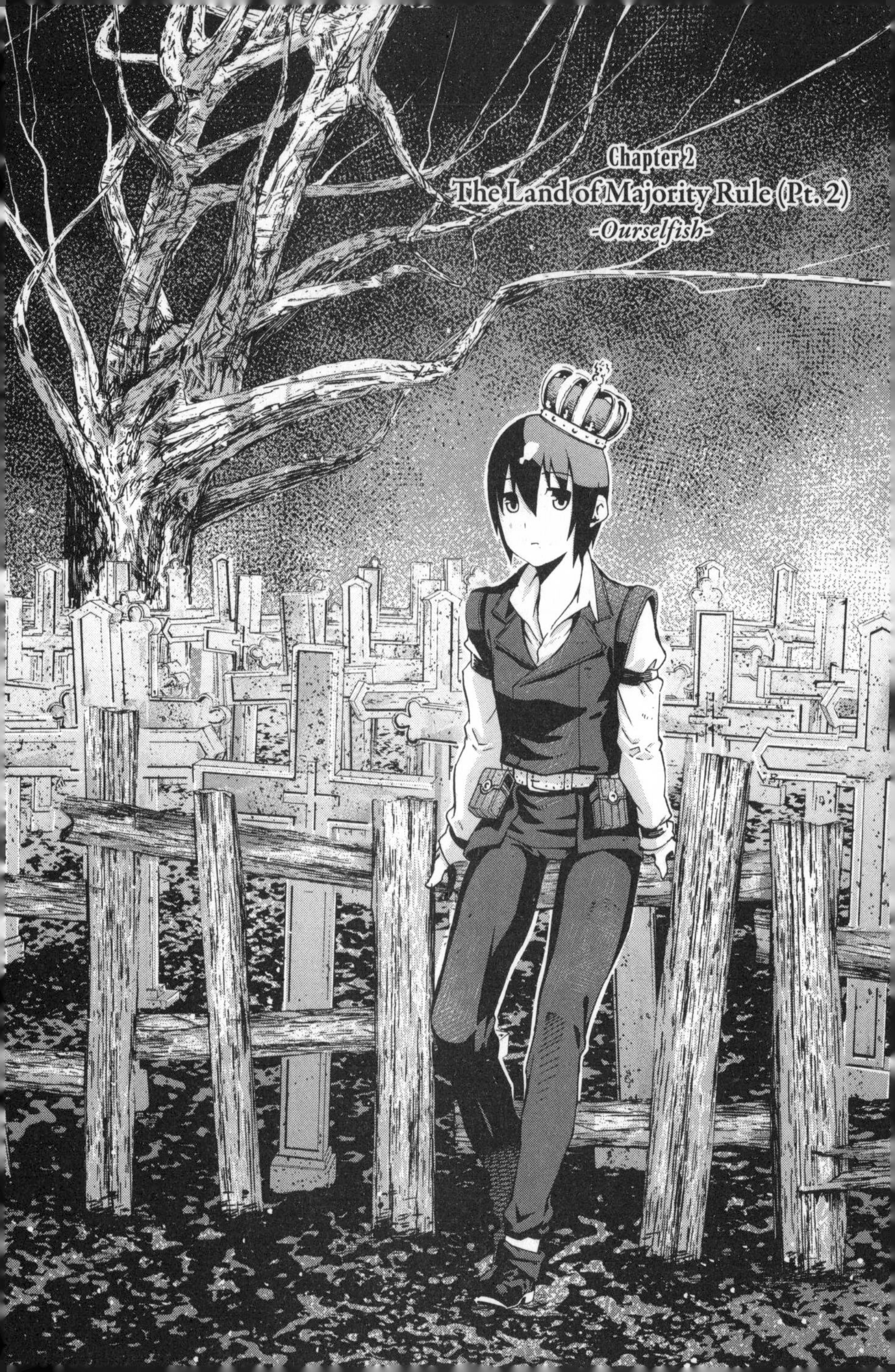
Chapter 2
The Land of Majority Rule (Pt. 2)
-Ourselfish-

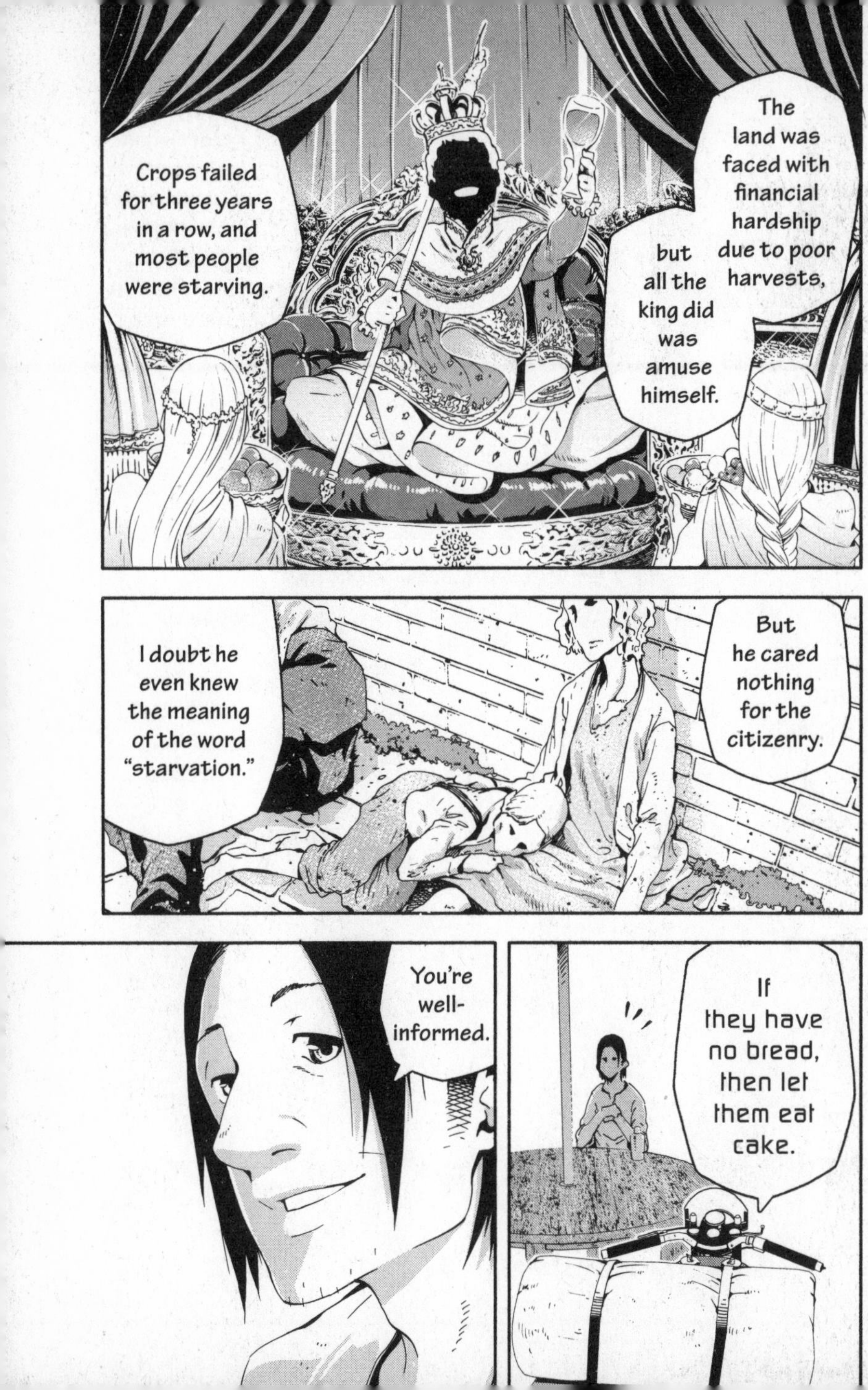
The land was faced with financial hardship due to poor harvests,
but all the king did was amuse himself.
Crops failed for three years in a row, and most people were starving.
But he cared nothing for the citizenry.
I doubt he even knew the meaning of the word "starvation."
If they have no bread, then let them eat cake.
You're well-informed.

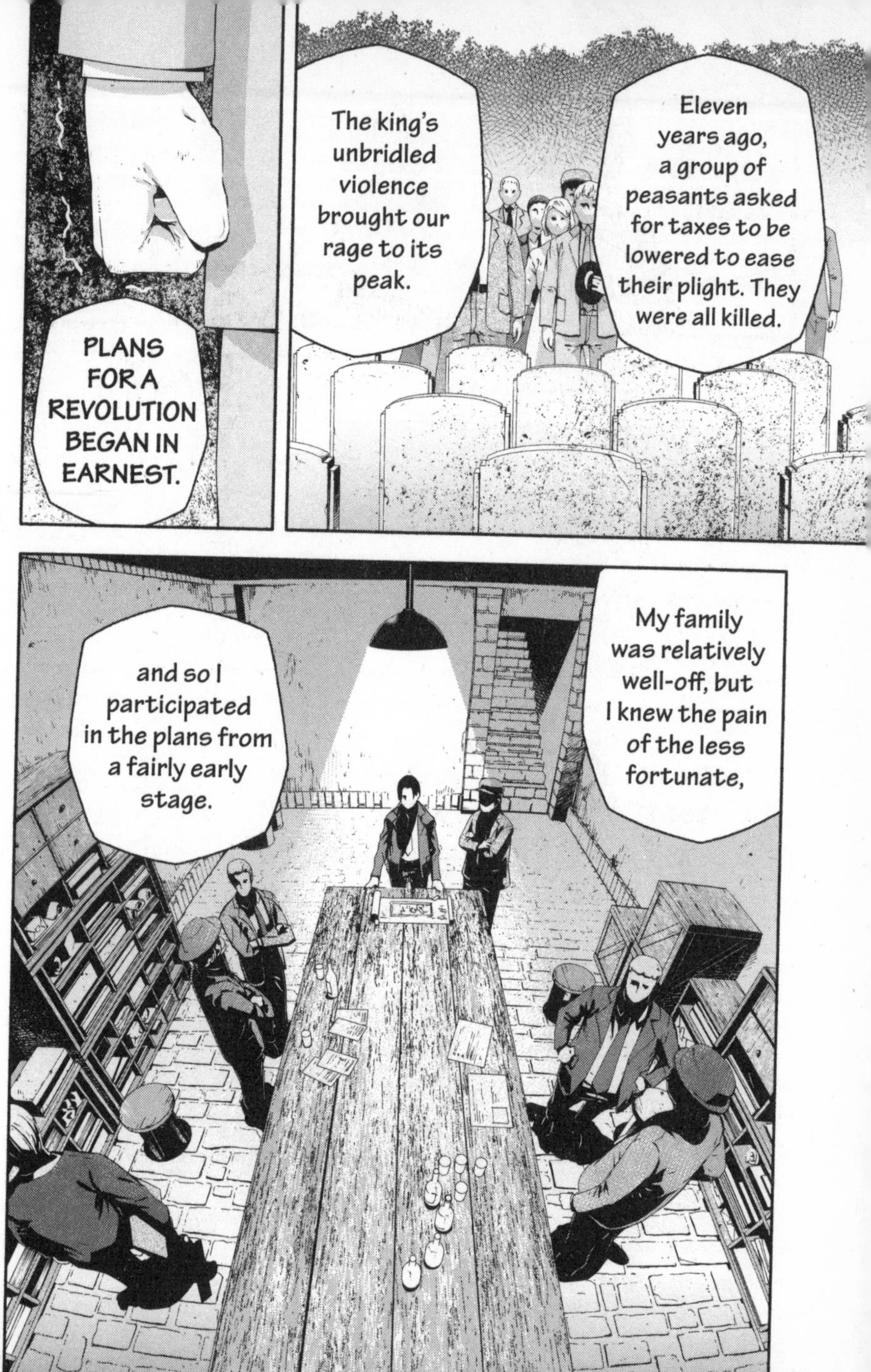
Eleven years ago, a group of peasants asked for taxes to be lowered to ease their plight. They were all killed.
The king's unbridled violence brought our rage to its peak.
PLANS FOR A REVOLUTION BEGAN IN EARNEST.
My family was relatively well-off, but I knew the pain of the less fortunate,
and so I participated in the plans from a fairly early stage.

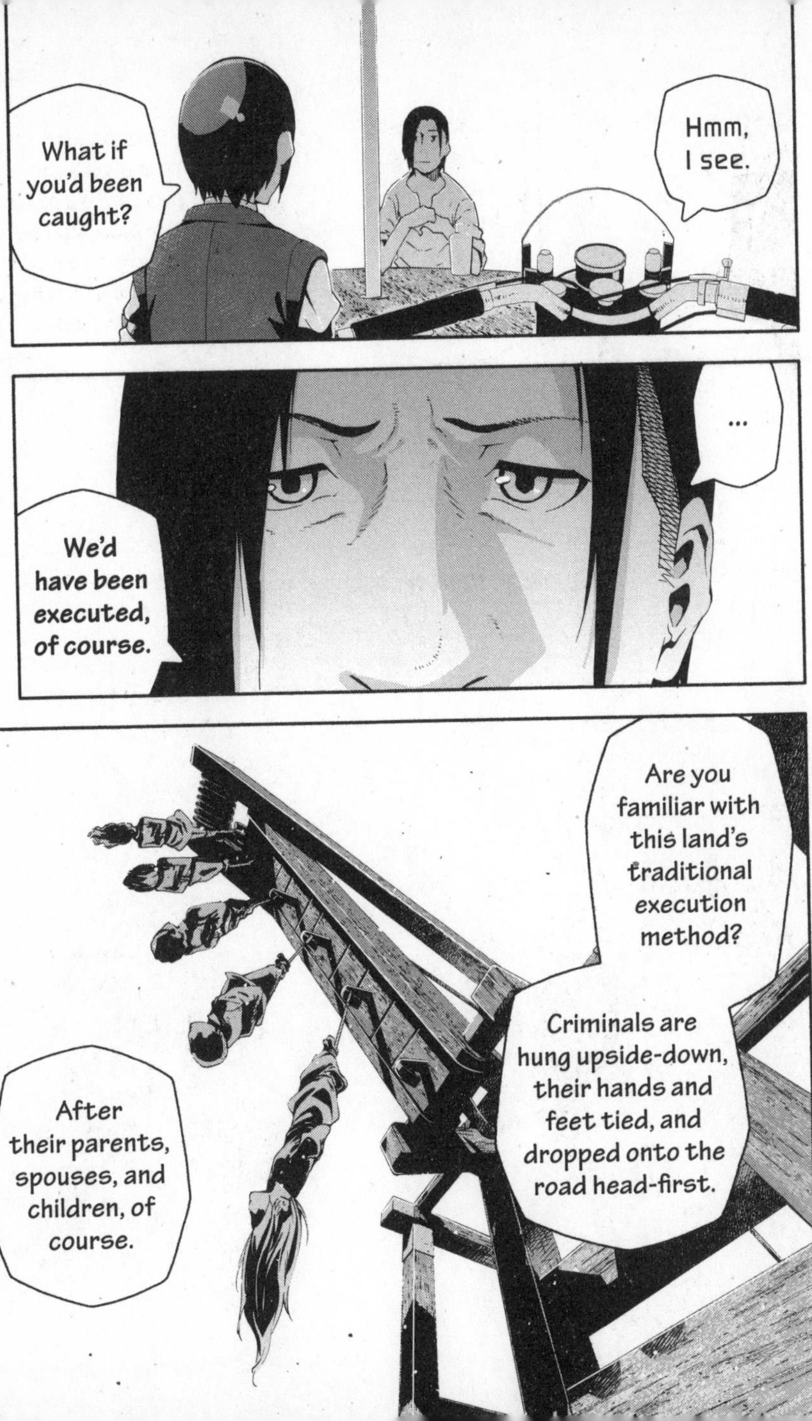
Hmm, I see.
What if you'd been caught?
...
We'd have been executed, of course.
Are you familiar with this land's traditional execution method?
Criminals are hung upside-down, their hands and feet tied, and dropped onto the road head-first.
After their parents, spouses, and children, of course.

I saw many of my comrades publically executed in this way.

KRUNCH

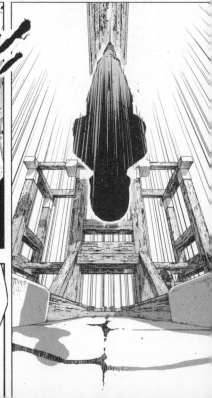

...

Many, many times...

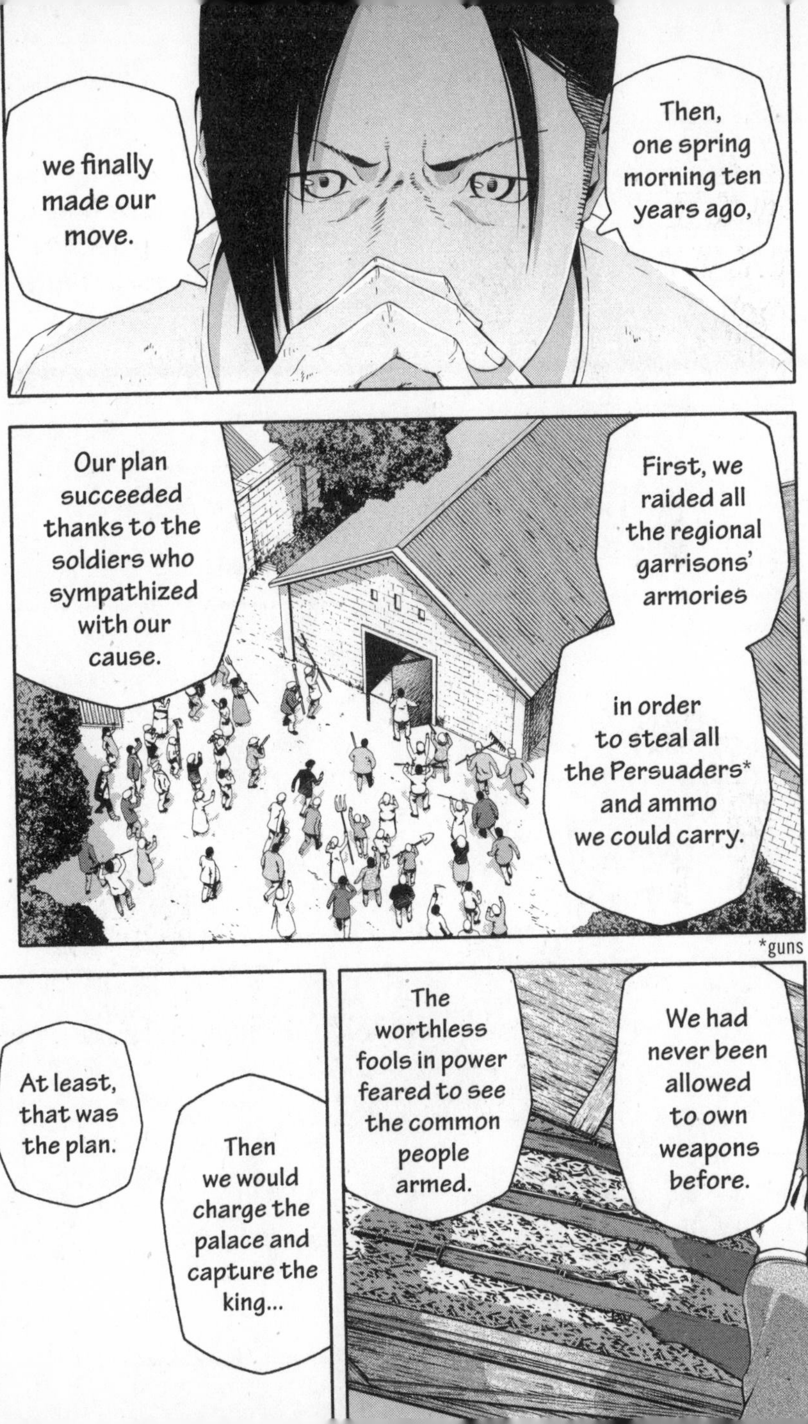
Then, one spring morning ten years ago,
we finally made our move.
First, we raided all the regional garrisons' armories
in order to steal all the Persuaders* and ammo we could carry.
Our plan succeeded thanks to the soldiers who sympathized with our cause.
We had never been allowed to own weapons before.
The worthless fools in power feared to see the common people armed.
Then we would charge the palace and capture the king...
At least, that was the plan.

*guns

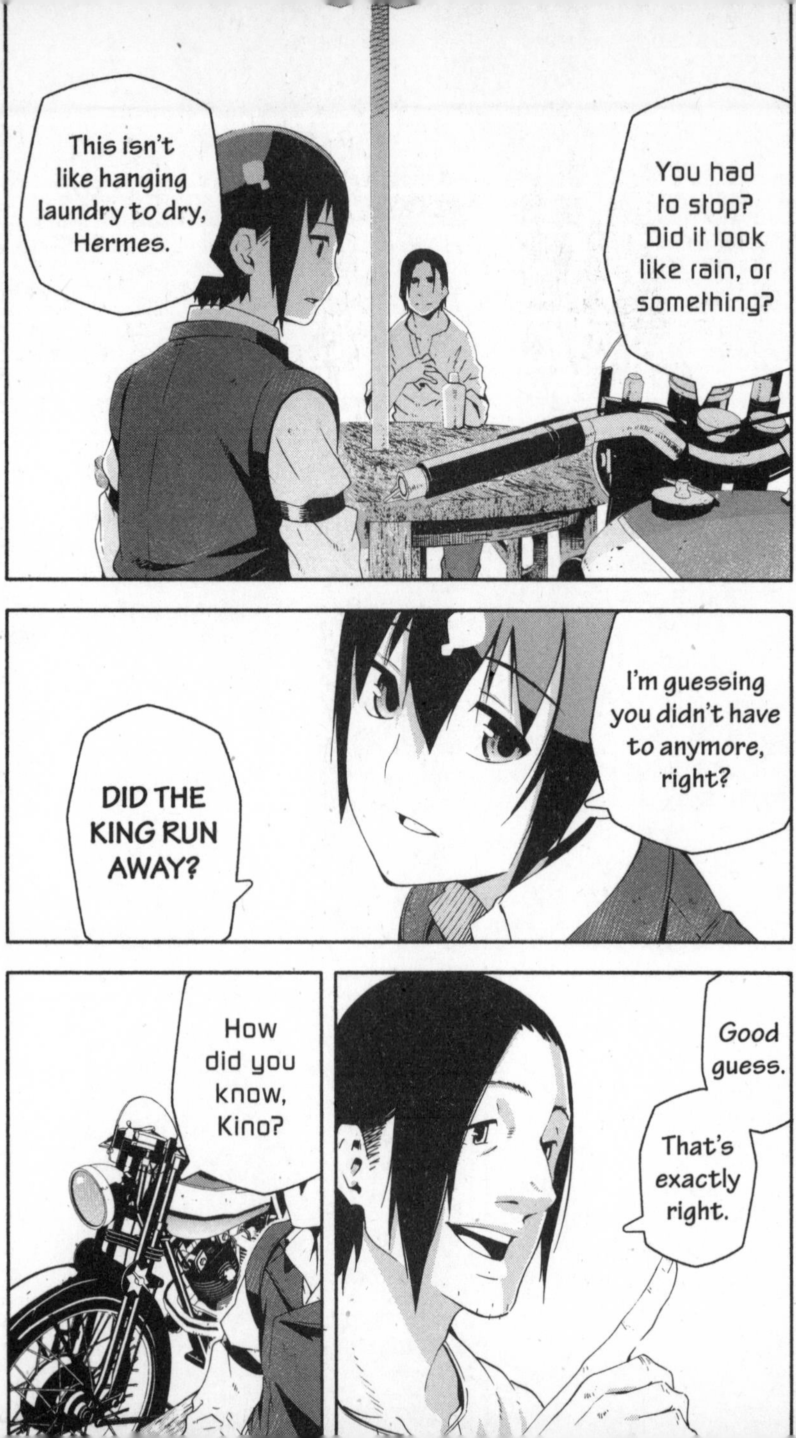
You had to stop? Did it look like rain, or something?
This isn't like hanging laundry to dry, Hermes.
I'm guessing you didn't have to anymore, right?
DID THE KING RUN AWAY?
Good guess.
That's exactly right.
How did you know, Kino?

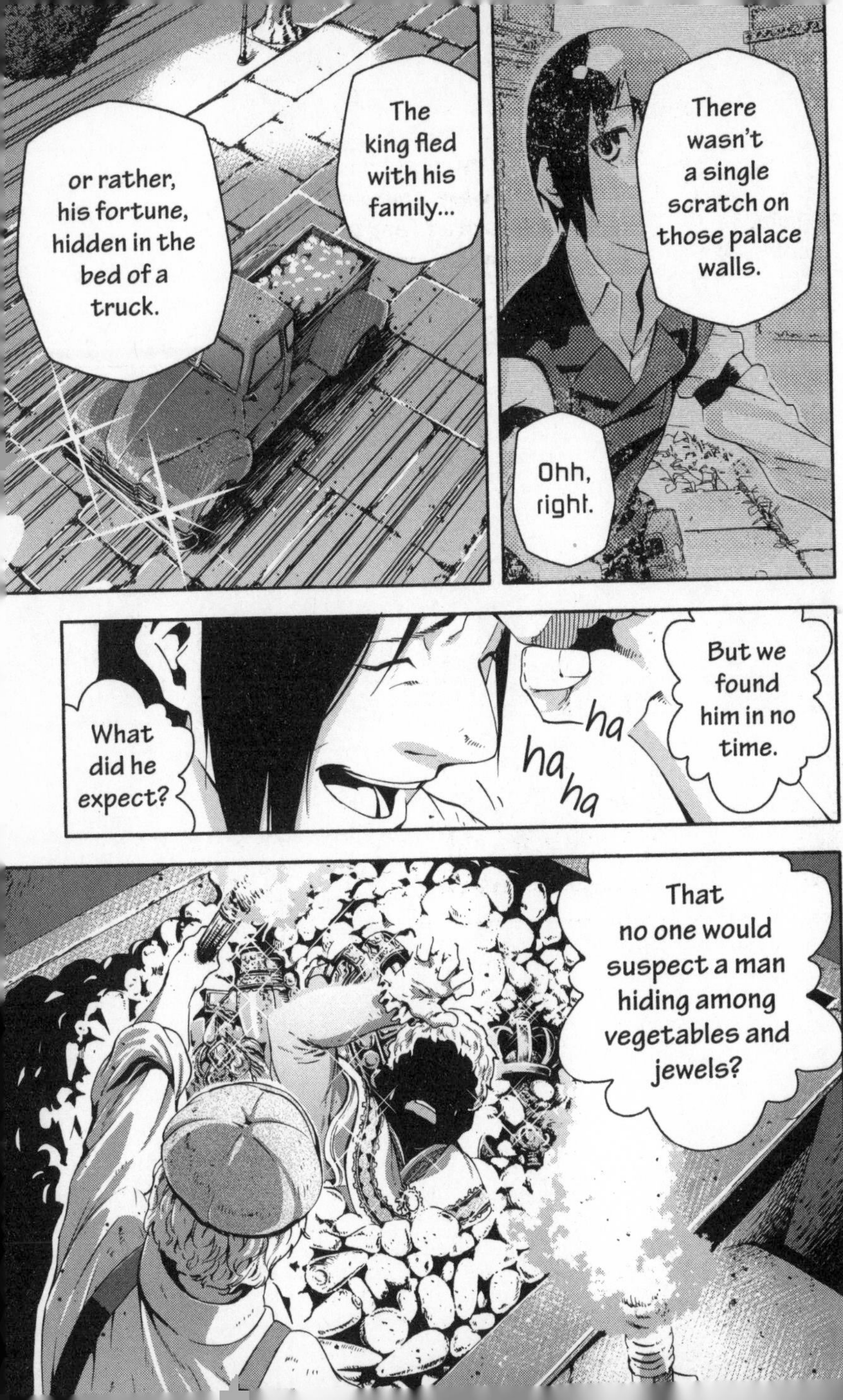
There wasn't a single scratch on those palace walls.
Ohh, right.
The king fled with his family...
or rather, his fortune, hidden in the bed of a truck.
But we found him in no time.
ha ha ha
What did he expect?
That no one would suspect a man hiding among vegetables and jewels?

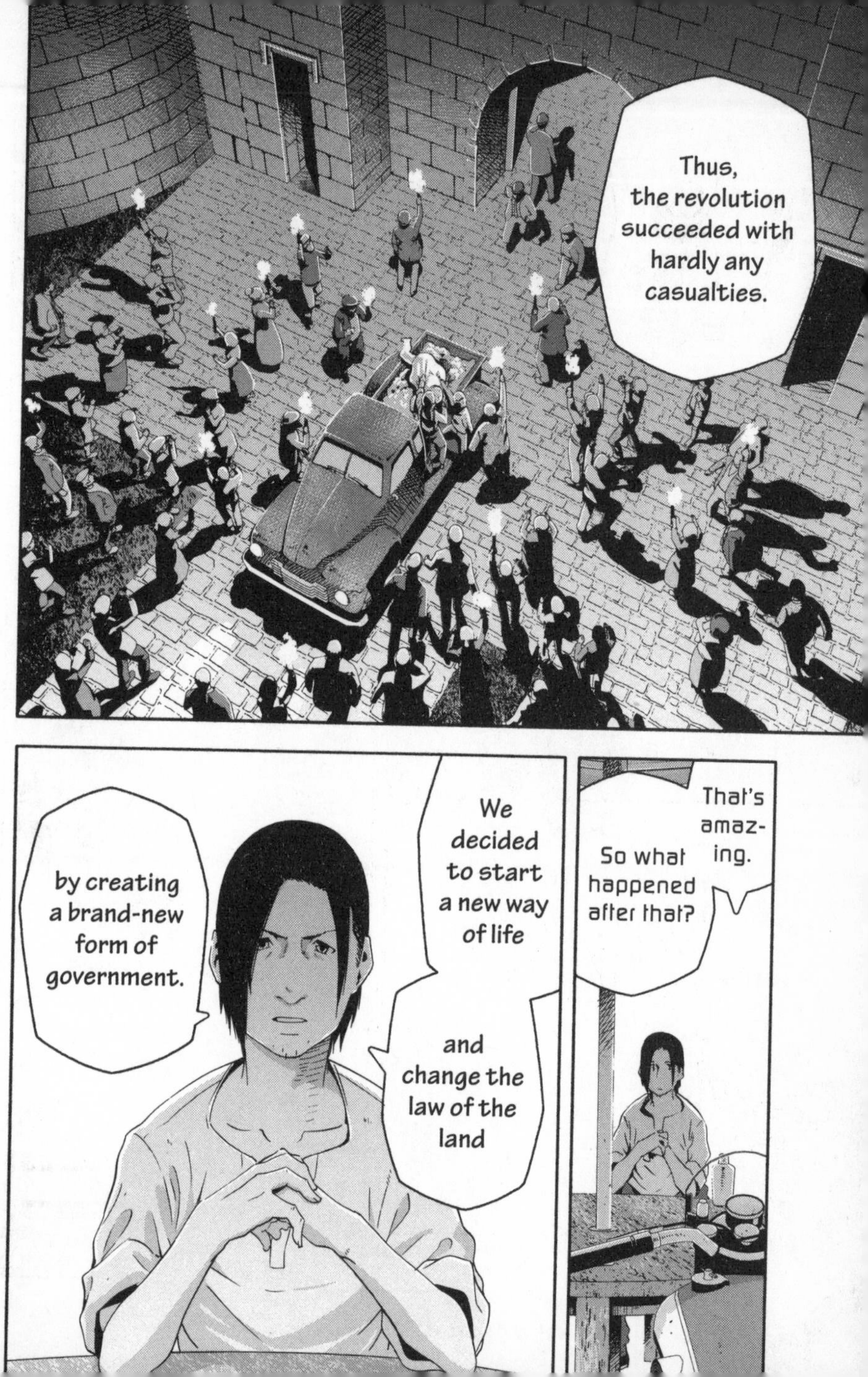
Thus, the revolution succeeded with hardly any casualties.
That's amaz-ing.
So what happened after that?
We decided to start a new way of life
and change the law of the land
by creating a brand-new form of government.

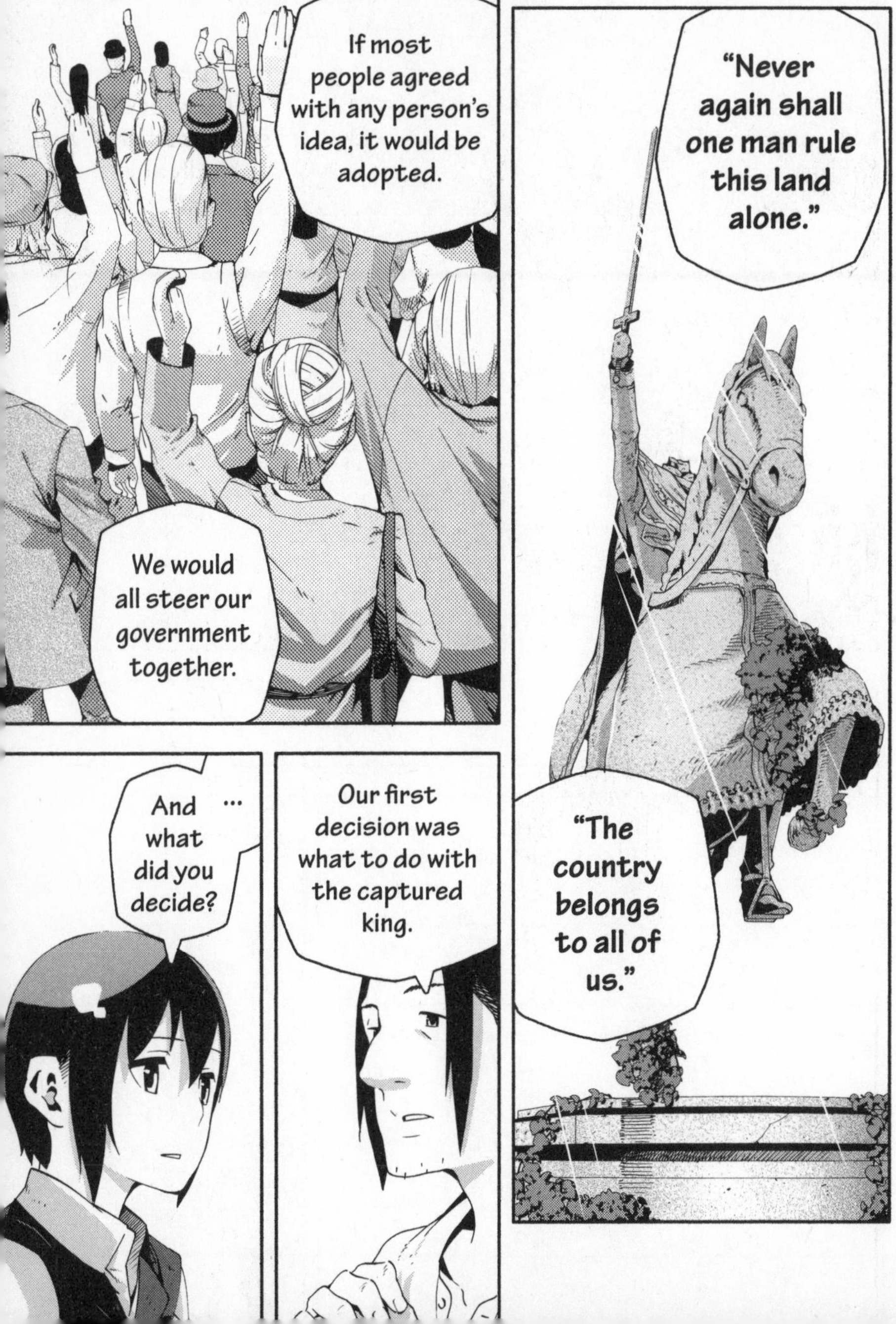
"Never again shall one man rule this land alone."
"The country belongs to all of us."
If most people agreed with any person's idea, it would be adopted.
We would all steer our government together.
Our first decision was what to do with the captured king.
And ... what did you decide?

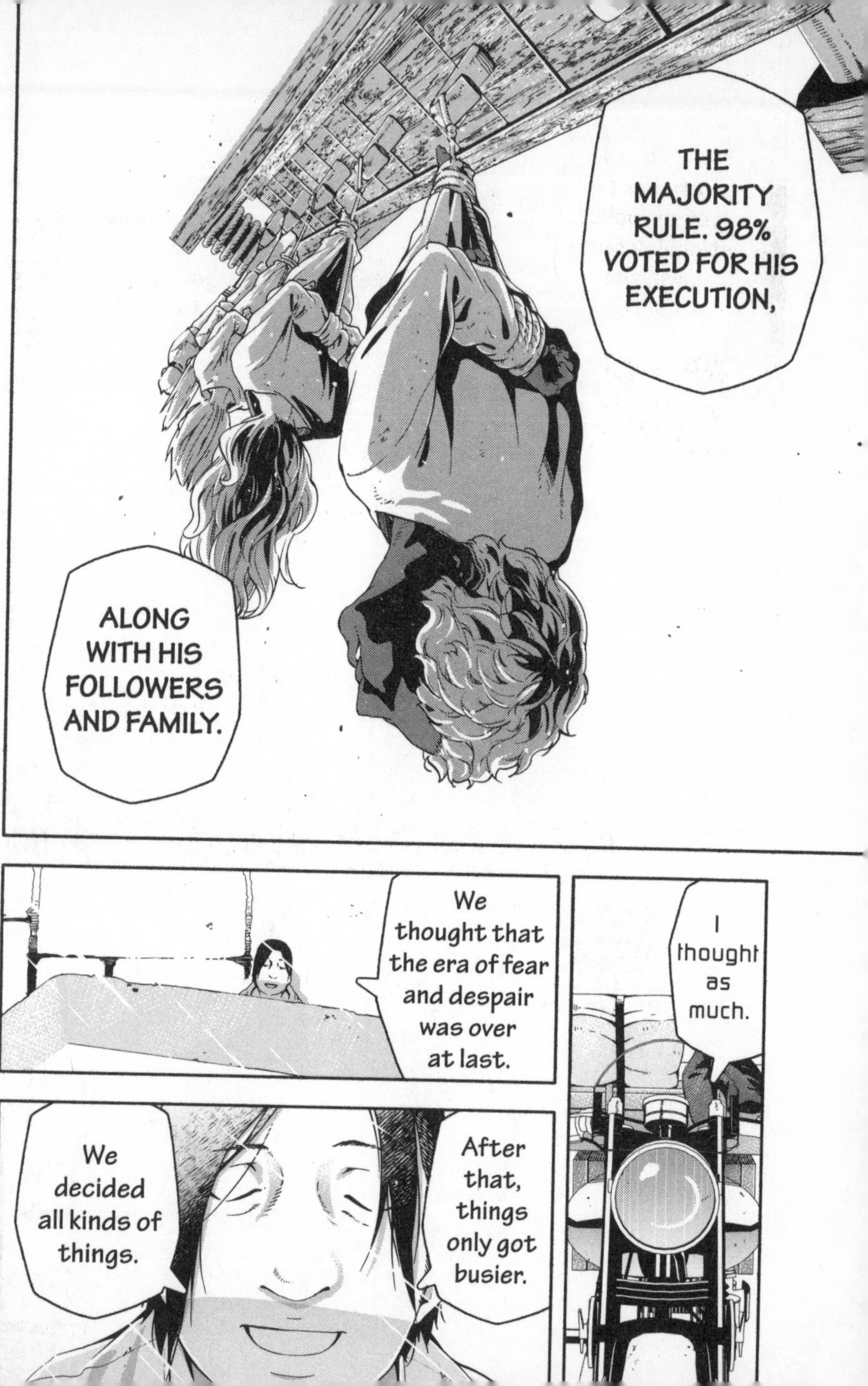
THE MAJORITY RULE. 98% VOTED FOR HIS EXECUTION,
ALONG WITH HIS FOLLOWERS AND FAMILY.
I thought as much.
We thought that the era of fear and despair was over at last.
After that, things only got busier.
We decided all kinds of things.

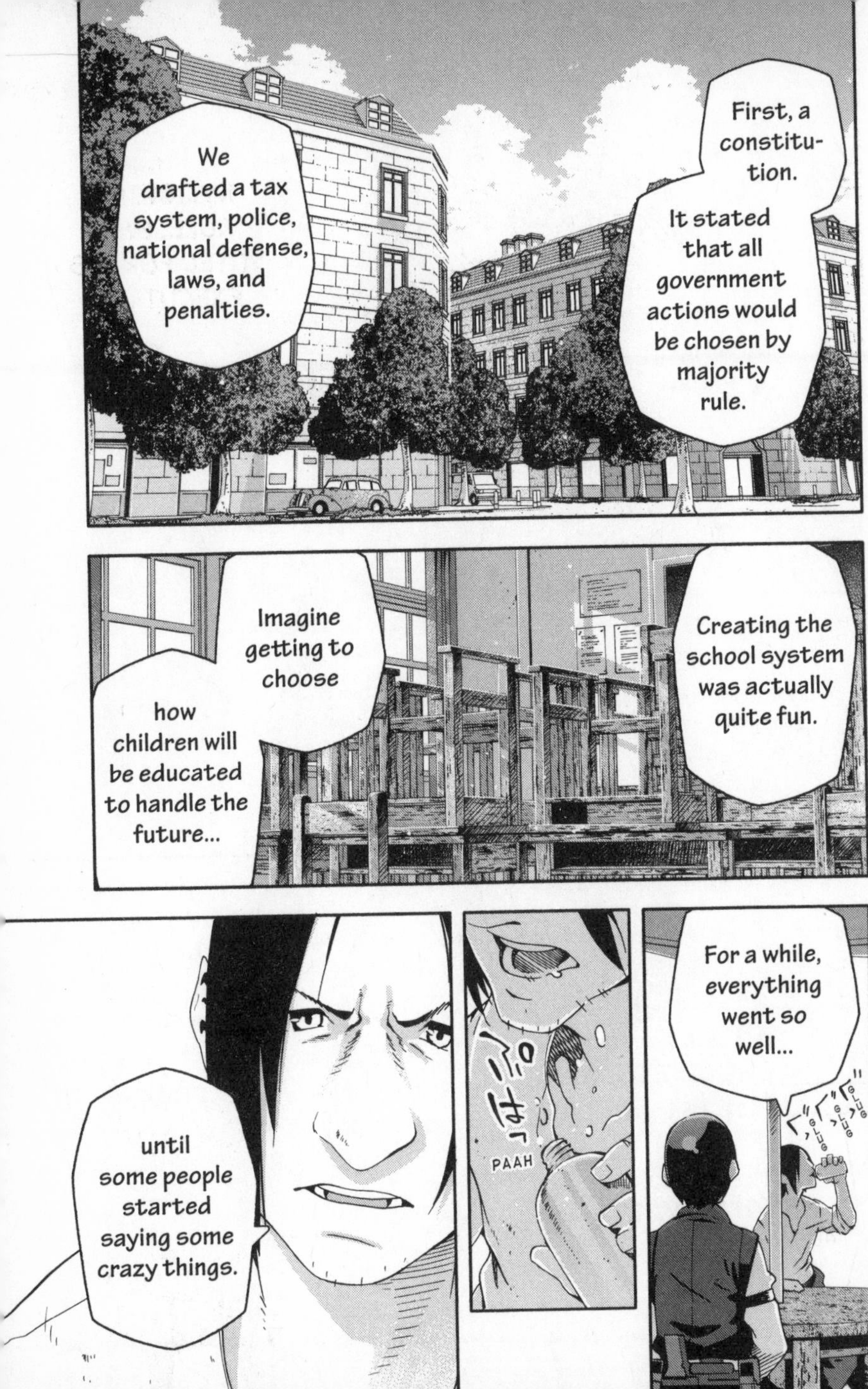
First, a constitution.
It stated that all government actions would be chosen by majority rule.
We drafted a tax system, police, national defense, laws, and penalties.
Creating the school system was actually quite fun.
Imagine getting to choose
how children will be educated to handle the future...
For a while, everything went so well...
GLUG GLUG GLUG
PAAH
until some people started saying some crazy things.

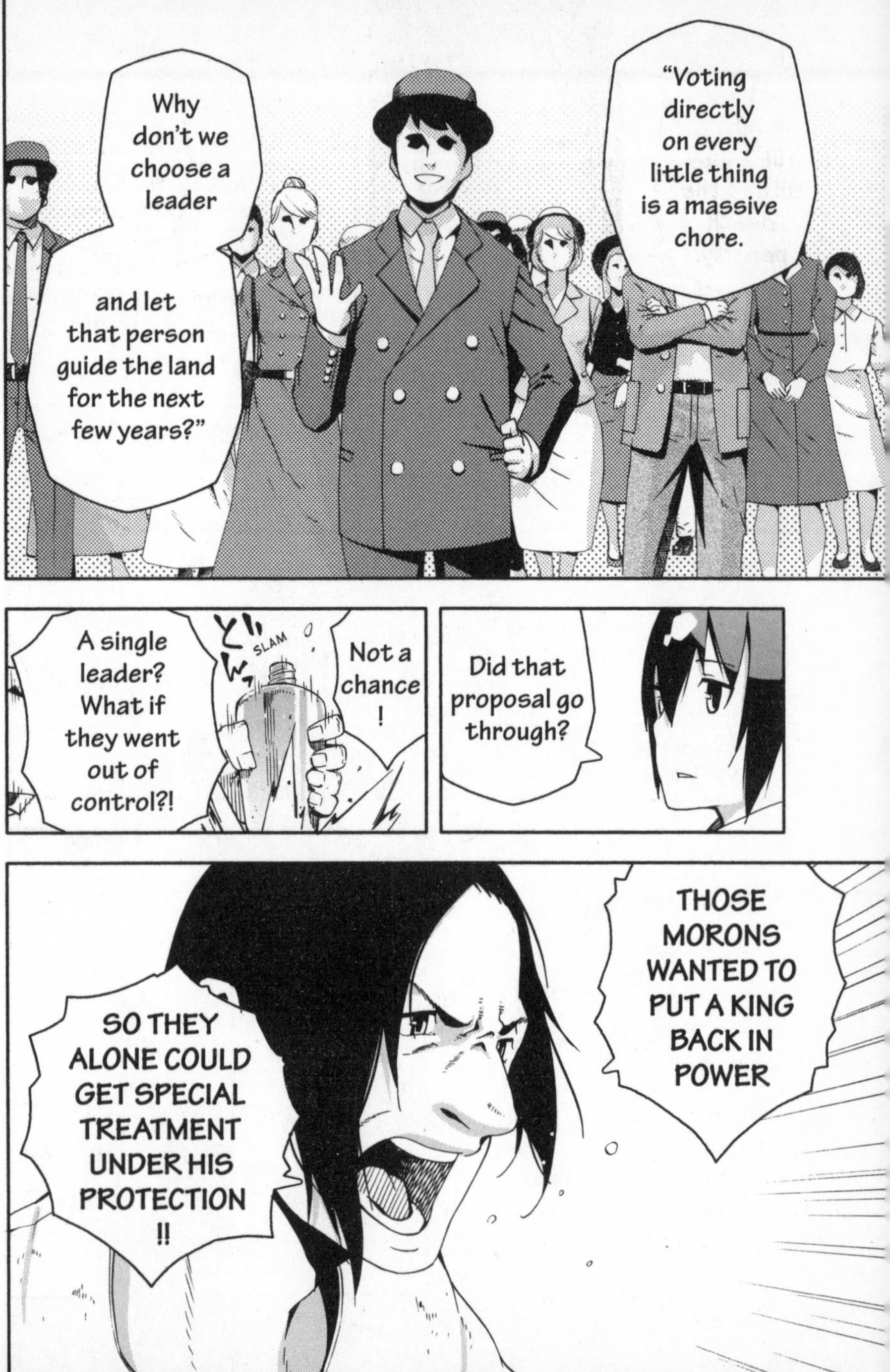
“Voting directly on every little thing is a massive chore.
Why don’t we choose a leader
and let that person guide the land for the next few years?”
Did that proposal go through?
Not a chance!
SLAM
A single leader? What if they went out of control?!
THOSE MORONS WANTED TO PUT A KING BACK IN POWER
SO THEY ALONE COULD GET SPECIAL TREATMENT UNDER HIS PROTECTION!!

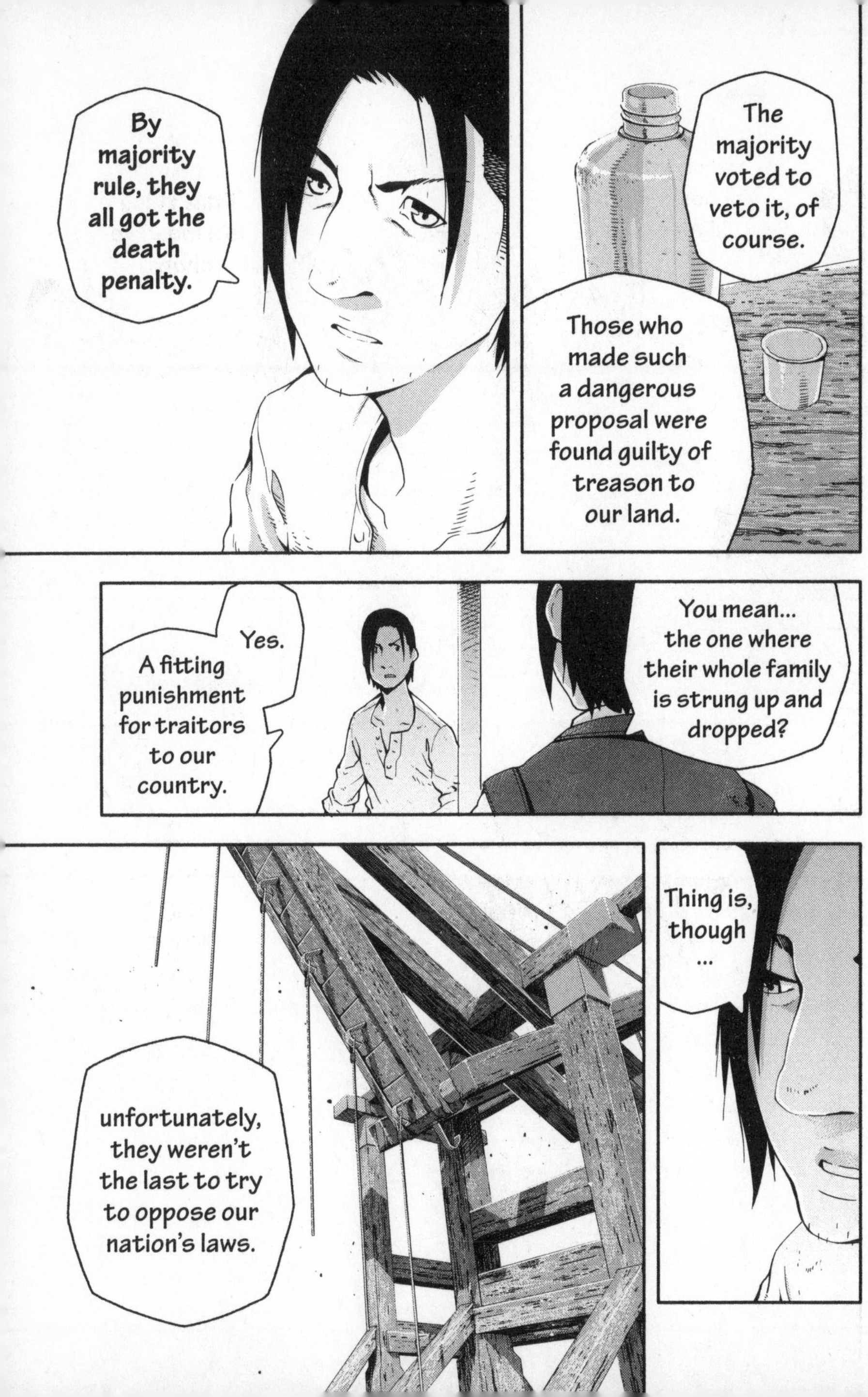
The majority voted to veto it, of course.
Those who made such a dangerous proposal were found guilty of treason to our land.
By majority rule, they all got the death penalty.
You mean... the one where their whole family is strung up and dropped?
Yes.
A fitting punishment for traitors to our country.
Thing is, though ...
unfortunately, they weren't the last to try to oppose our nation's laws.

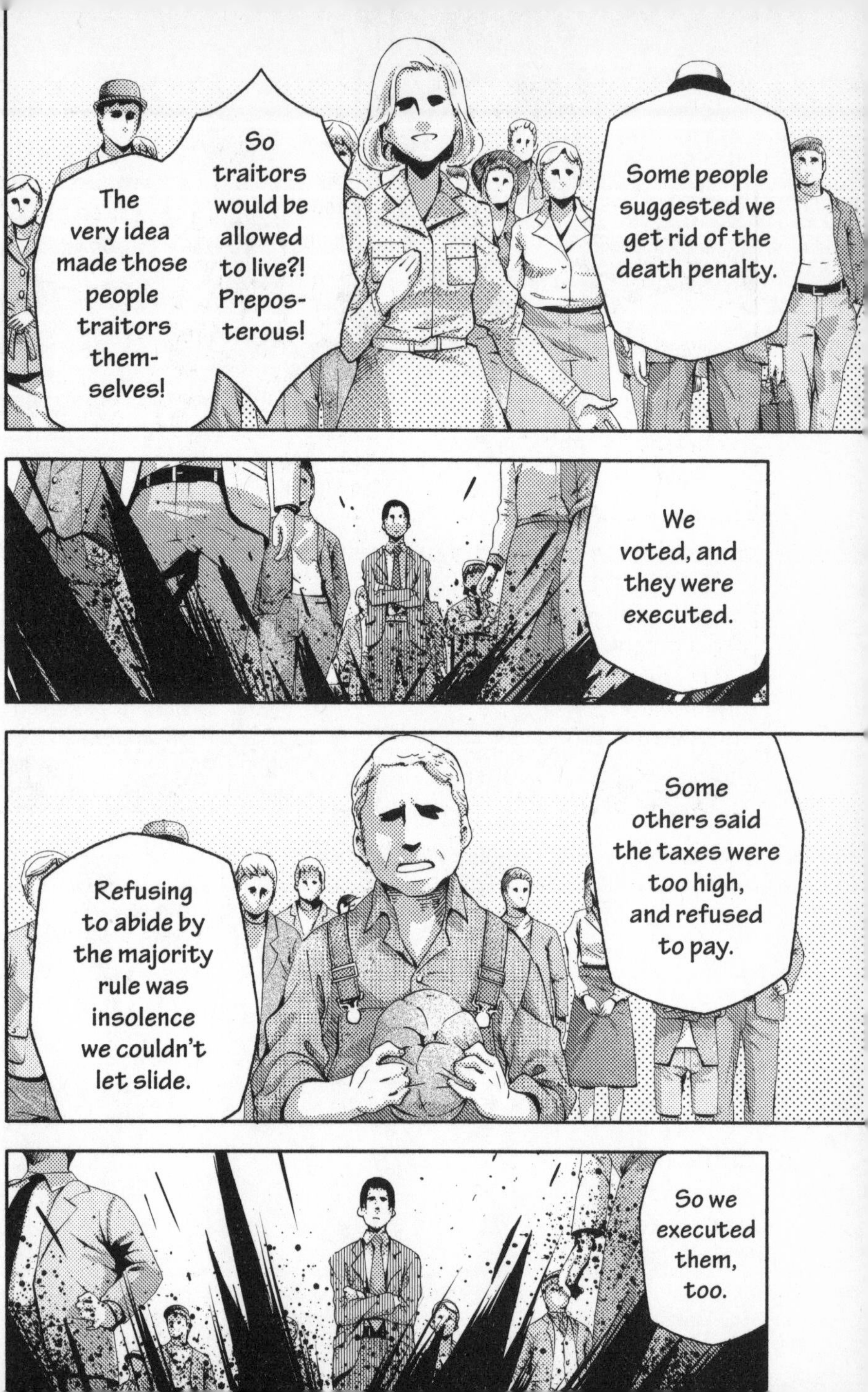
Some people suggested we get rid of the death penalty.
So traitors would be allowed to live?! Prepos-terous!
The very idea made those people traitors them-selves!
We voted, and they were executed.
Some others said the taxes were too high, and refused to pay.
Refusing to abide by the majority rule was insolence we couldn't let slide.
So we executed them, too.

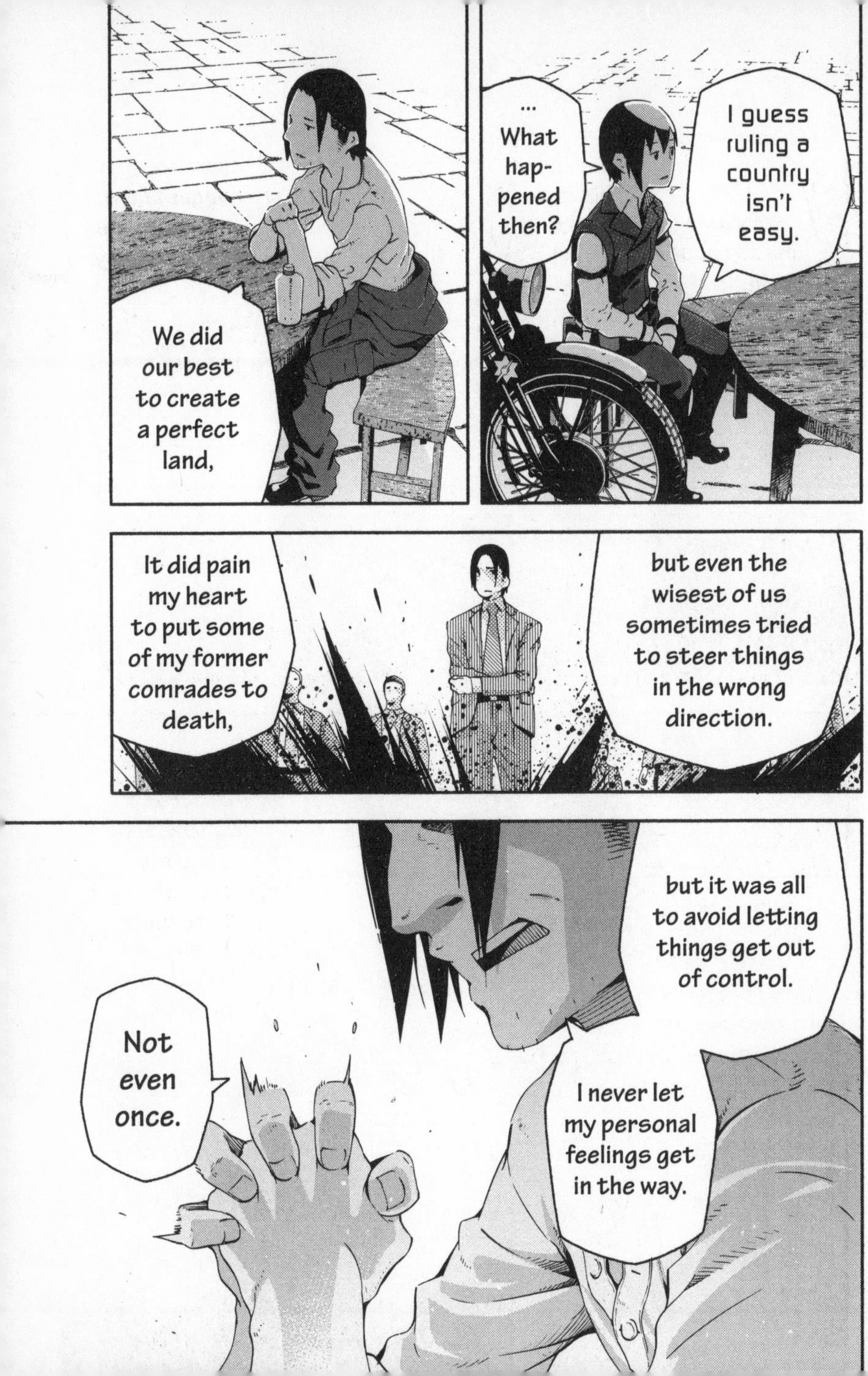
I guess ruling a country isn't easy.
... What hap-pened then?
We did our best to create a perfect land,
but even the wisest of us sometimes tried to steer things in the wrong direction.
It did pain my heart to put some of my former comrades to death,
but it was all to avoid letting things get out of control.
I never let my personal feelings get in the way.
Not even once.

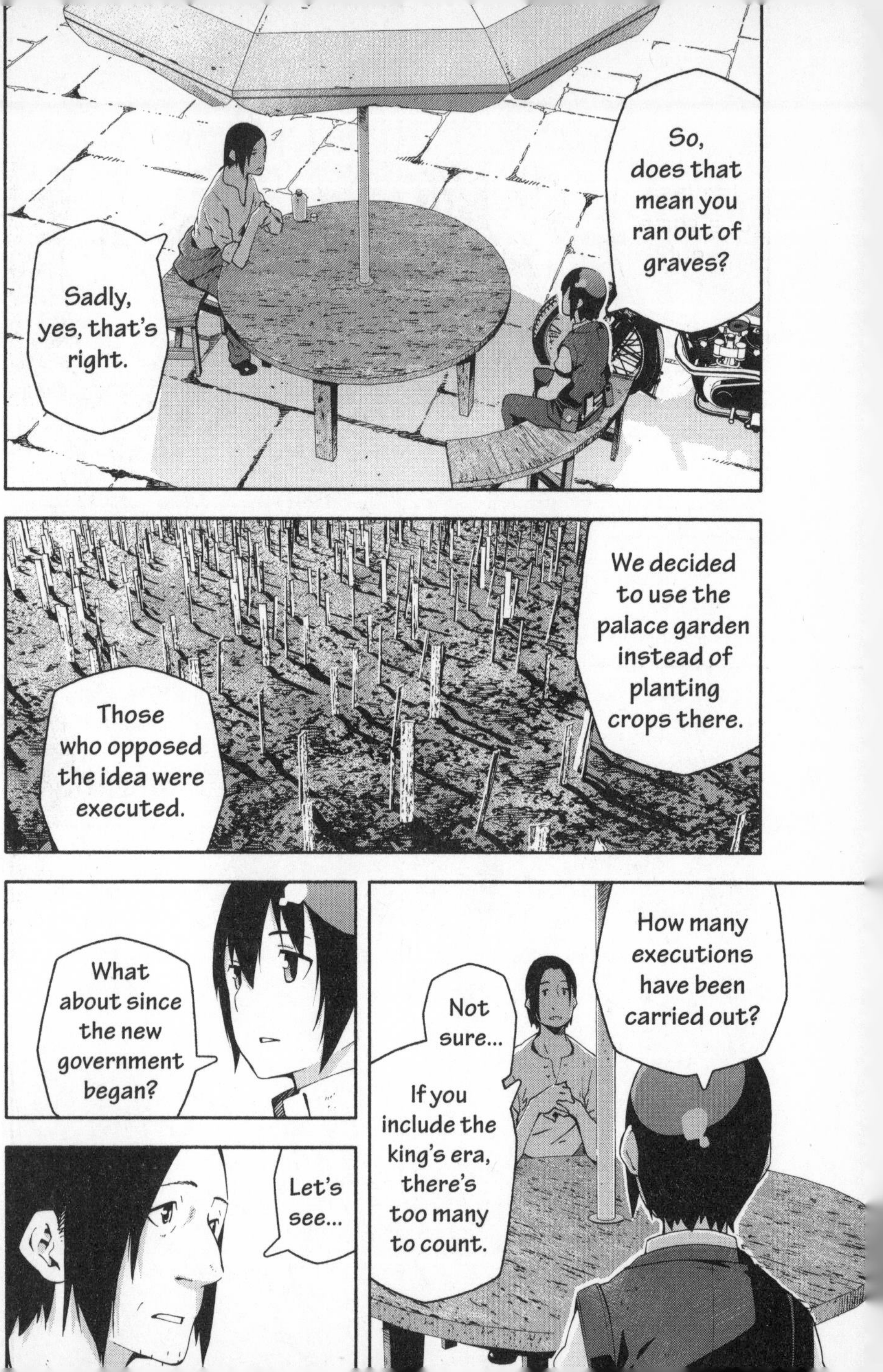
So, does that mean you ran out of graves?
Sadly, yes, that's right.
We decided to use the palace garden instead of planting crops there.
Those who opposed the idea were executed.
How many executions have been carried out?
Not sure...
If you include the king's era, there's too many to count.
What about since the new government began?
Let's see...

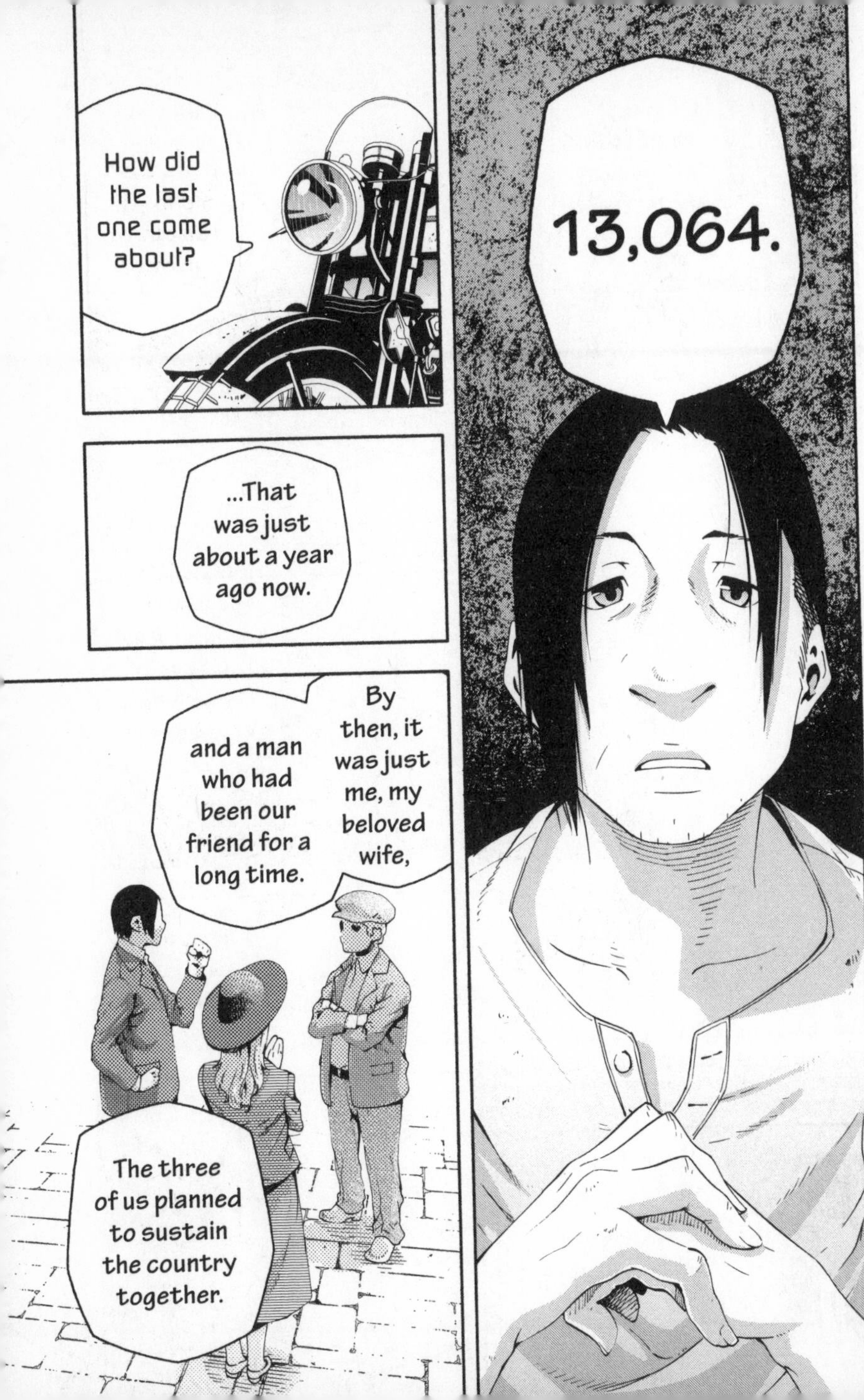
13,064.
How did the last one come about?
...That was just about a year ago now.
By then, it was just me, my beloved wife,
and a man who had been our friend for a long time.
The three of us planned to sustain the country together.

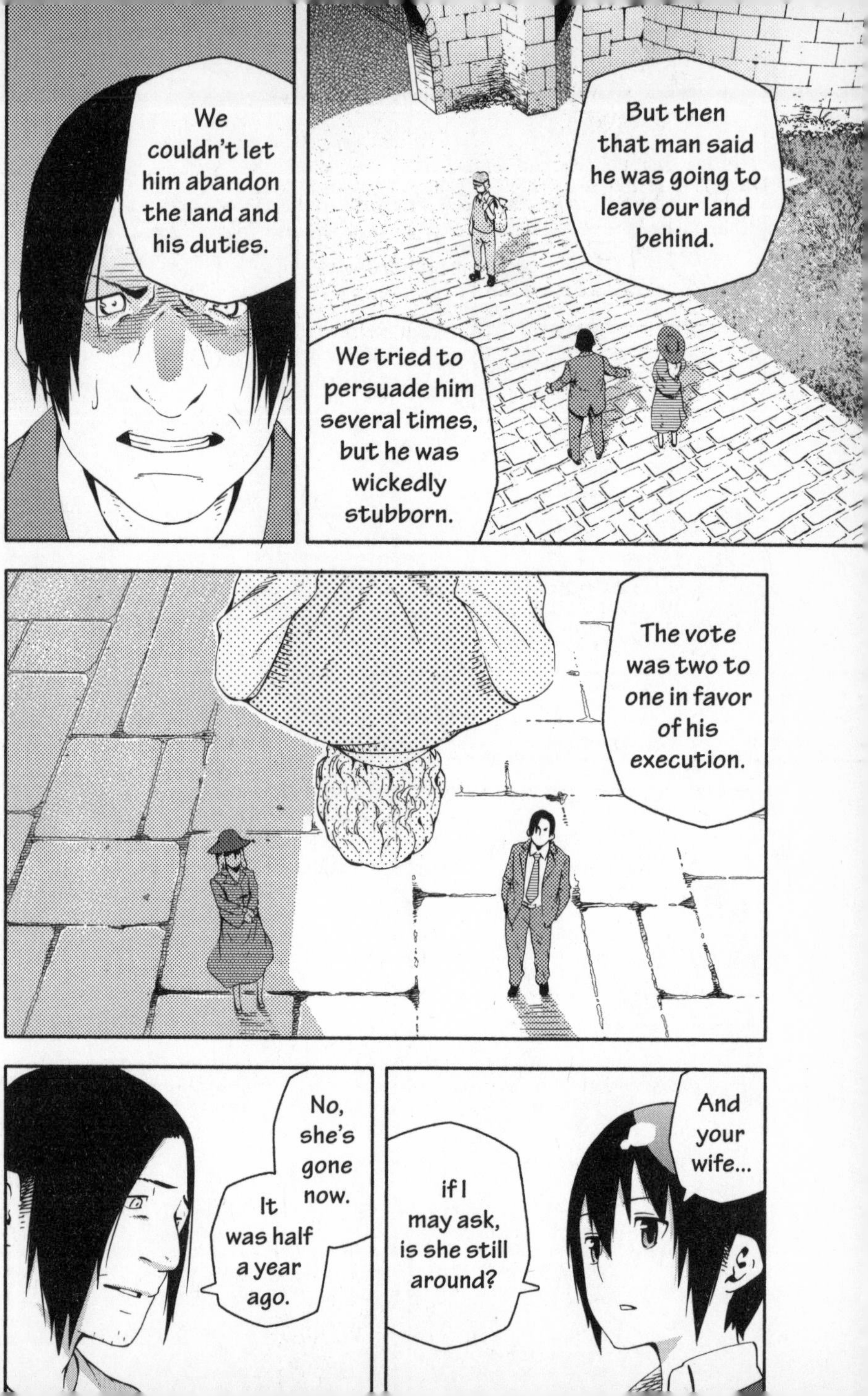
But then that man said he was going to leave our land behind.
We tried to persuade him several times, but he was wickedly stubborn.
We couldn't let him abandon the land and his duties.
The vote was two to one in favor of his execution.
And your wife...
if I may ask, is she still around?
No, she's gone now.
It was half a year ago.

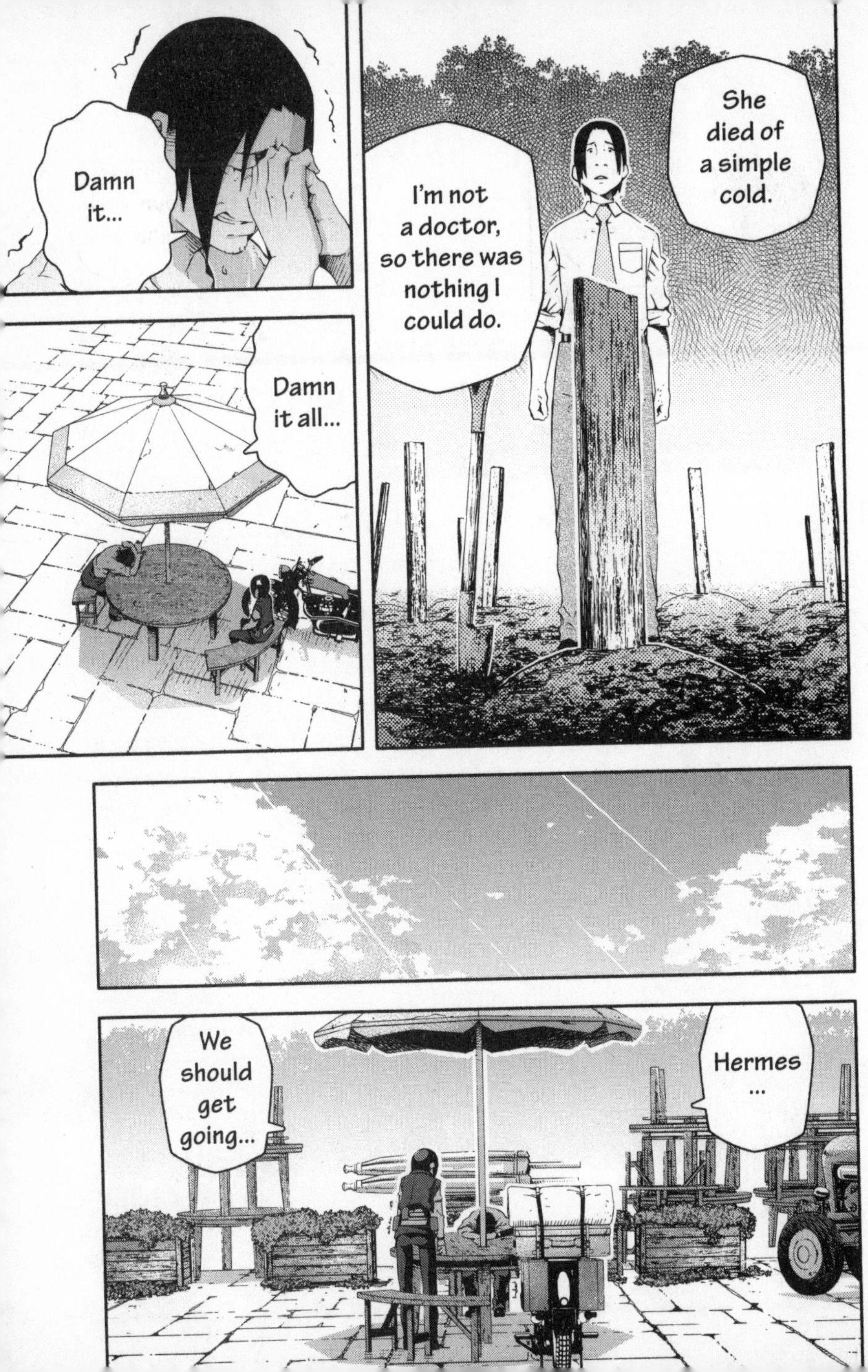
She died of a simple cold.
I'm not a doctor, so there was nothing I could do.
Damn it...
Damn it all...
Hermes ...
We should get going...

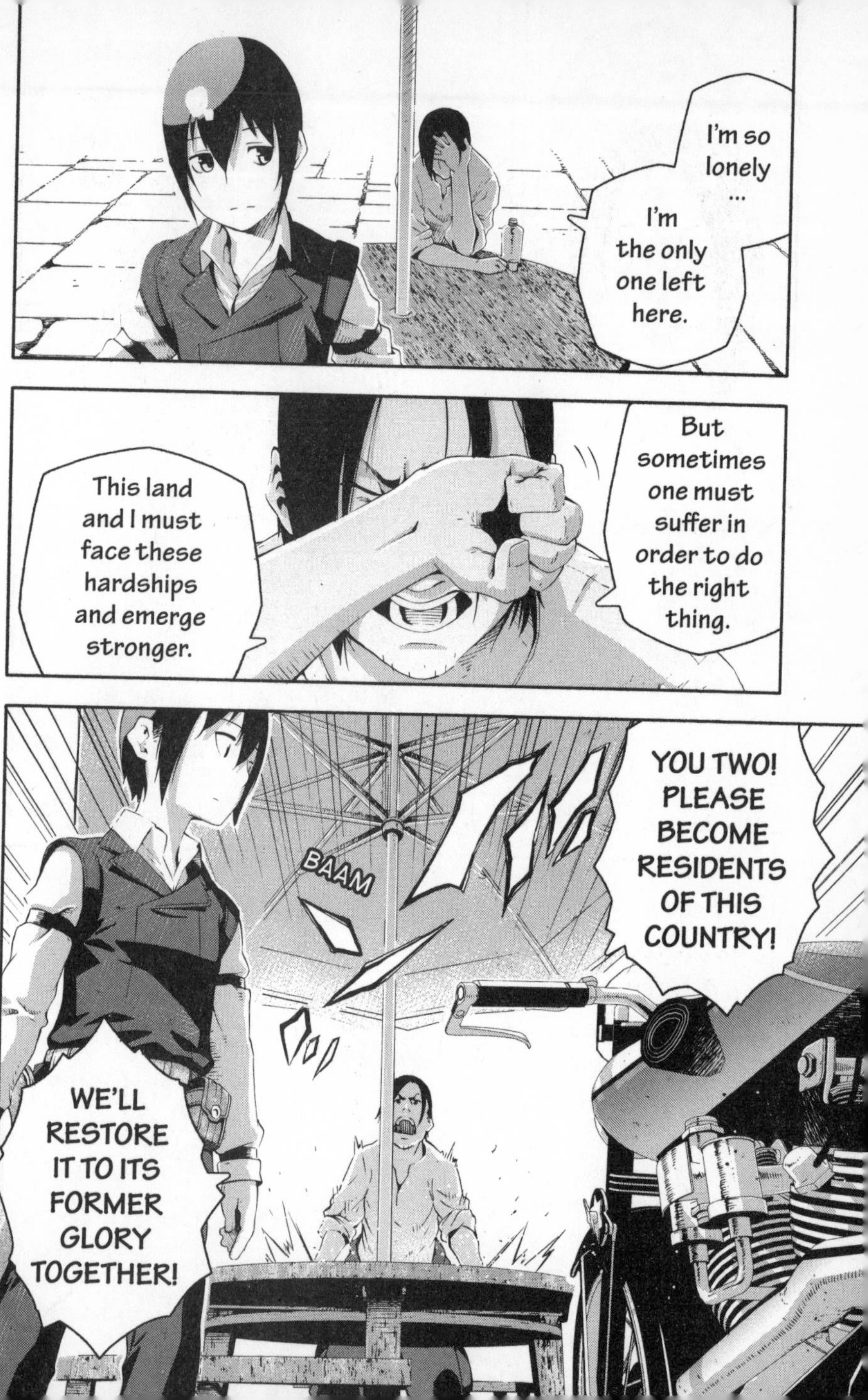
I'm so lonely ...
I'm the only one left here.
But sometimes one must suffer in order to do the right thing.
This land and I must face these hardships and emerge stronger.
YOU TWO! PLEASE BECOME RESIDENTS OF THIS COUNTRY!
BAAM
WE'LL RESTORE IT TO ITS FORMER GLORY TOGETHER!

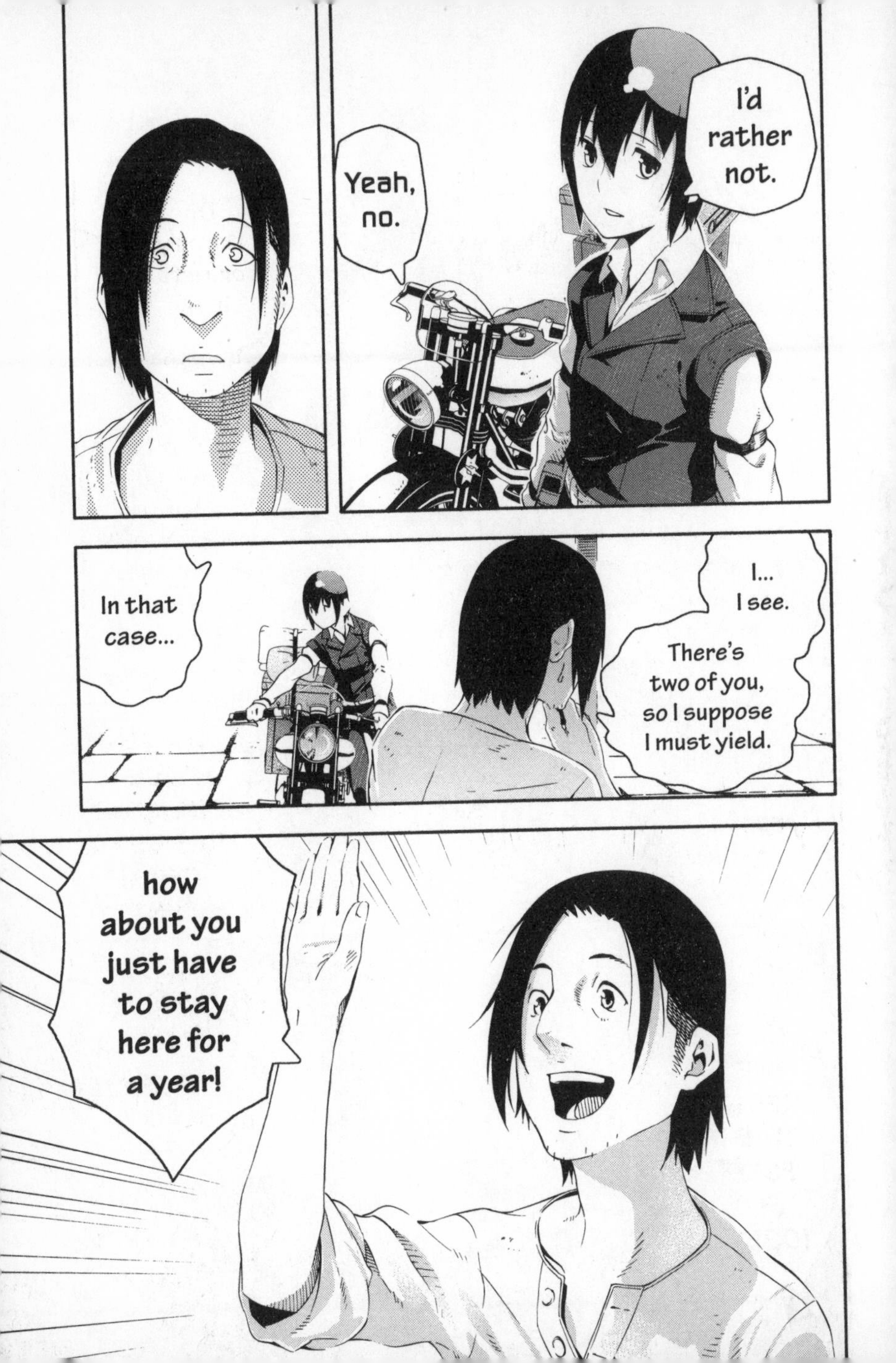
I'd rather not.
Yeah, no.
I... I see.
There's two of you, so I suppose I must yield.
In that case...
how about you just have to stay here for a year!

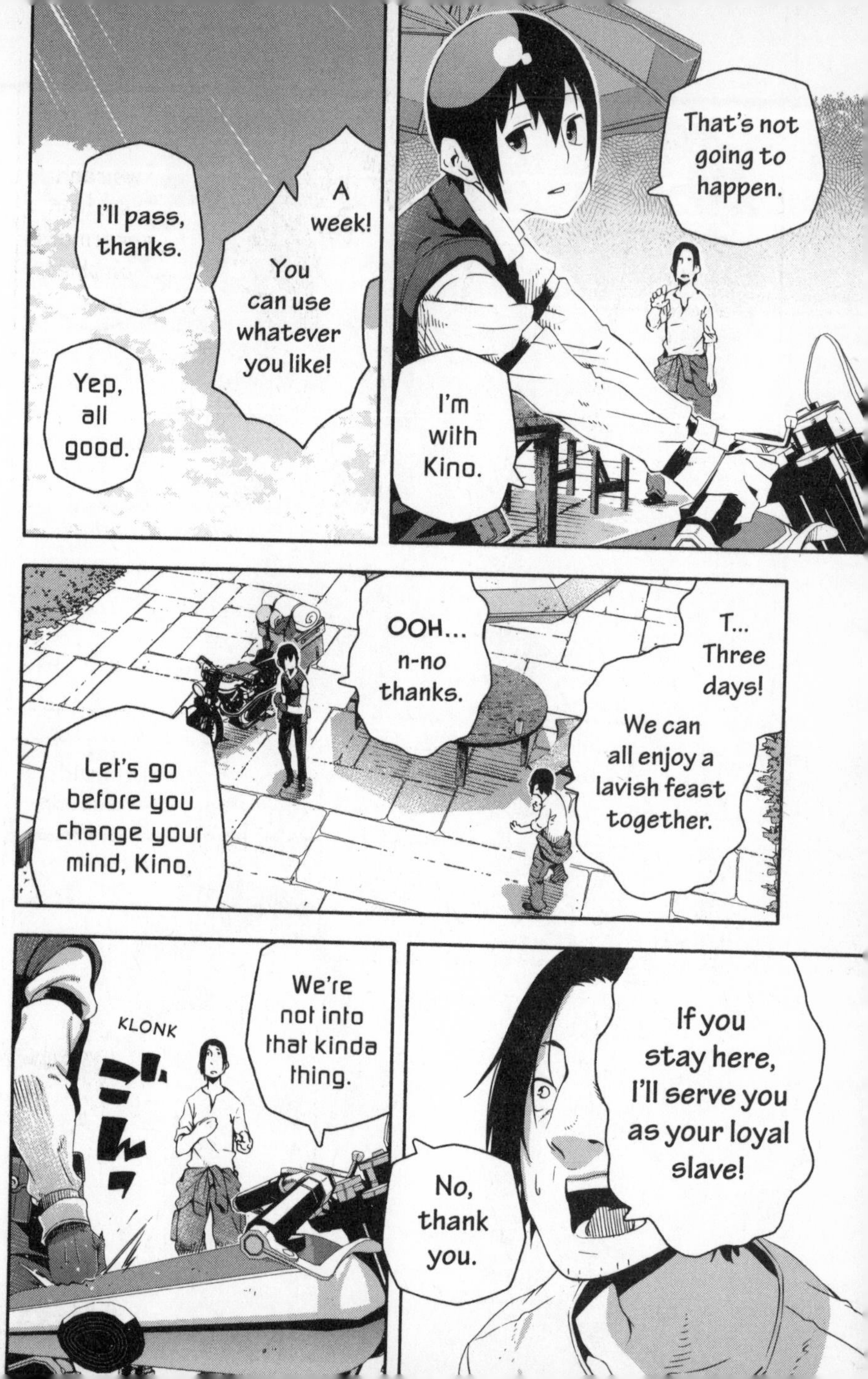
That's not going to happen.
I'm with Kino.
A week!
You can use whatever you like!
I'll pass, thanks.
Yep, all good.
T... Three days!
We can all enjoy a lavish feast together.
OOH... n-no thanks.
Let's go before you change your mind, Kino.
If you stay here, I'll serve you as your loyal slave!
No, thank you.
We're not into that kinda thing.
KLONK

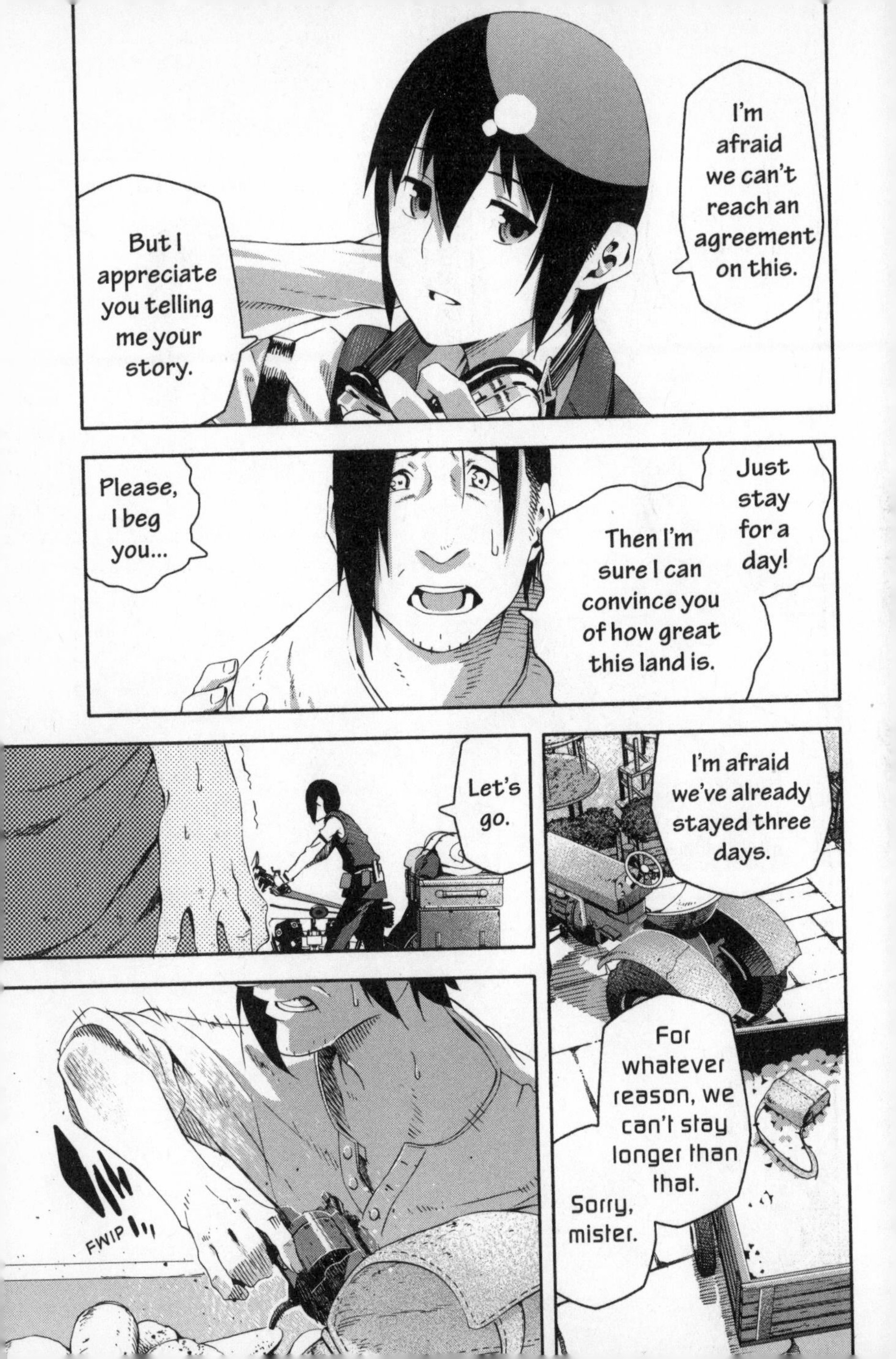
I'm afraid we can't reach an agreement on this.
But I appreciate you telling me your story.
Just stay for a day!
Then I'm sure I can convince you of how great this land is.
Please, I beg you...
I'm afraid we've already stayed three days.
For whatever reason, we can't stay longer than that.
Sorry, mister.
Let's go.
FWIP

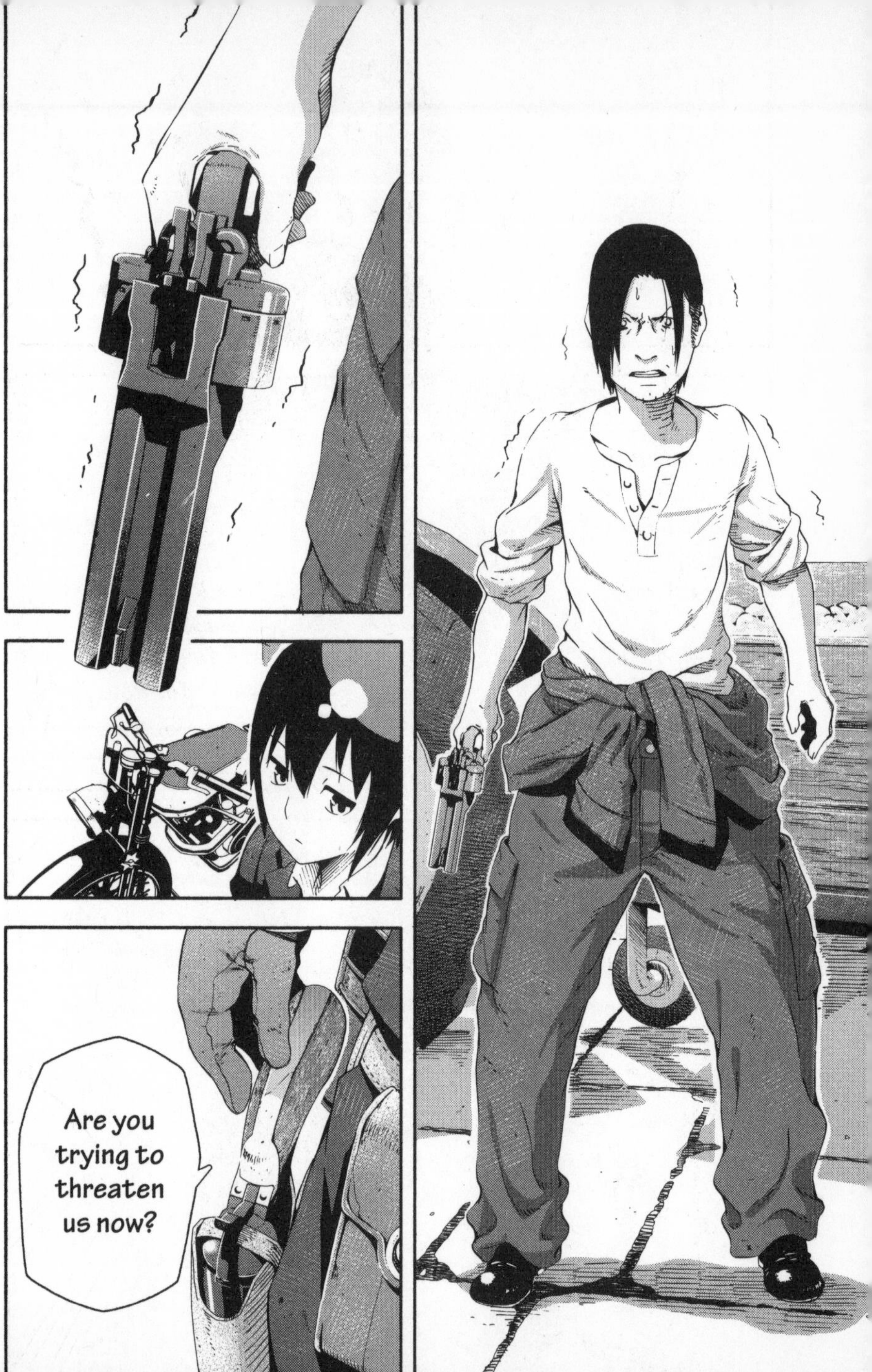
Are you trying to threaten us now?

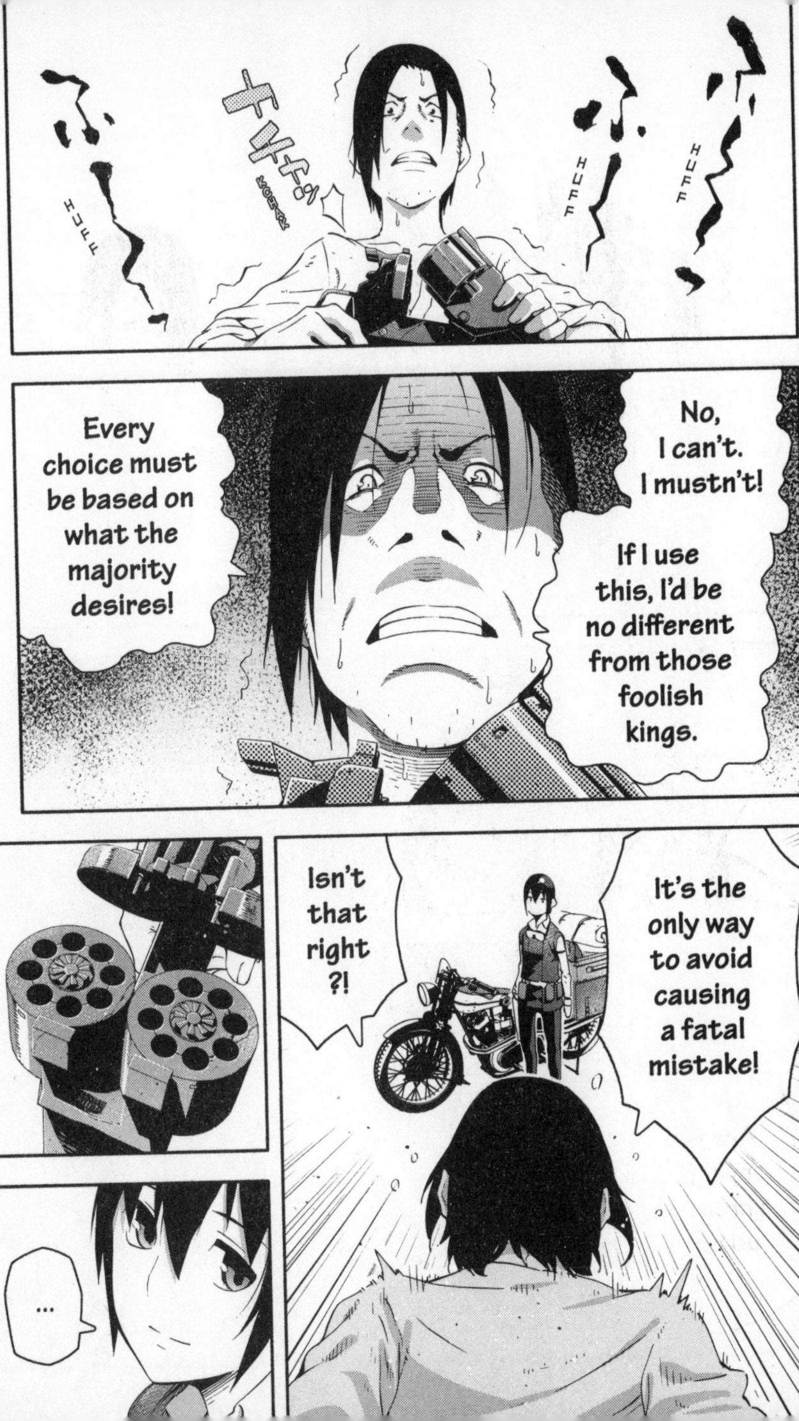
HUFF
HUFF
KCHAK
HUFF
No, I can't. I mustn't!
If I use this, I'd be no different from those foolish kings.
Every choice must be based on what the majority desires!
It's the only way to avoid causing a fatal mistake!
Isn't that right?!
...

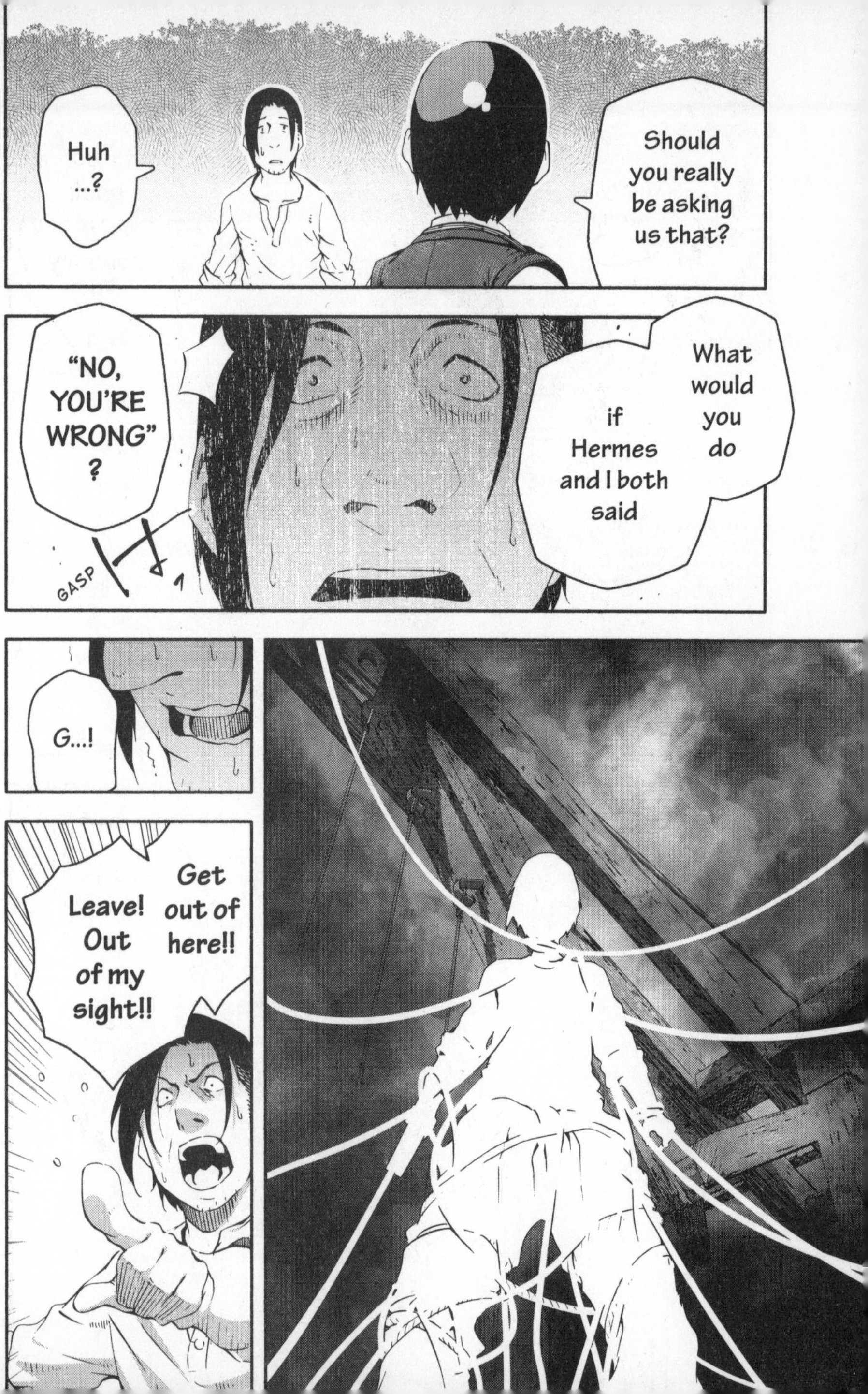
Should you really be asking us that?
Huh ...?
What would you do if Hermes and I both said
"NO, YOU'RE WRONG"?
GASP
G...!
Get out of here!! Leave! Out of my sight!!

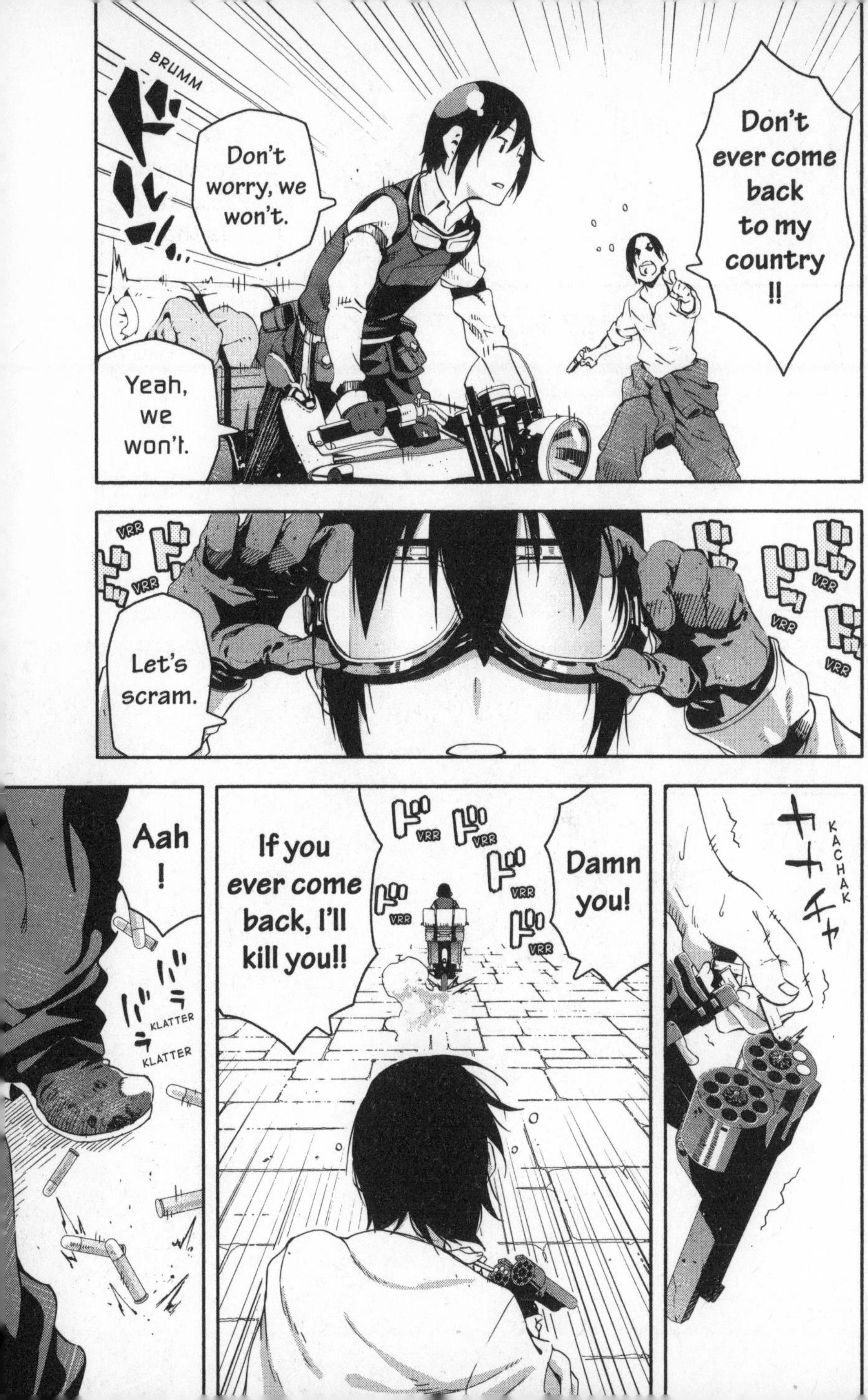

Don't ever come back to my country!!
BRUMM
Don't worry, we won't.
Yeah, we won't.
VRR
Let's scram.
KACHAK
Damn you!
If you ever come back, I'll kill you!!
VRR
Aah!
KLATTER
KLATTER

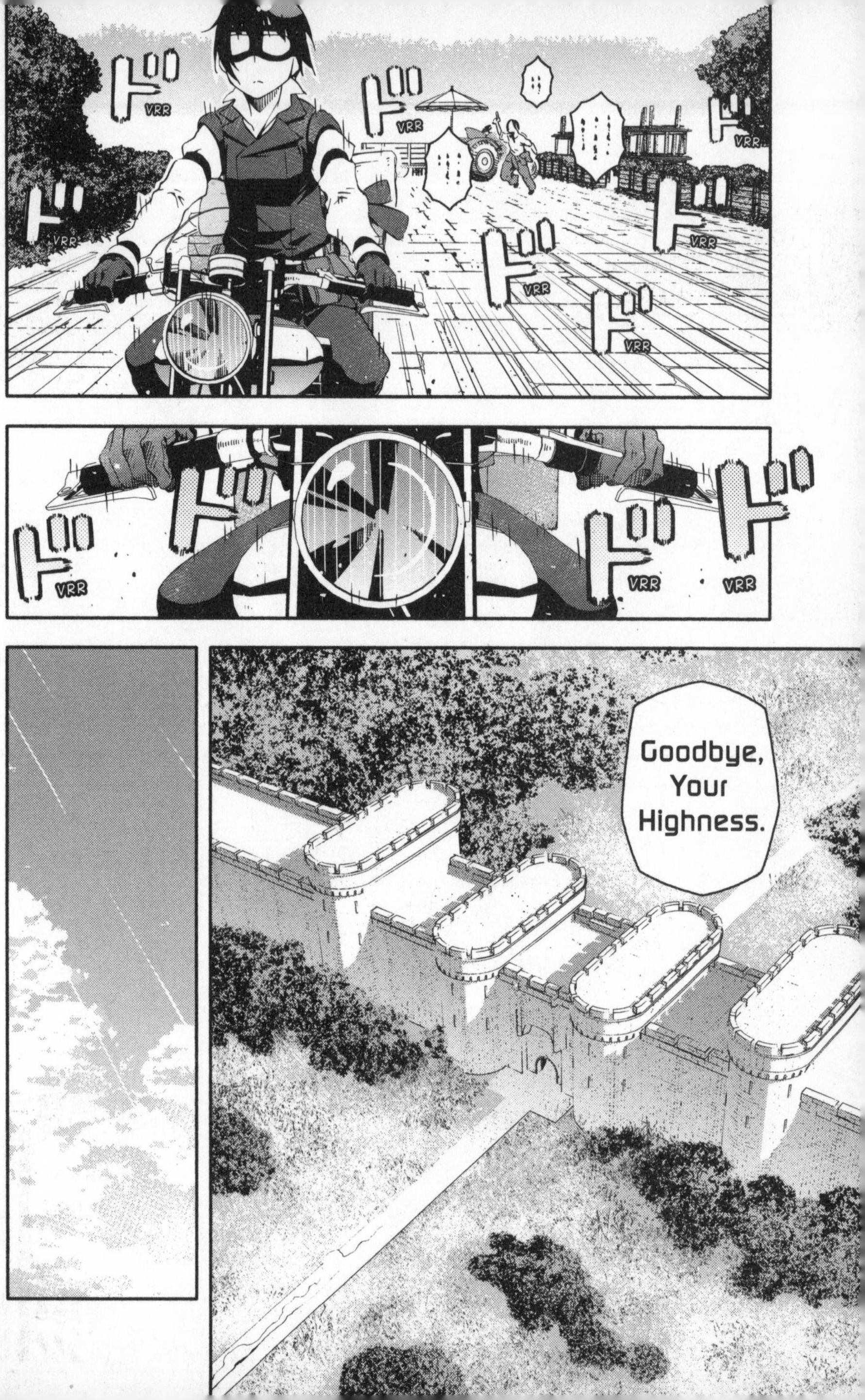
VRR
VRR
VRR
VRR
VRR
VRR
VRR
VRR
VRR
VRR
Goodbye, Your Highness.

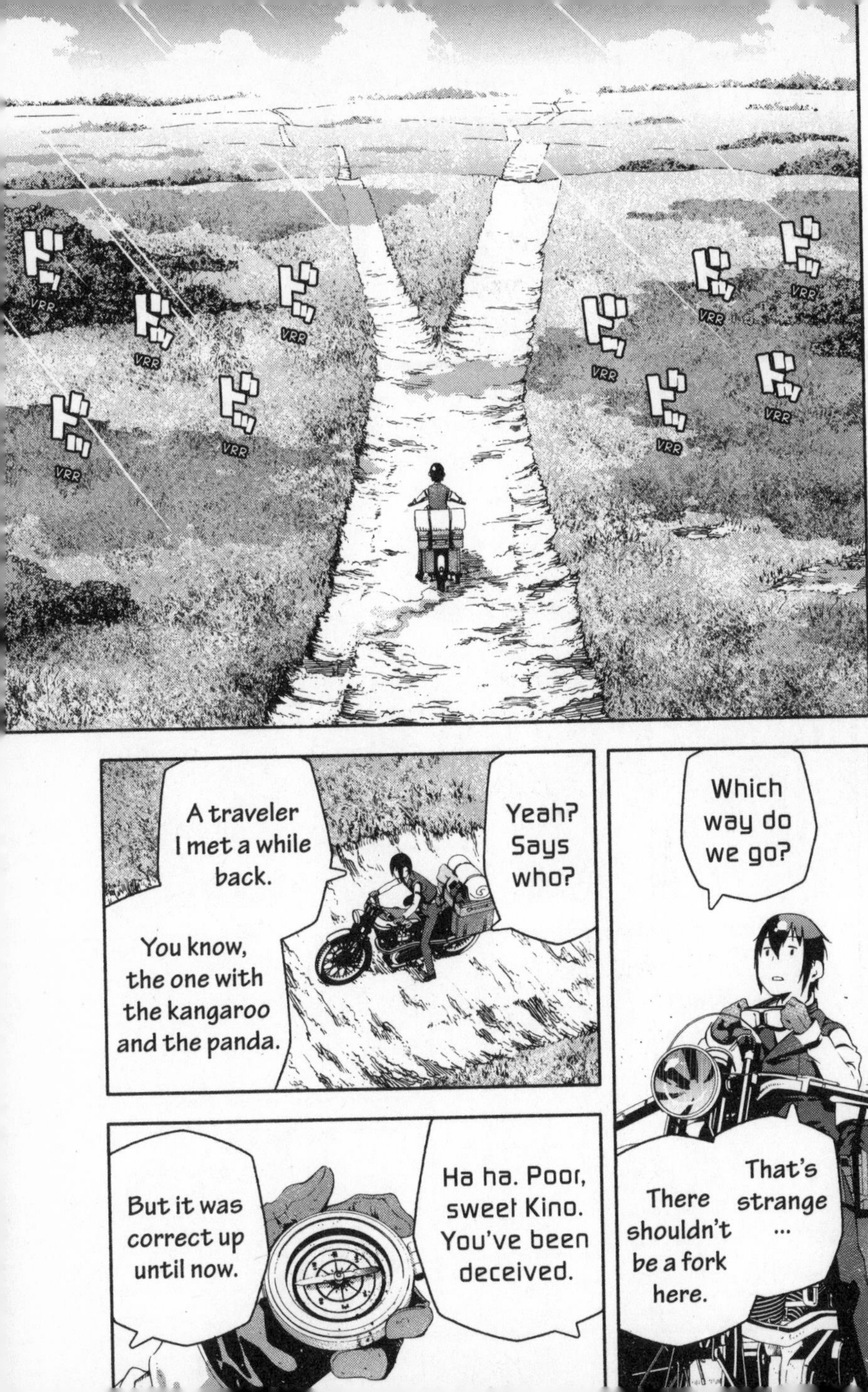
ドッ VRR
ドッ VRR
ドッ VRR
ドッ VRR
ドッ VRR
ドッ VRR
ドッ VRR
ドッ VRR
ドッ VRR
Which way do we go?
That's strange ...
There shouldn't be a fork here.
Yeah? Says who?
A traveler I met a while back.
You know, the one with the kangaroo and the panda.
Ha ha. Poor, sweet Kino. You've been deceived.
But it was correct up until now.

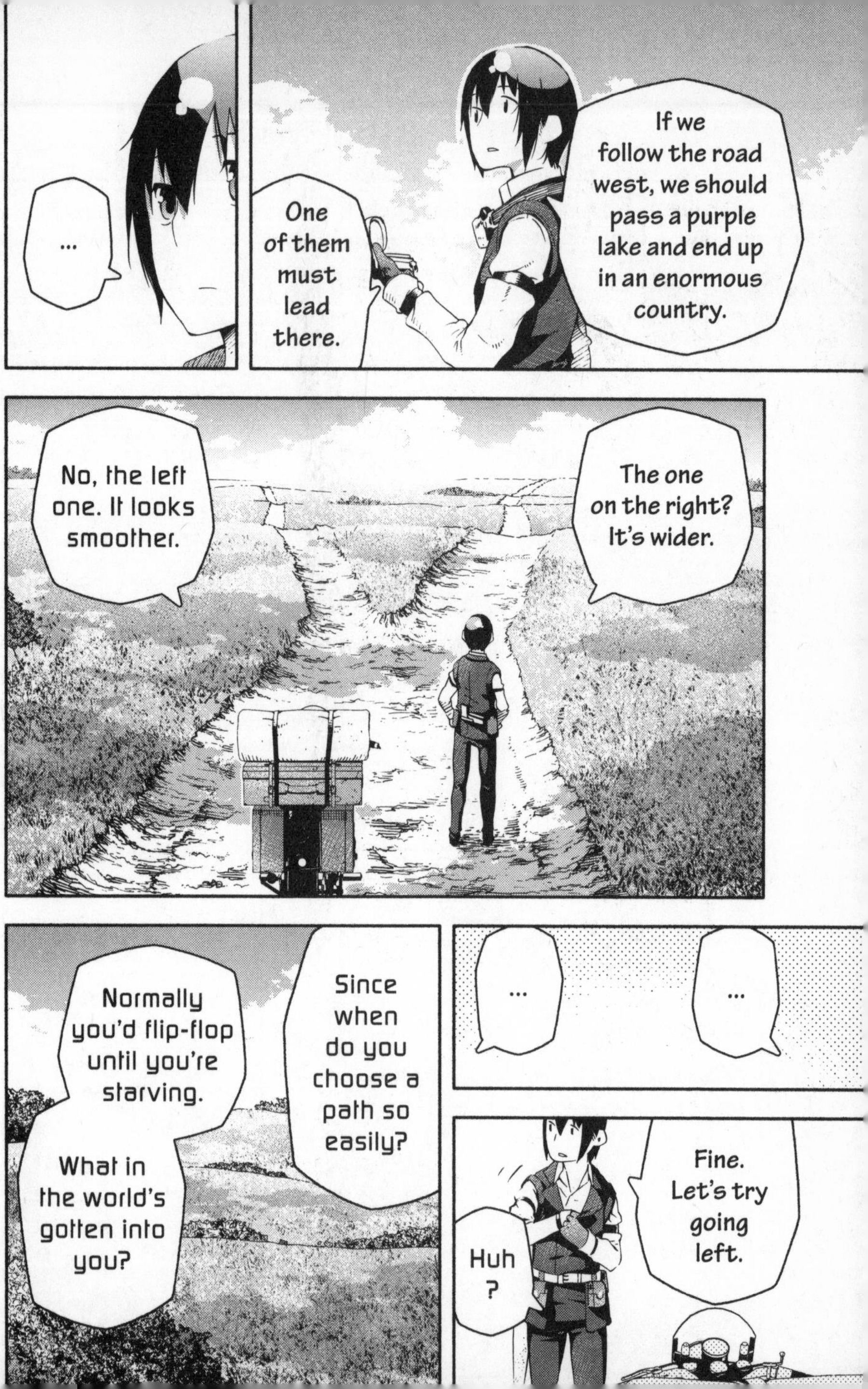
If we follow the road west, we should pass a purple lake and end up in an enormous country.
One of them must lead there.
...
The one on the right? It's wider.
No, the left one. It looks smoother.
...
...
Fine. Let's try going left.
Huh?
Since when do you choose a path so easily?
Normally you'd flip-flop until you're starving.
What in the world's gotten into you?

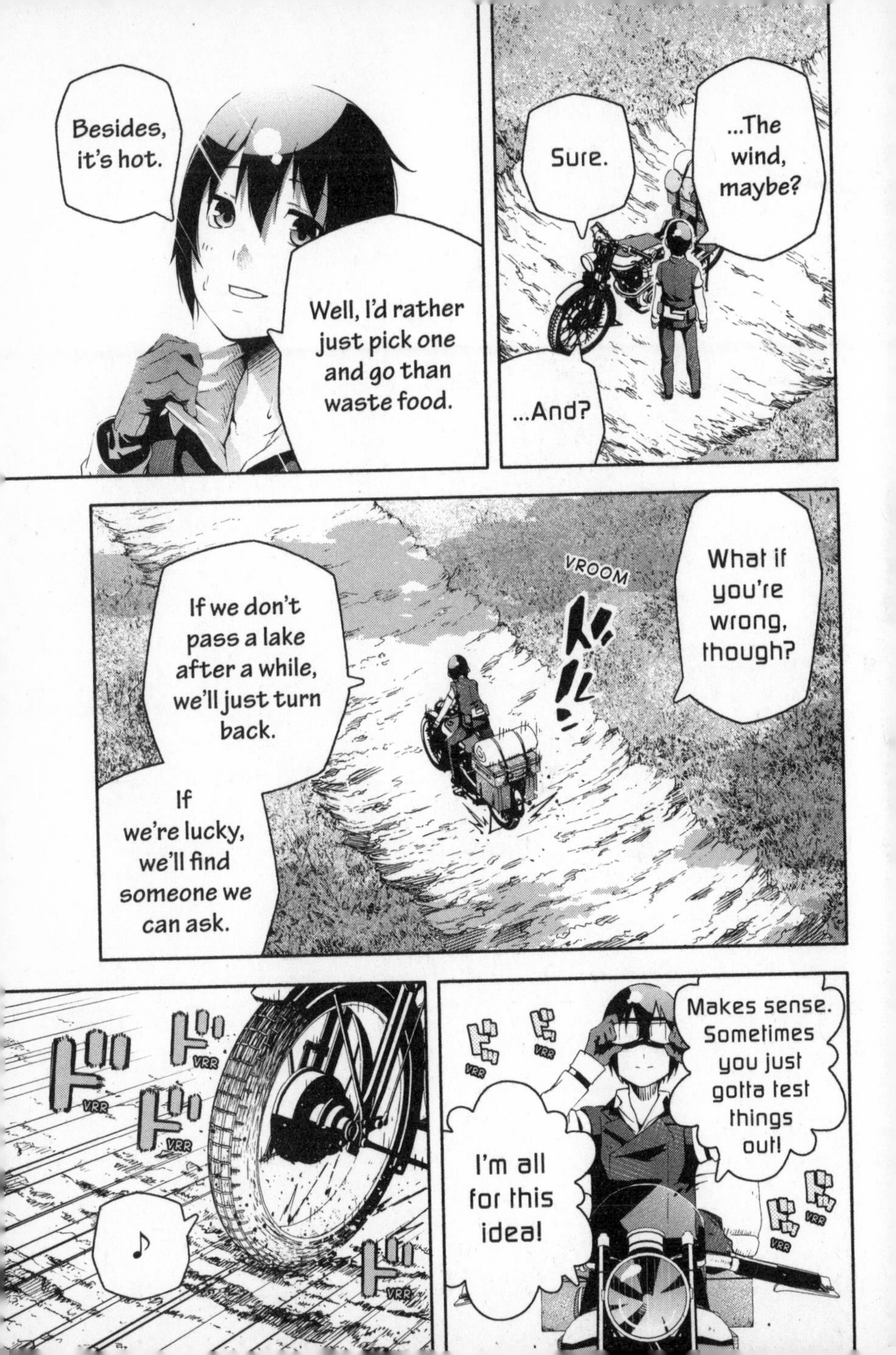
...The wind, maybe?
Sure.
...And?
Well, I'd rather just pick one and go than waste food.
Besides, it's hot.
What if you're wrong, though?
VROOM
If we don't pass a lake after a while, we'll just turn back.
If we're lucky, we'll find someone we can ask.
Makes sense. Sometimes you just gotta test things out!
I'm all for this idea!
VRR
VRR
VRR
VRR
VRR
VRR
VRR
♪

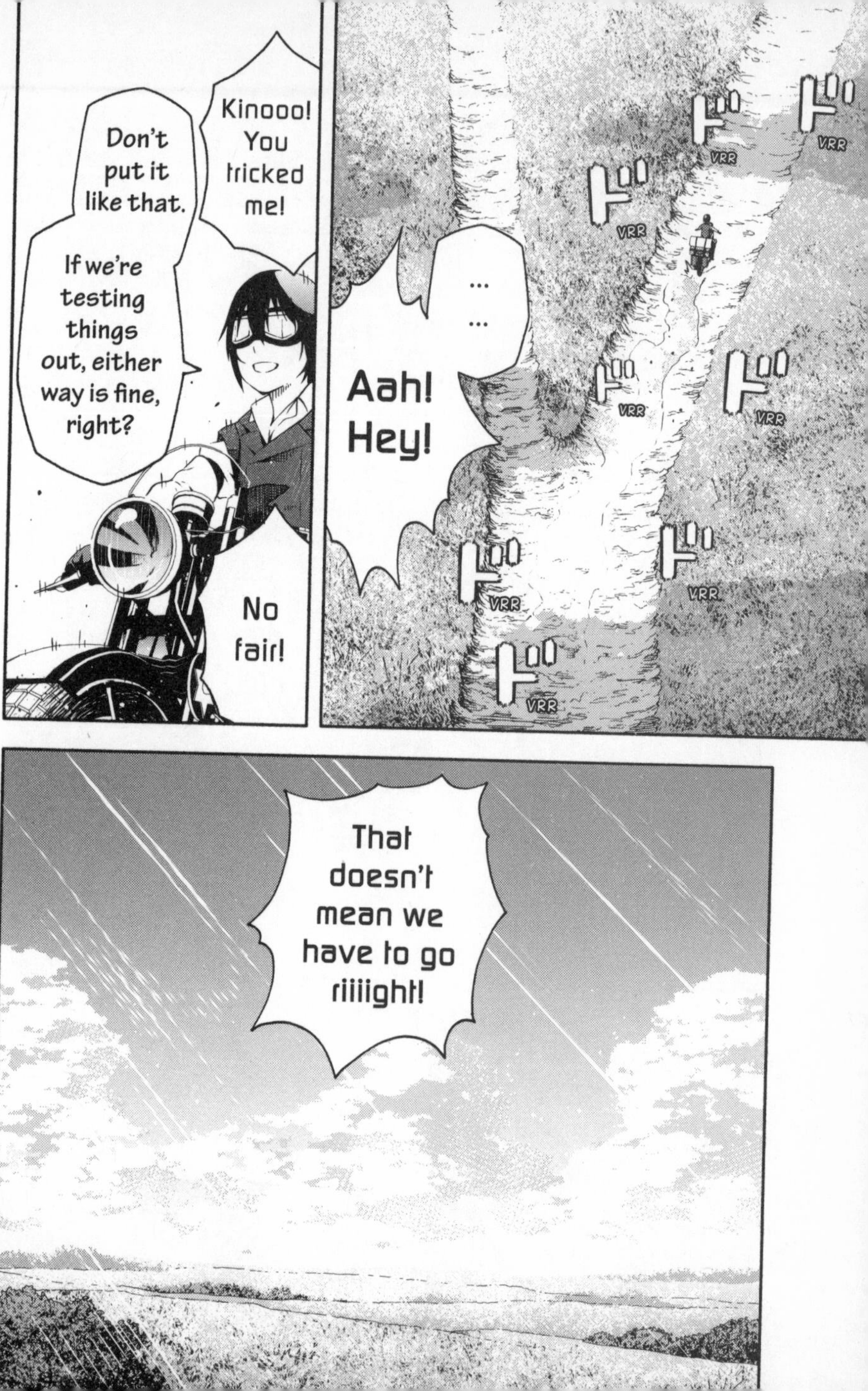
VRR
VRR
VRR
VRR
VRR
VRR
VRR
...
...
Aah! Hey!
Kinooo! You tricked me!
Don't put it like that.
If we're testing things out, either way is fine, right?
No fair!
That doesn't mean we have to go riiiight!

Kino's Journey

—→ The Beautiful World ←—

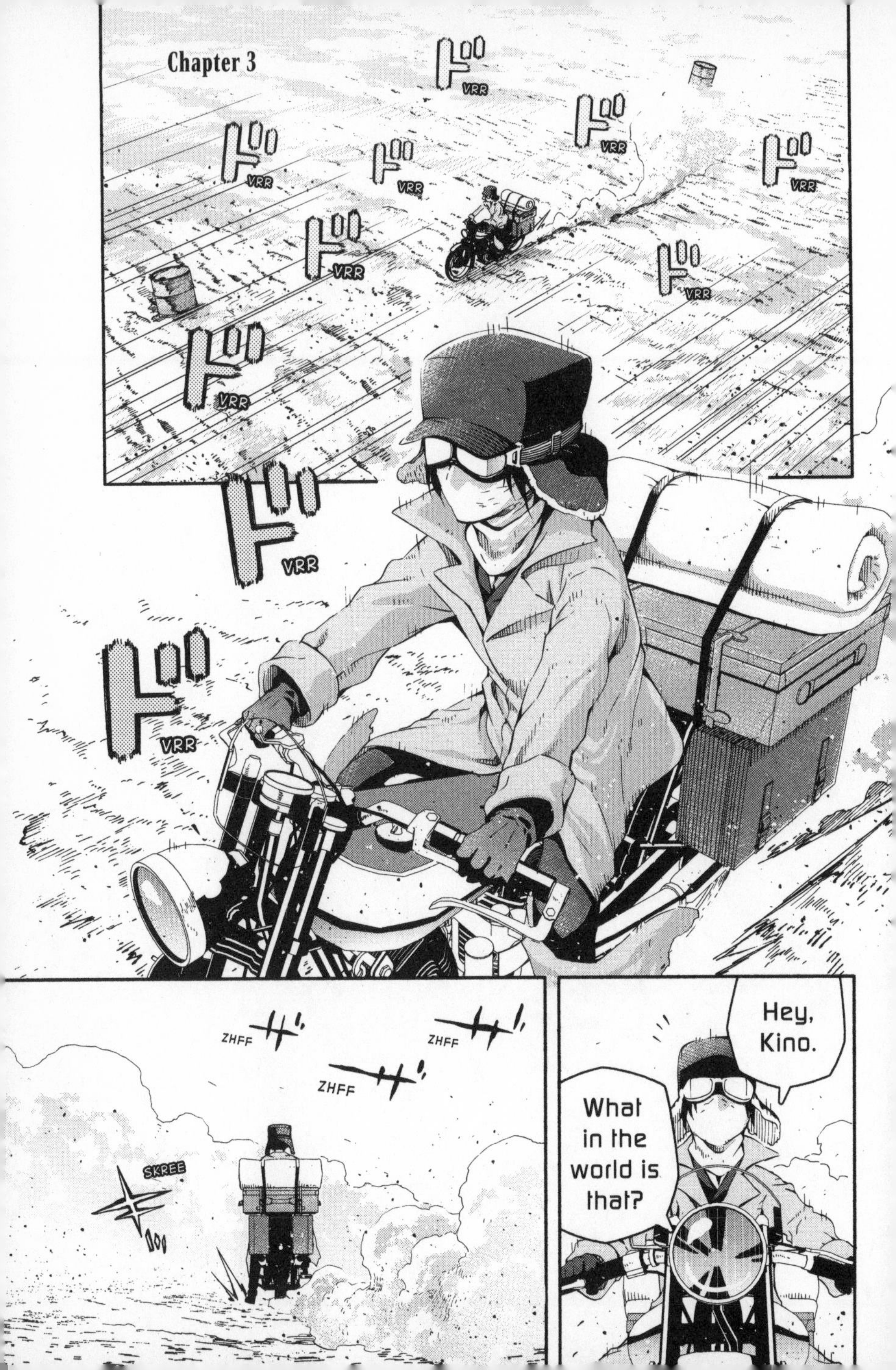
Chapter 3
VRR
VRR
VRR
VRR
VRR
VRR
VRR
VRR
VRR
VRR
Hey, Kino.
What in the world is that?
ZHFF
ZHFF
ZHFF
SKREE

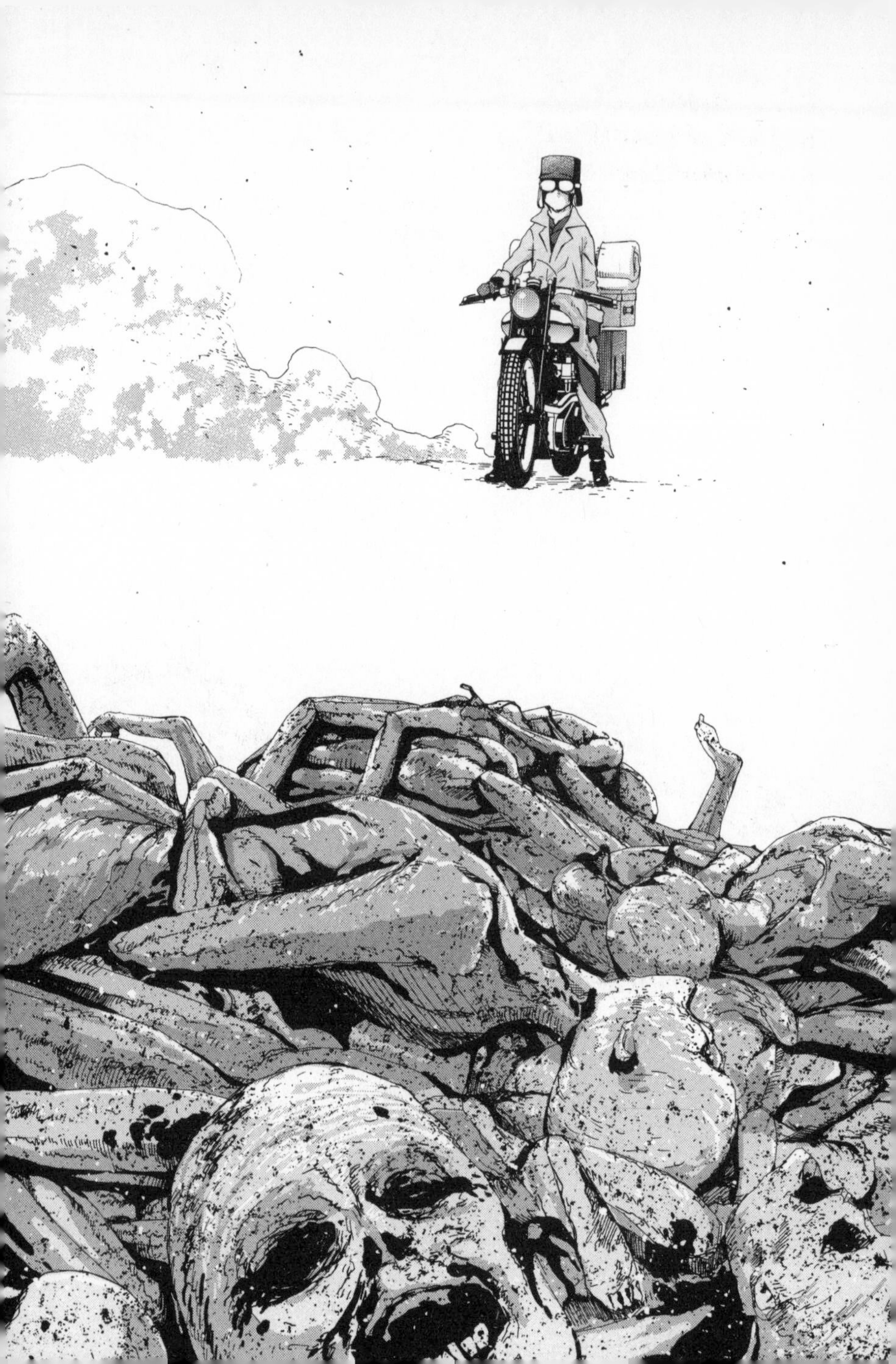

Chapter 3
The Land of Peace (Pt. 1)
-Mother's Love-

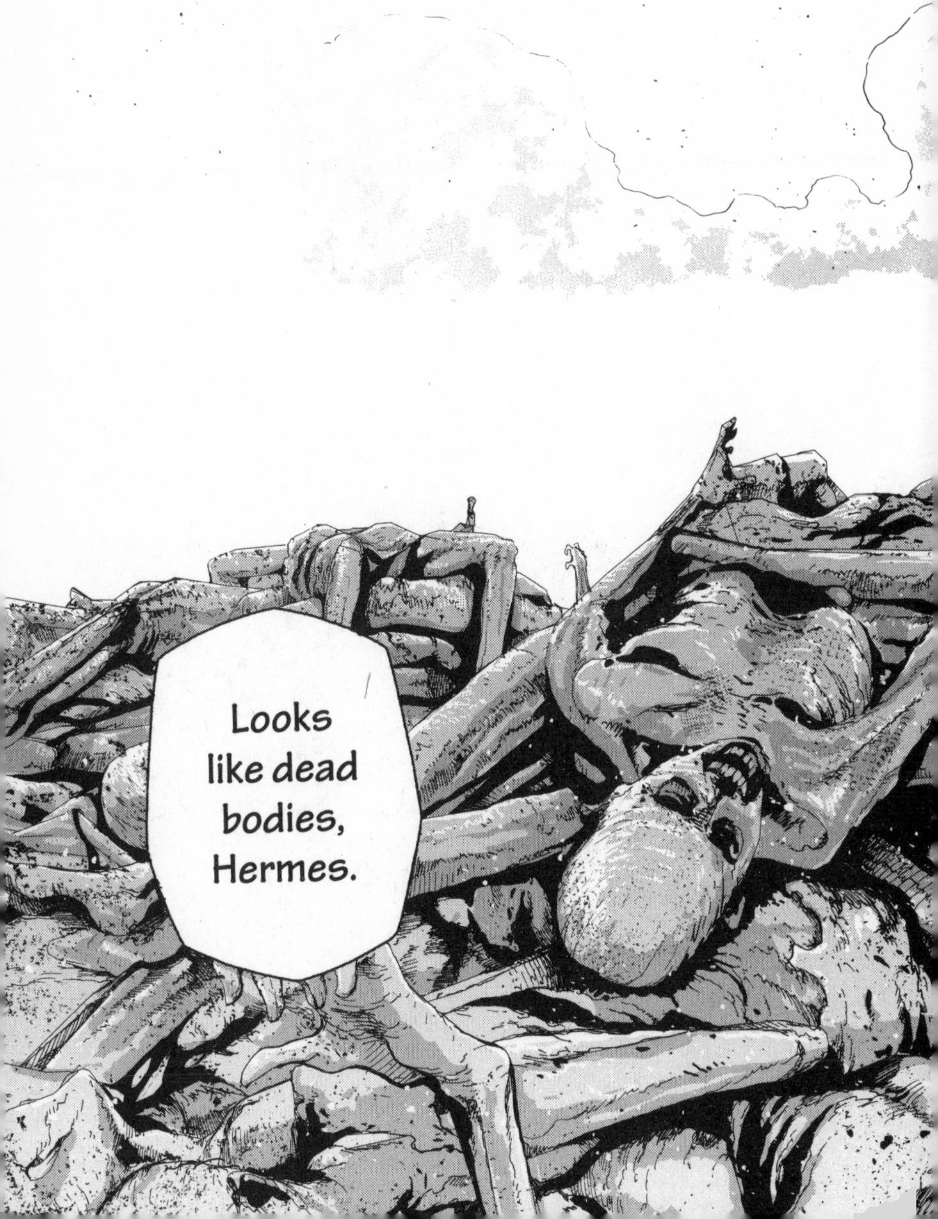
Looks like dead bodies, Hermes.

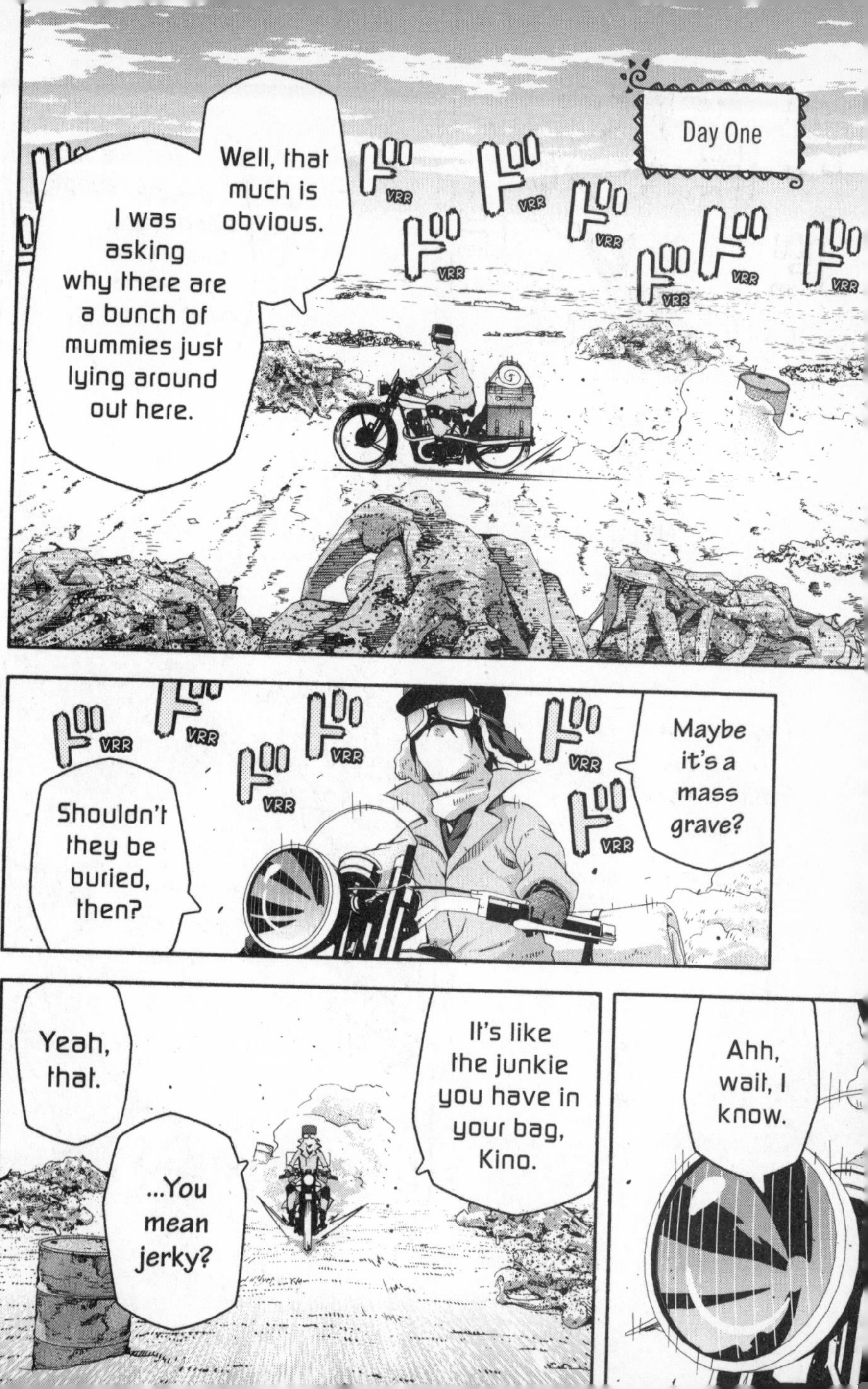
Day One
VRR
VRR
VRR
VRR
VRR
VRR
VRR
Well, that much is obvious.
I was asking why there are a bunch of mummies just lying around out here.
VRR
VRR
Maybe it's a mass grave?
VRR
VRR
VRR
VRR
Shouldn't they be buried, then?
Ahh, wait, I know.
It's like the junkie you have in your bag, Kino.
...You mean jerky?
Yeah, that.

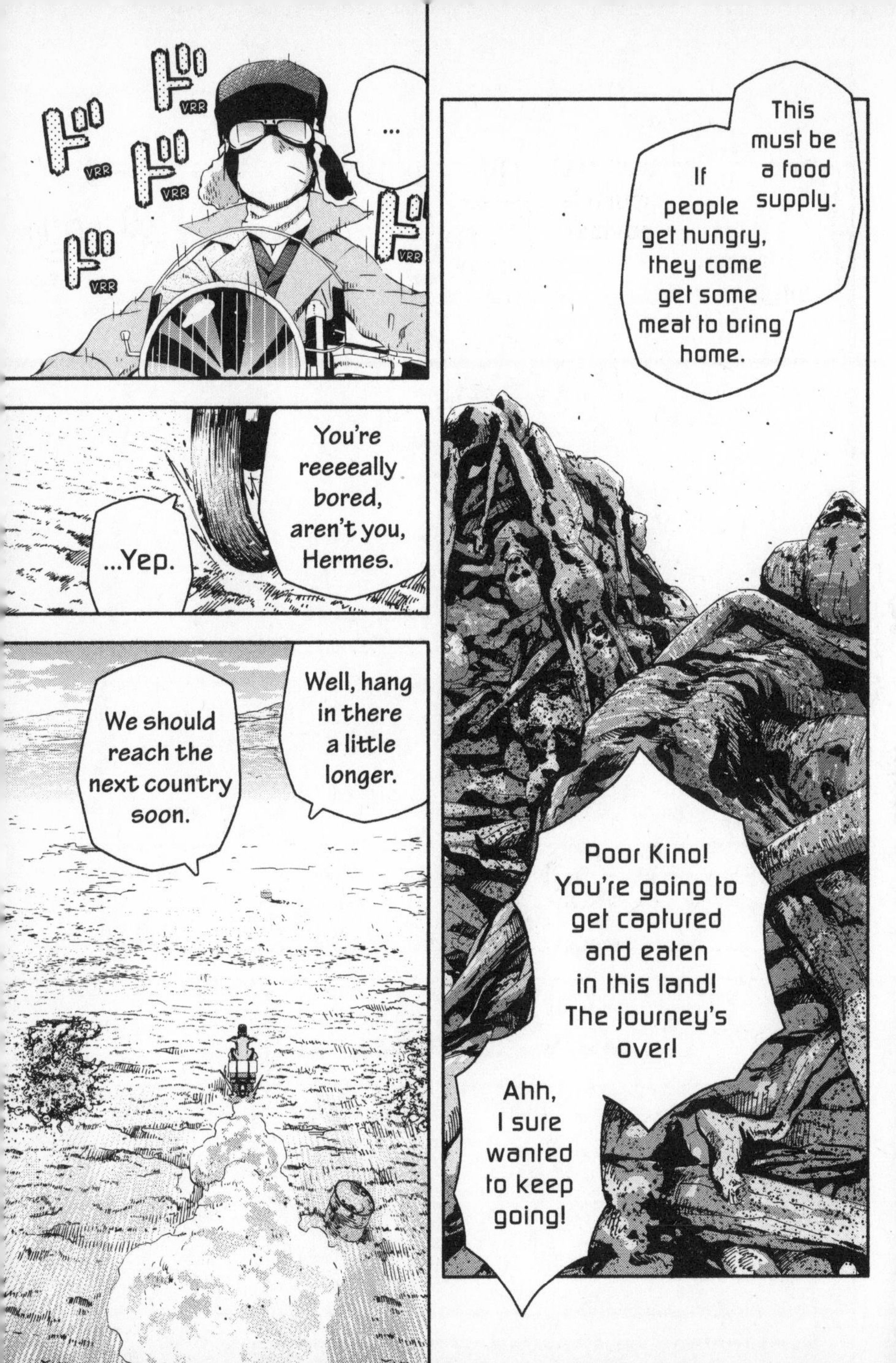
This must be a food supply.
If people get hungry, they come get some meat to bring home.
Poor Kino! You're going to get captured and eaten in this land! The journey's over!
Ahh, I sure wanted to keep going!
VRR
VRR
VRR
VRR
VRR
...
You're reeeeally bored, aren't you, Hermes.
...Yep.
Well, hang in there a little longer.
We should reach the next country soon.

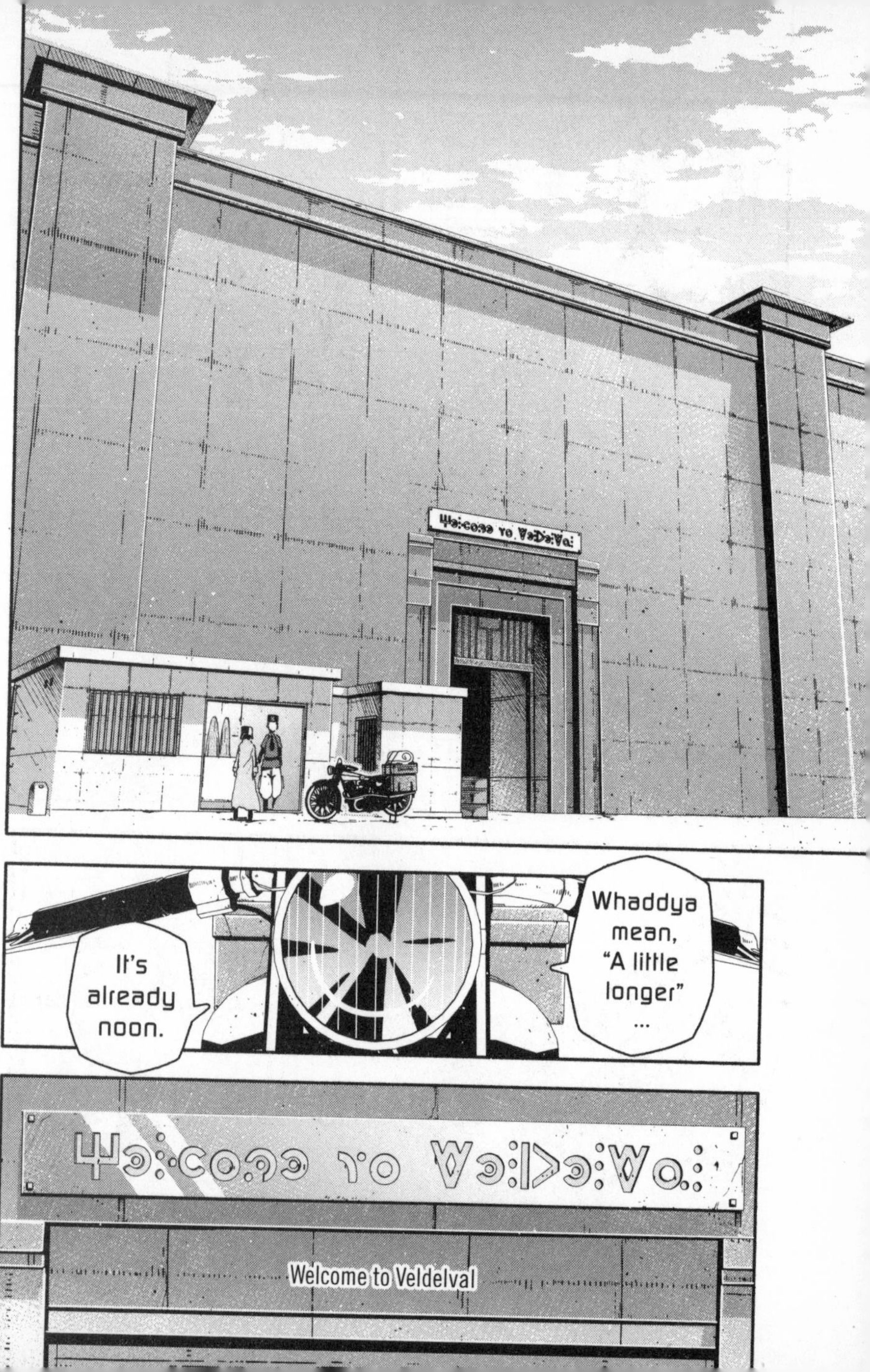
Whaddya mean, "A little longer" ...
It's already noon.
Welcome to Veldelval

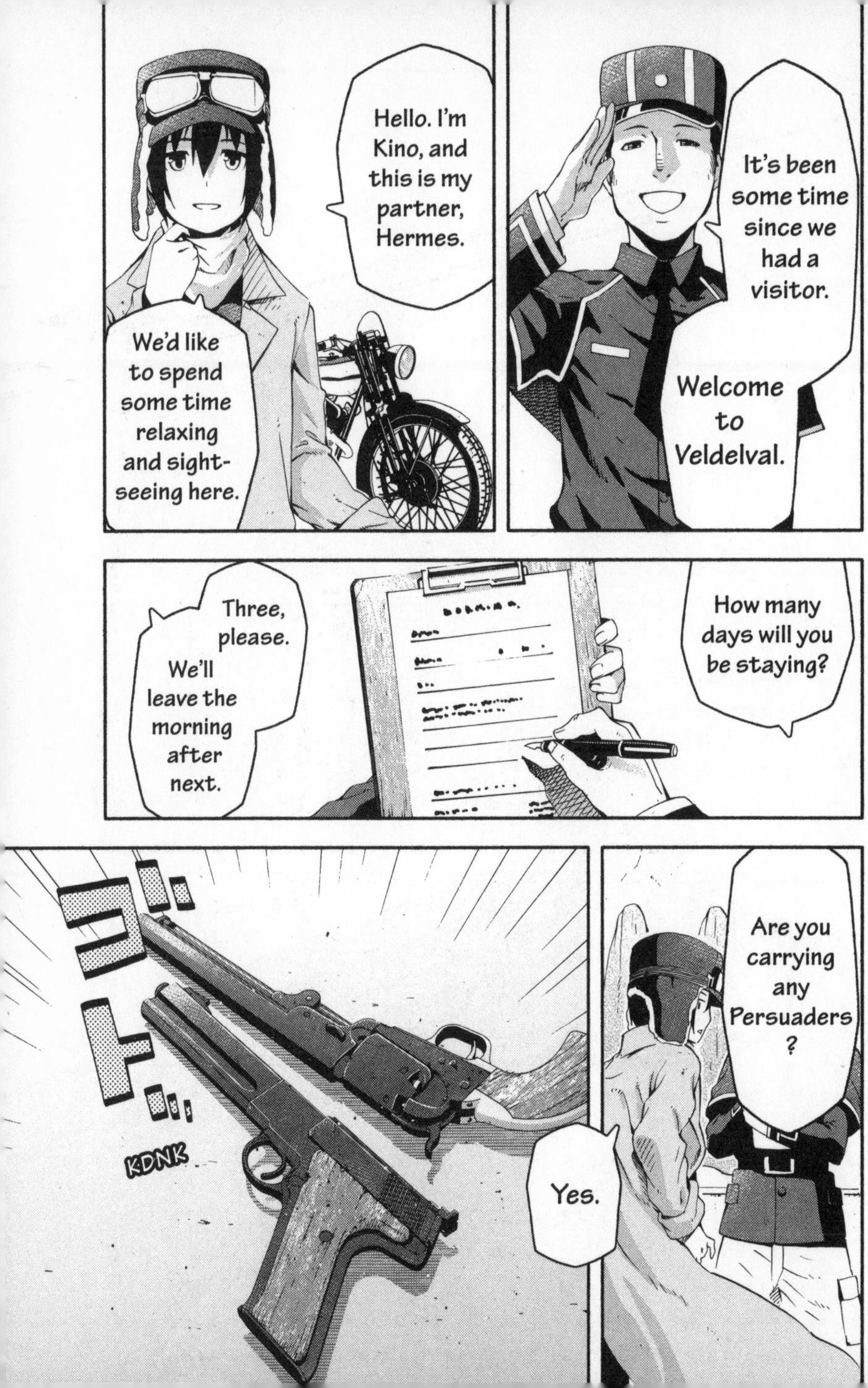
It's been some time since we had a visitor.
Welcome to Veldelval.
Hello. I'm Kino, and this is my partner, Hermes.
We'd like to spend some time relaxing and sight-seeing here.
How many days will you be staying?
Three, please.
We'll leave the morning after next.
Are you carrying any Persuaders?
Yes.
KDNK

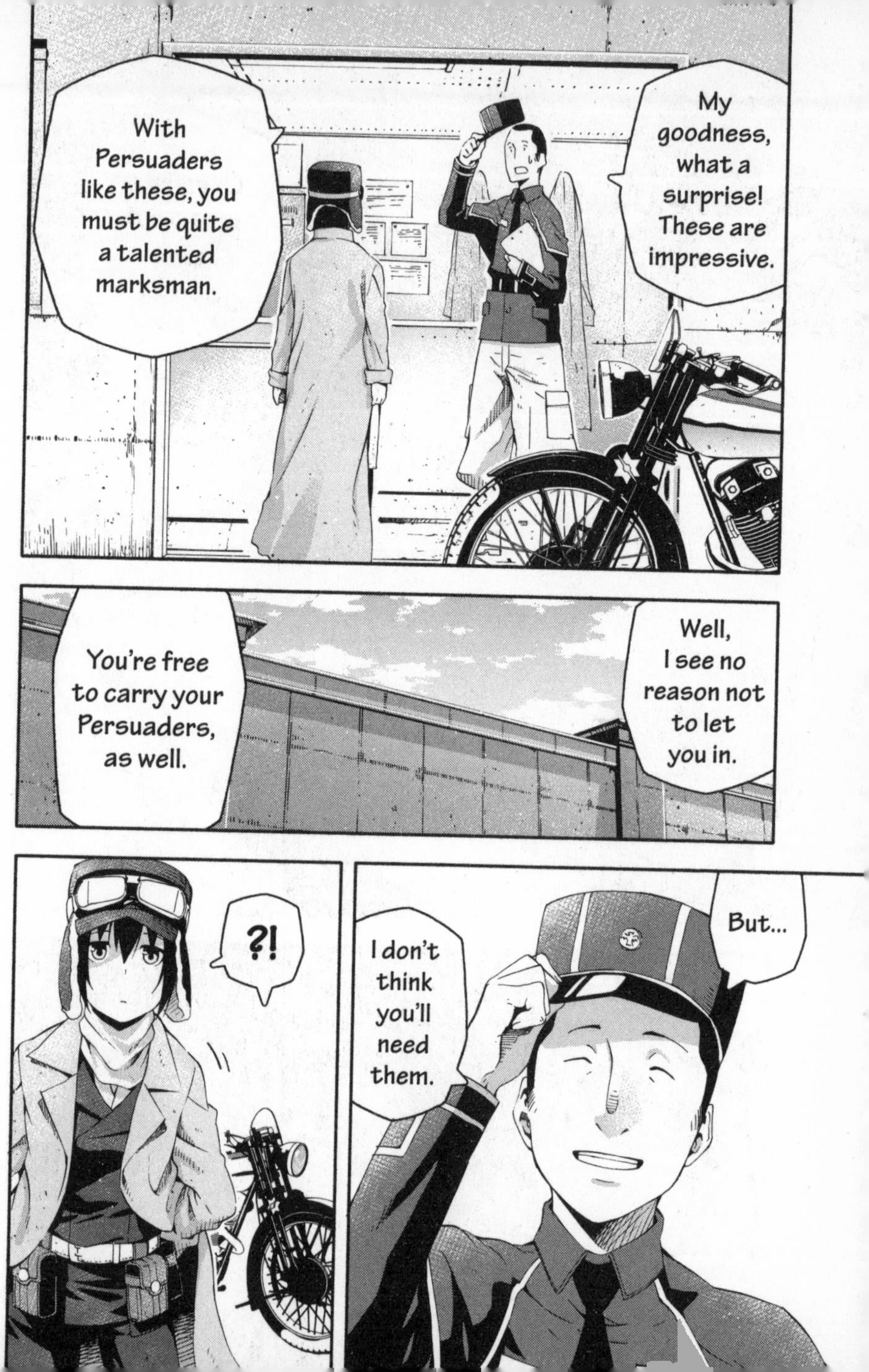
My goodness, what a surprise! These are impressive.
With Persuaders like these, you must be quite a talented marksman.
Well, I see no reason not to let you in.
You're free to carry your Persuaders, as well.
But...
I don't think you'll need them.
?!

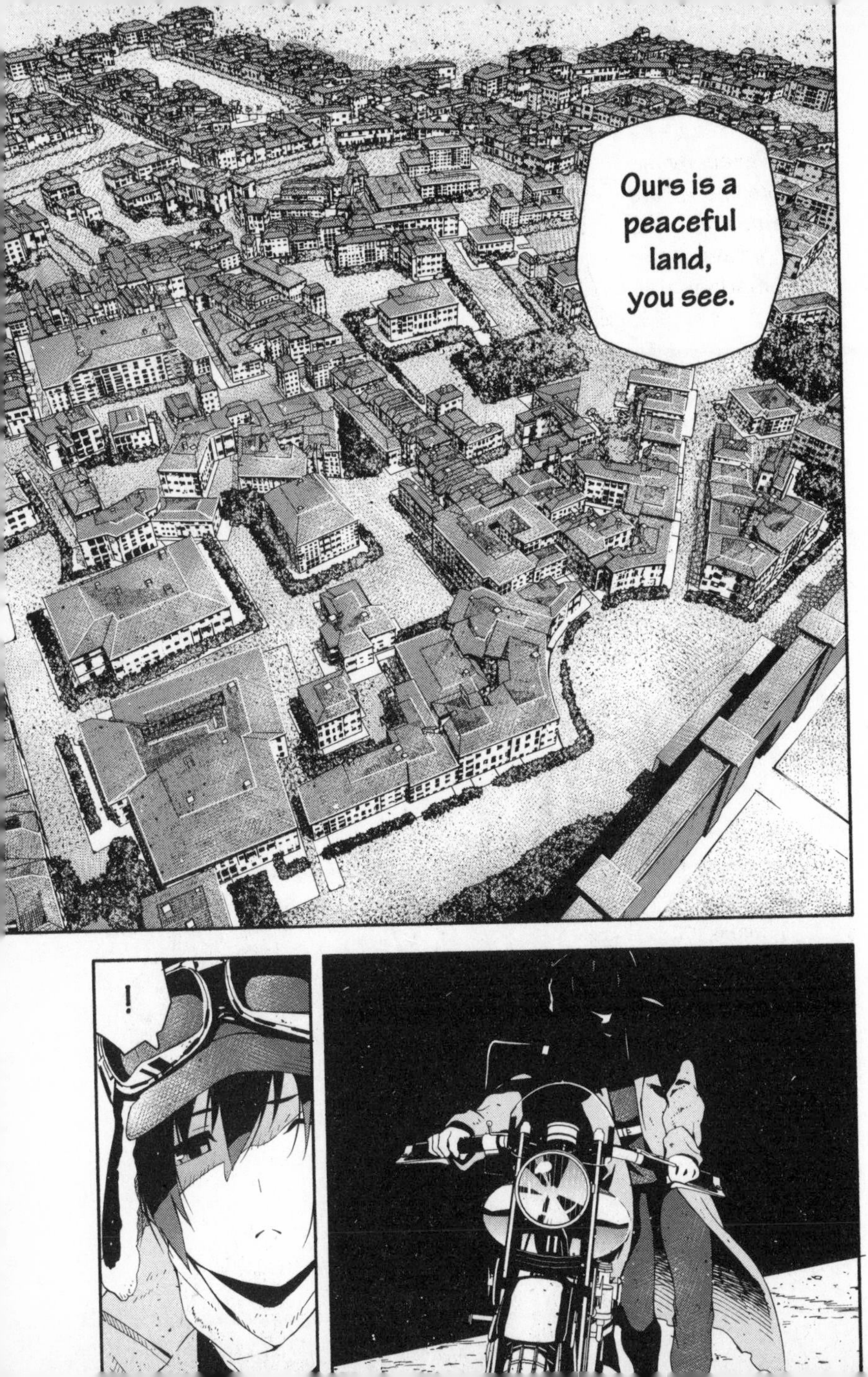
Ours is a peaceful land, you see.
!

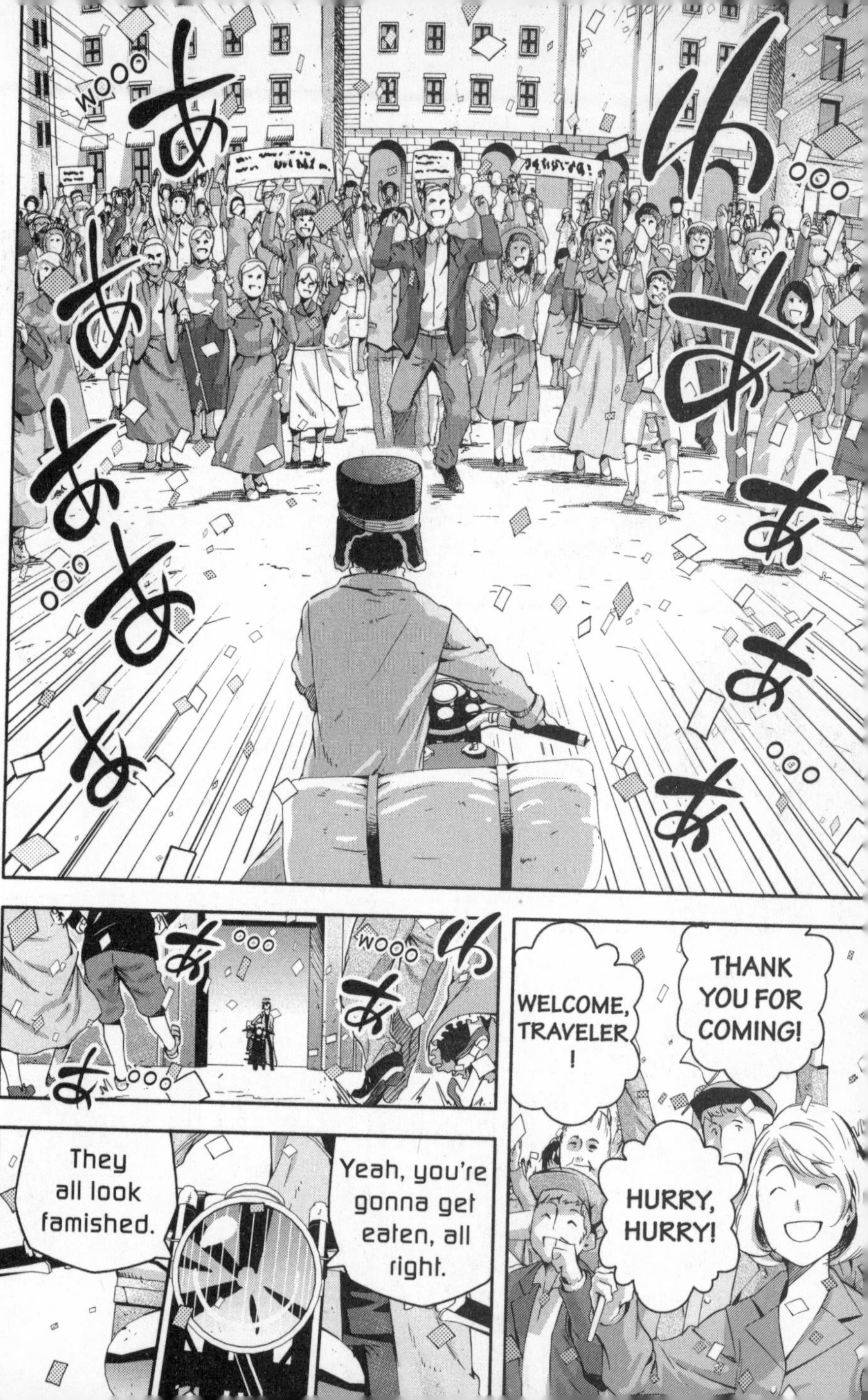

わあああああ
OOO
OOO
WOOO
あああああああ
OOO
THANK YOU FOR COMING!
WELCOME, TRAVELER!
HURRY, HURRY!
わあ
WOOO
あ
OOO
あ
OOO
They all look famished.
Yeah, you're gonna get eaten, all right.

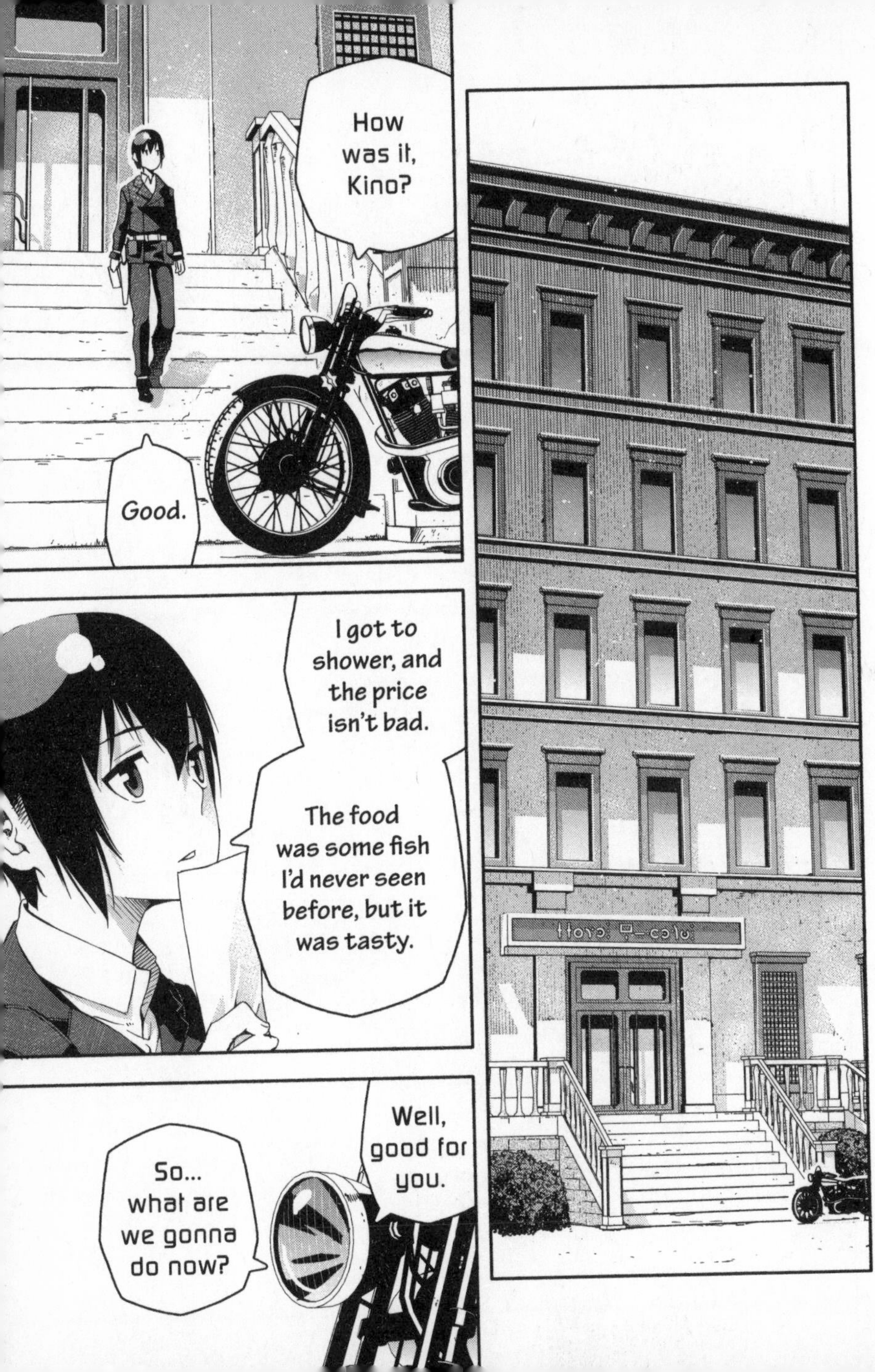
How was it, Kino?
Good.
I got to shower, and the price isn't bad.
The food was some fish I'd never seen before, but it was tasty.
Well, good for you.
So... what are we gonna do now?

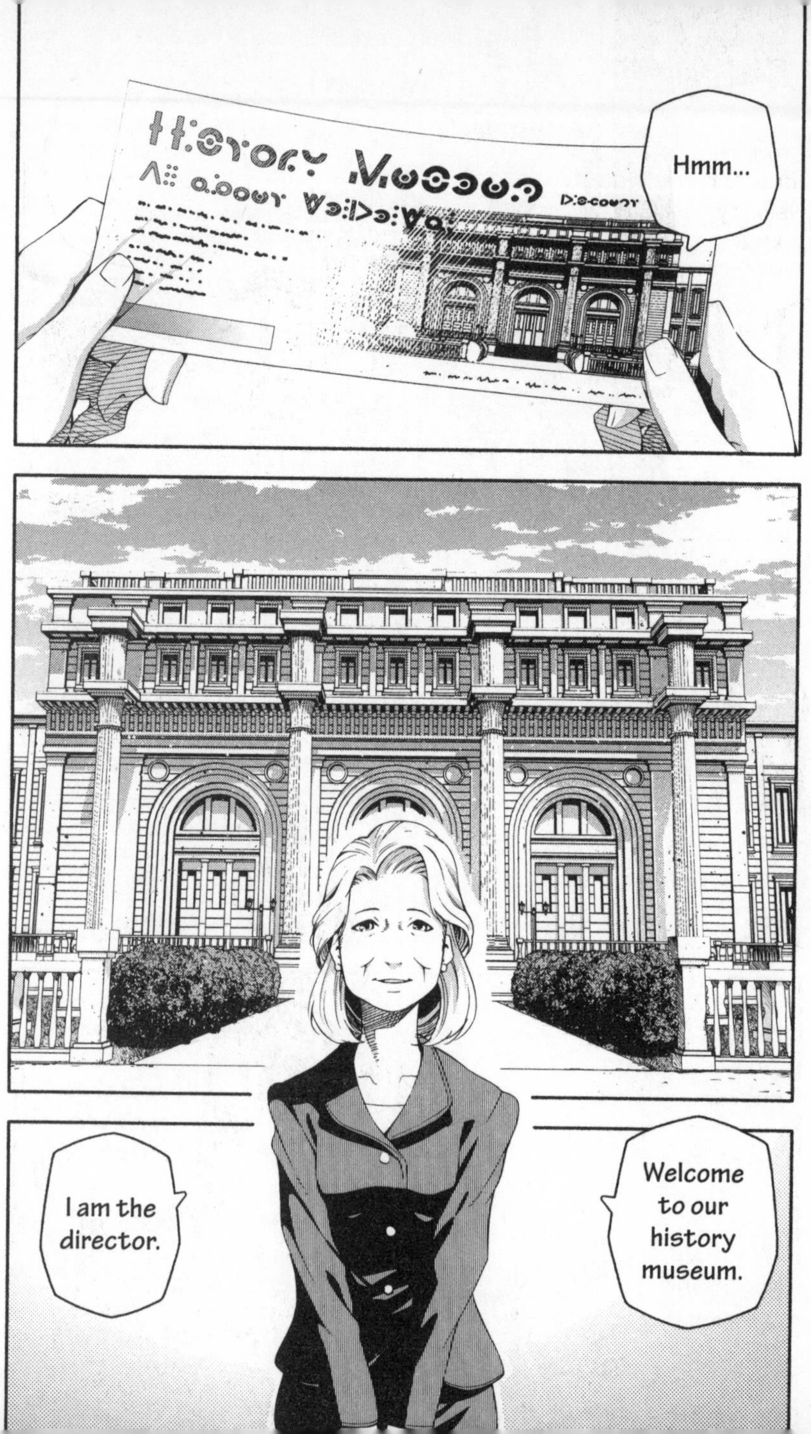
Hmm...
Welcome to our history museum.
I am the director.

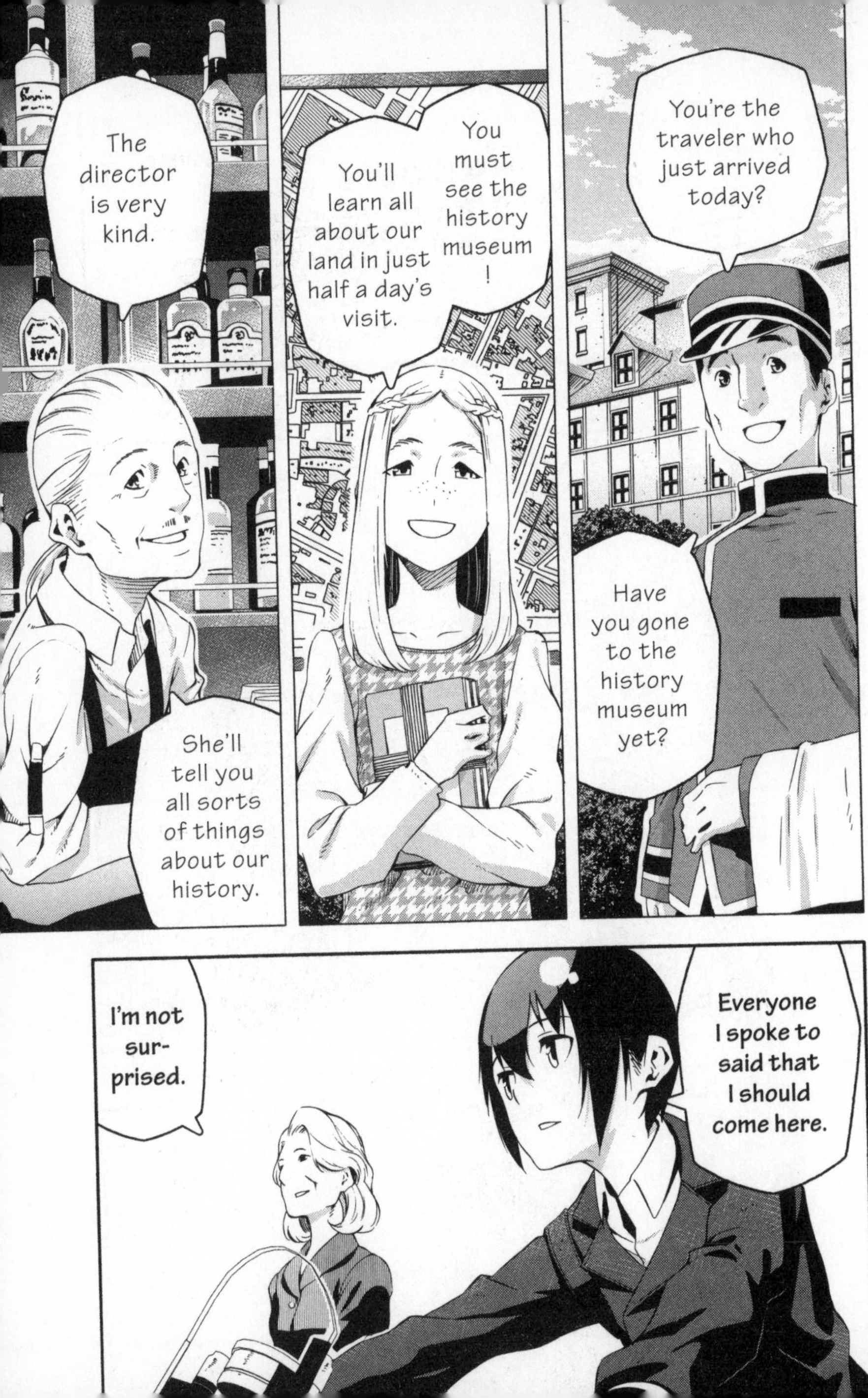
You're the traveler who just arrived today?
Have you gone to the history museum yet?
You must see the history museum!
You'll learn all about our land in just half a day's visit.
The director is very kind.
She'll tell you all sorts of things about our history.
Everyone I spoke to said that I should come here.
I'm not sur-prised.

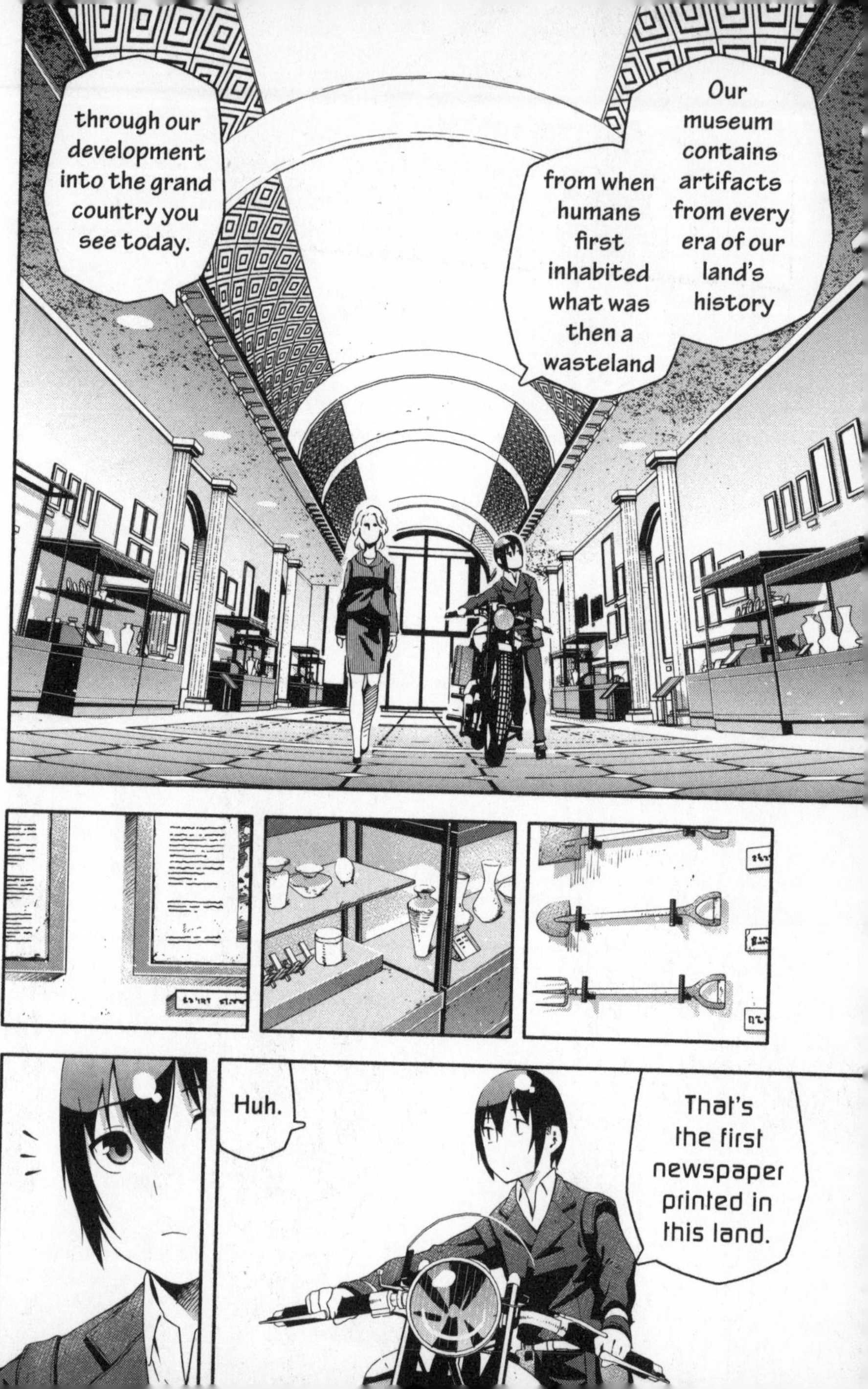
Our museum contains artifacts from every era of our land's history
from when humans first inhabited what was then a wasteland
through our development into the grand country you see today.
That's the first newspaper printed in this land.
Huh.

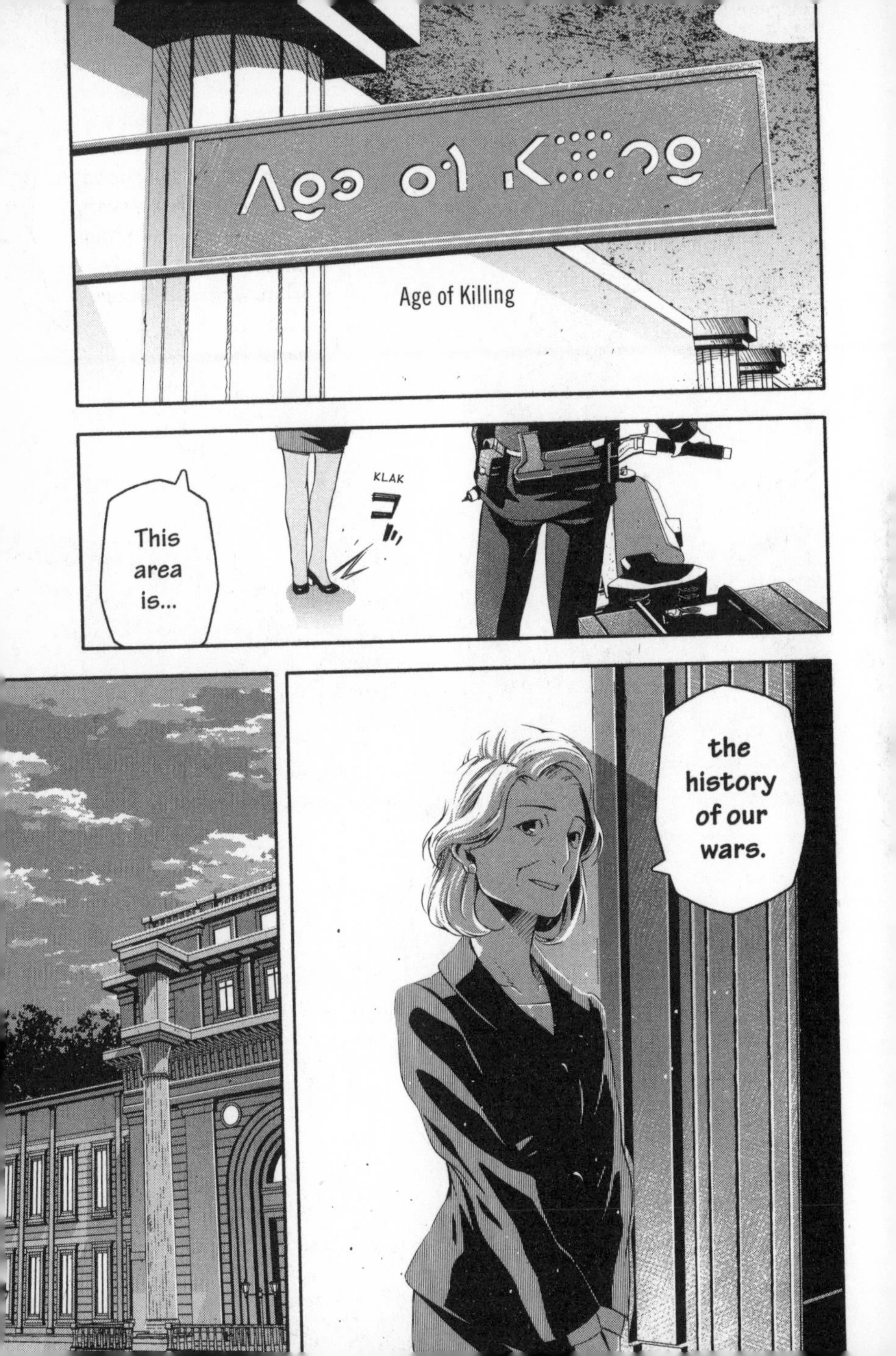
Age of Killing
KLAK
This area is...
the history of our wars.

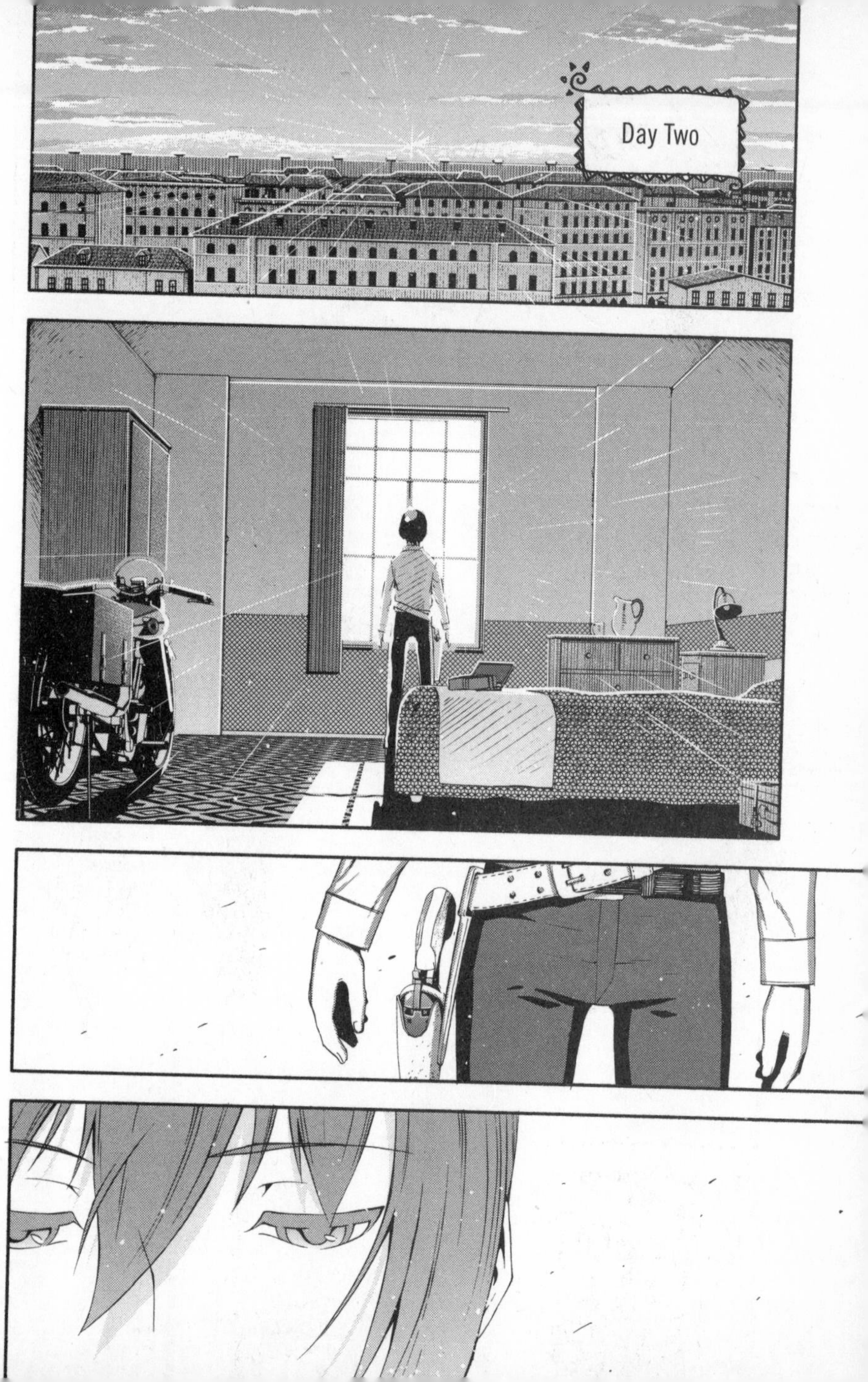
Day Two

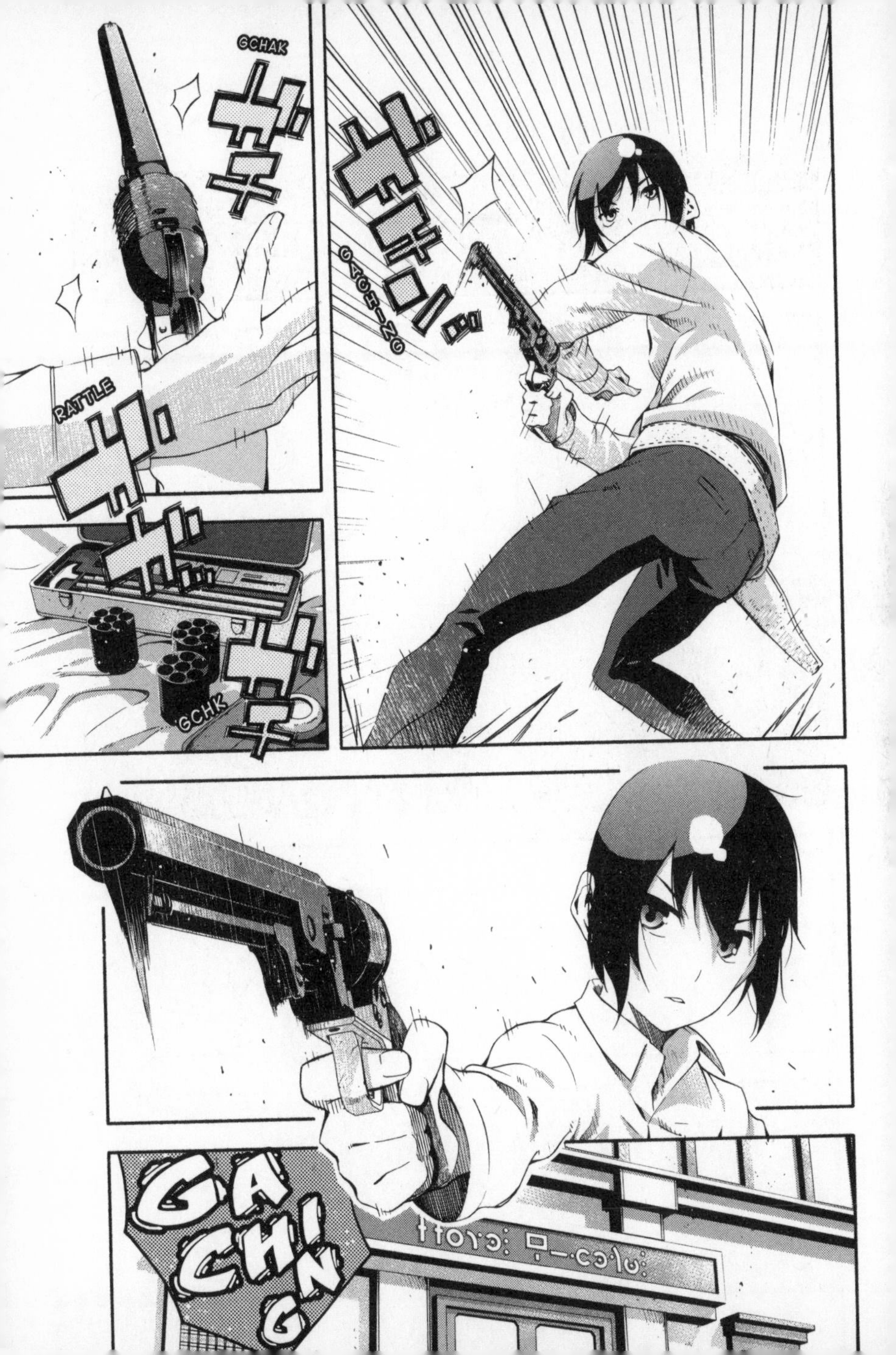
GACHING
GCHAK
RATTLE
GCHK
GACHING

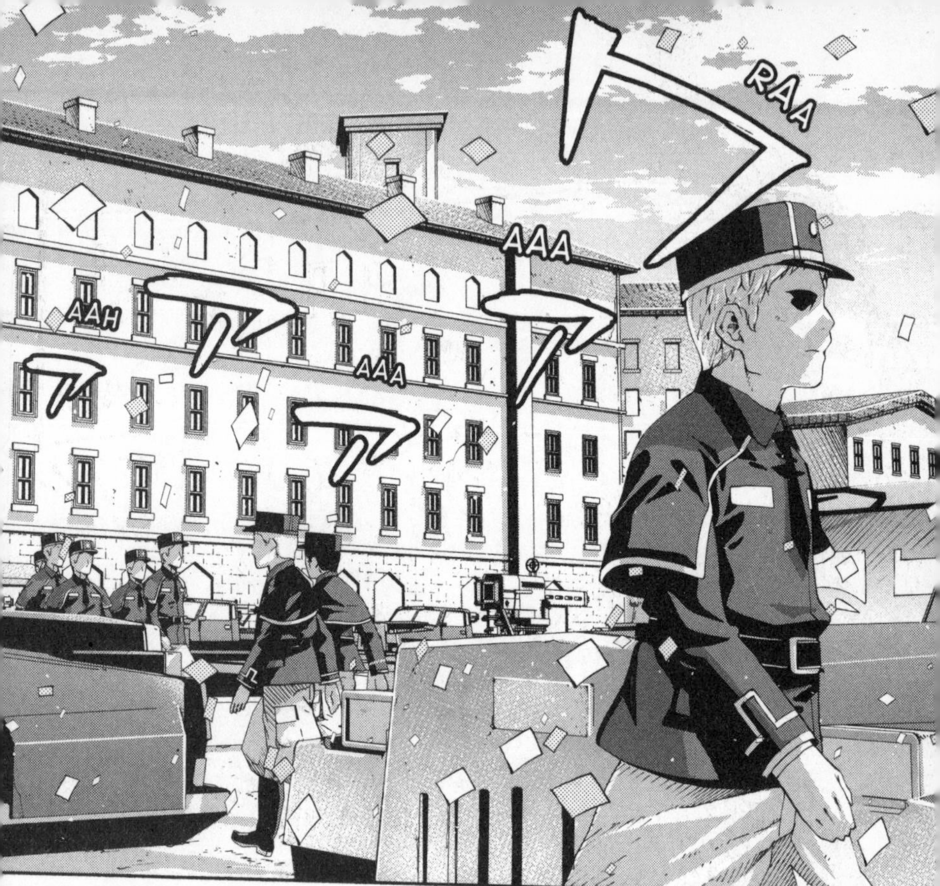
RAA
AAA
AAH
AAA

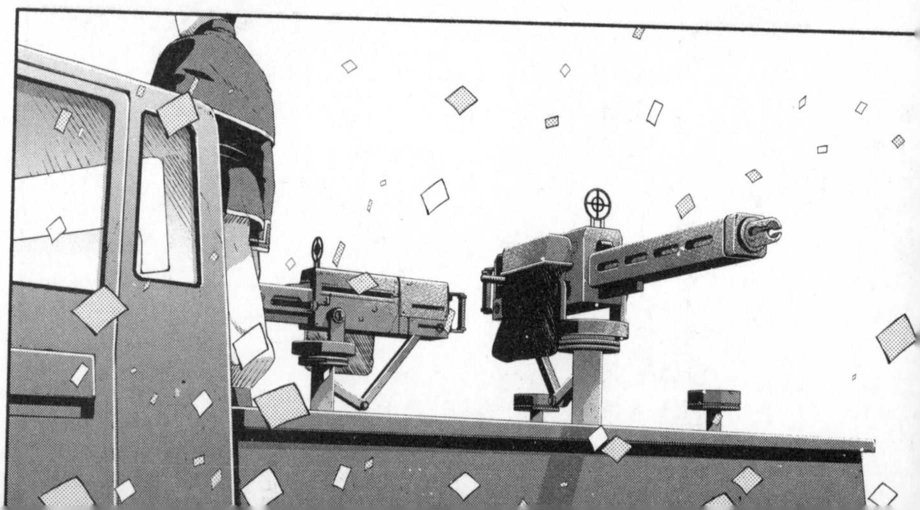

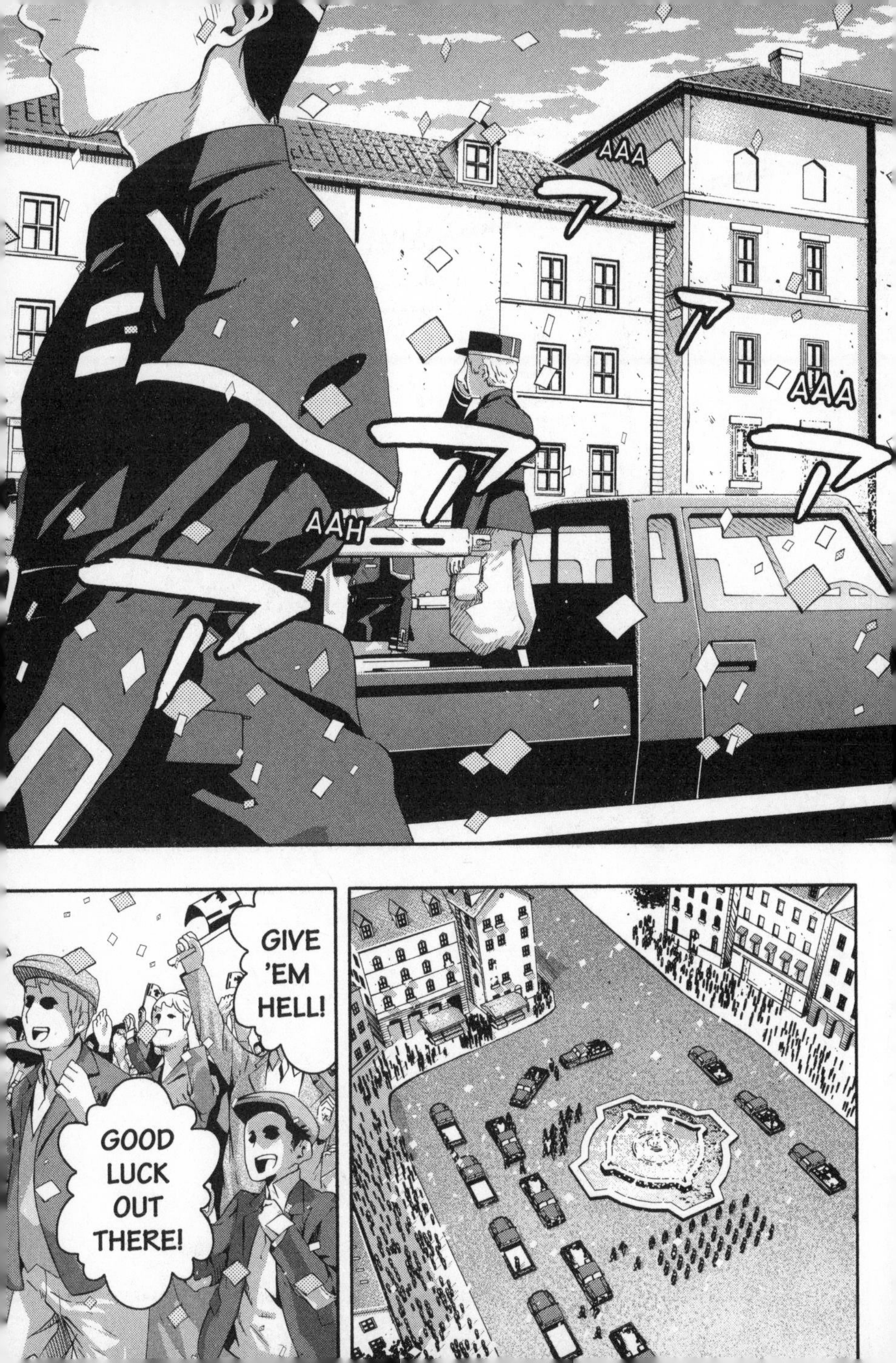
AAA
AAA
AAH
GIVE 'EM HELL!
GOOD LUCK OUT THERE!

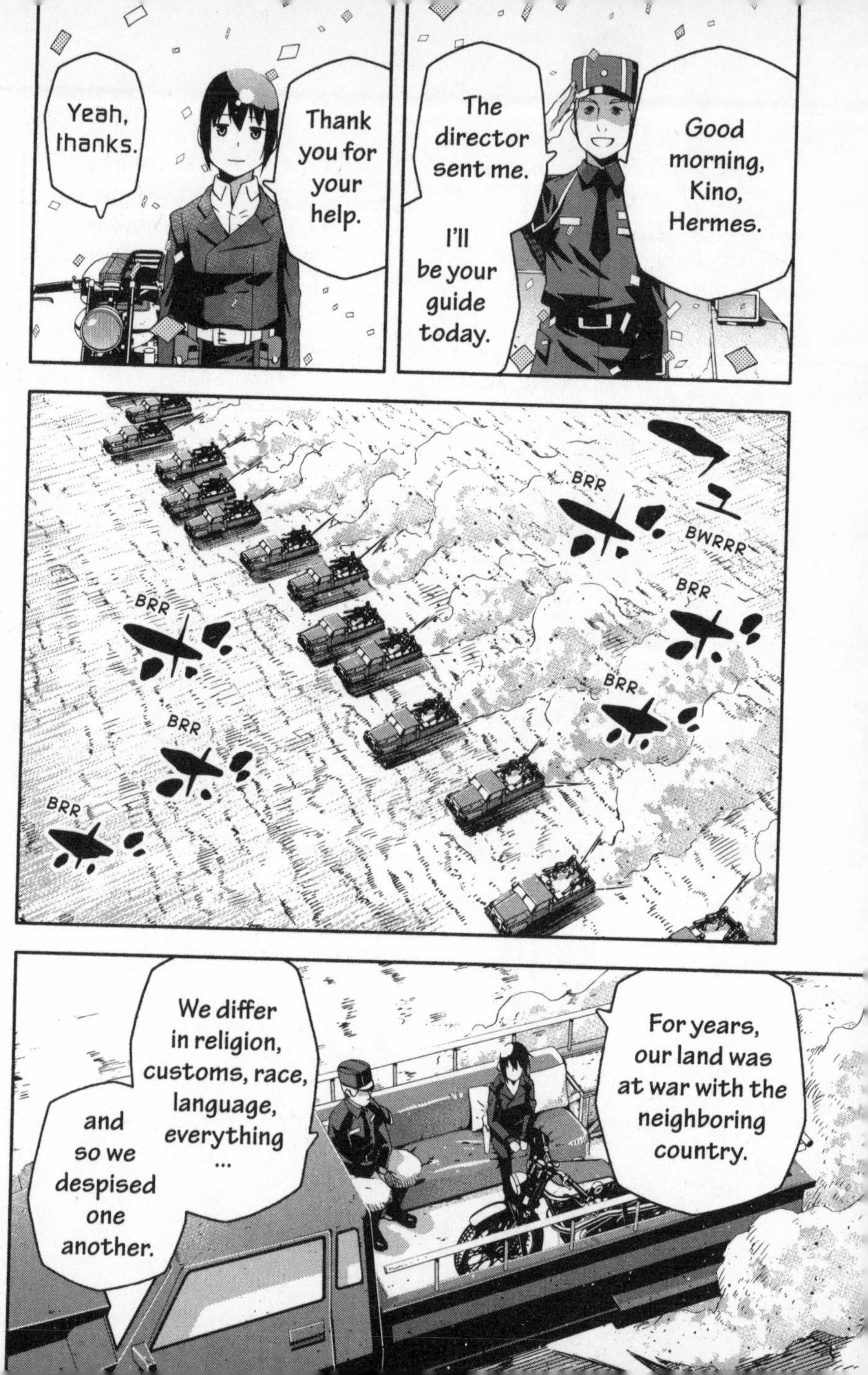
Good morning, Kino, Hermes.
The director sent me.
I'll be your guide today.
Thank you for your help.
Yeah, thanks.
BRR
BWRRR
BRR
BRR
BRR
BRR
BRR
For years, our land was at war with the neighboring country.
We differ in religion, customs, race, language, everything ...
and so we despised one another.

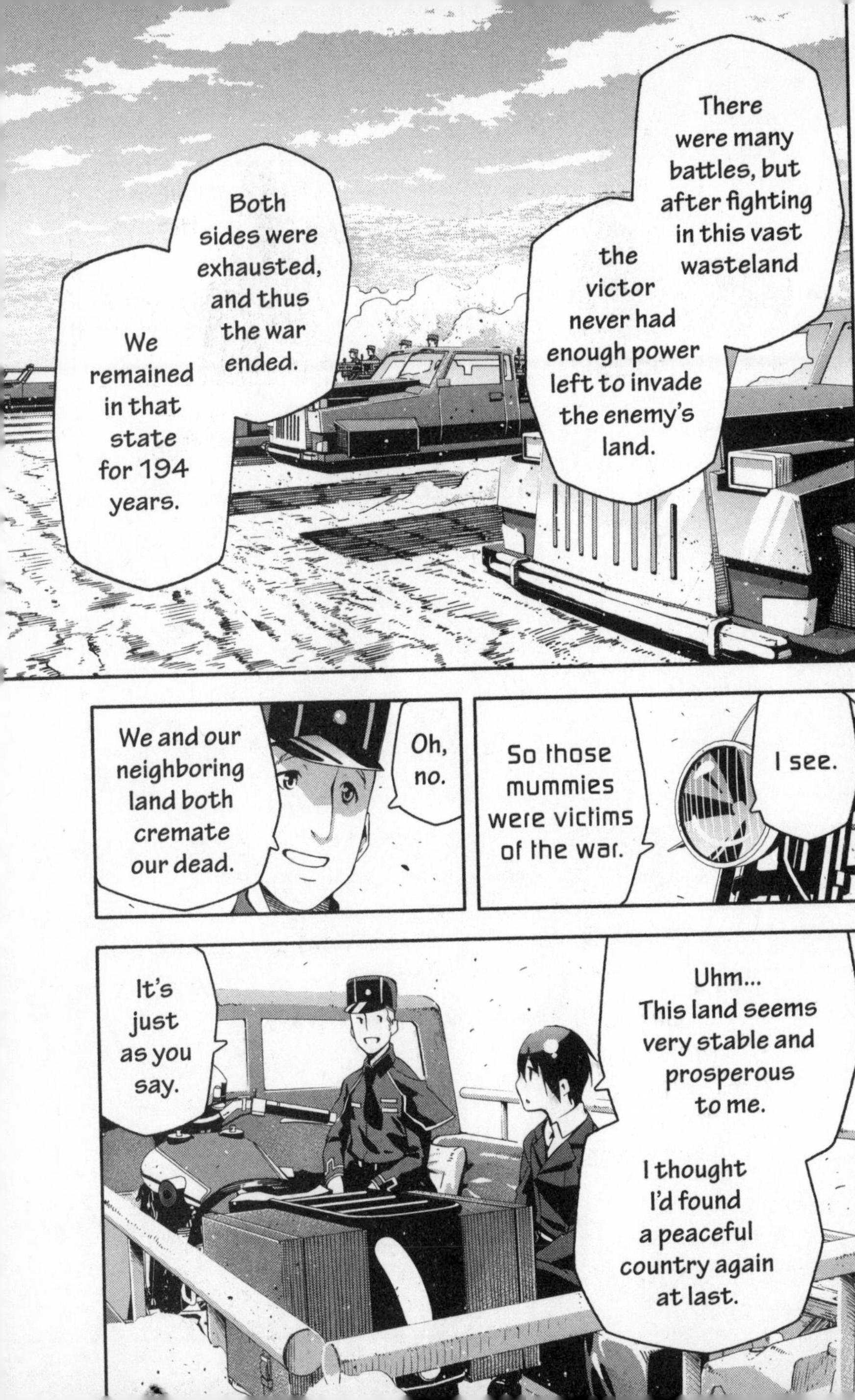
There were many battles, but after fighting in this vast wasteland
the victor never had enough power left to invade the enemy's land.
Both sides were exhausted, and thus the war ended.
We remained in that state for 194 years.
I see.
So those mummies were victims of the war.
Oh, no.
We and our neighboring land both cremate our dead.
Uhm... This land seems very stable and prosperous to me.
I thought I'd found a peaceful country again at last.
It's just as you say.

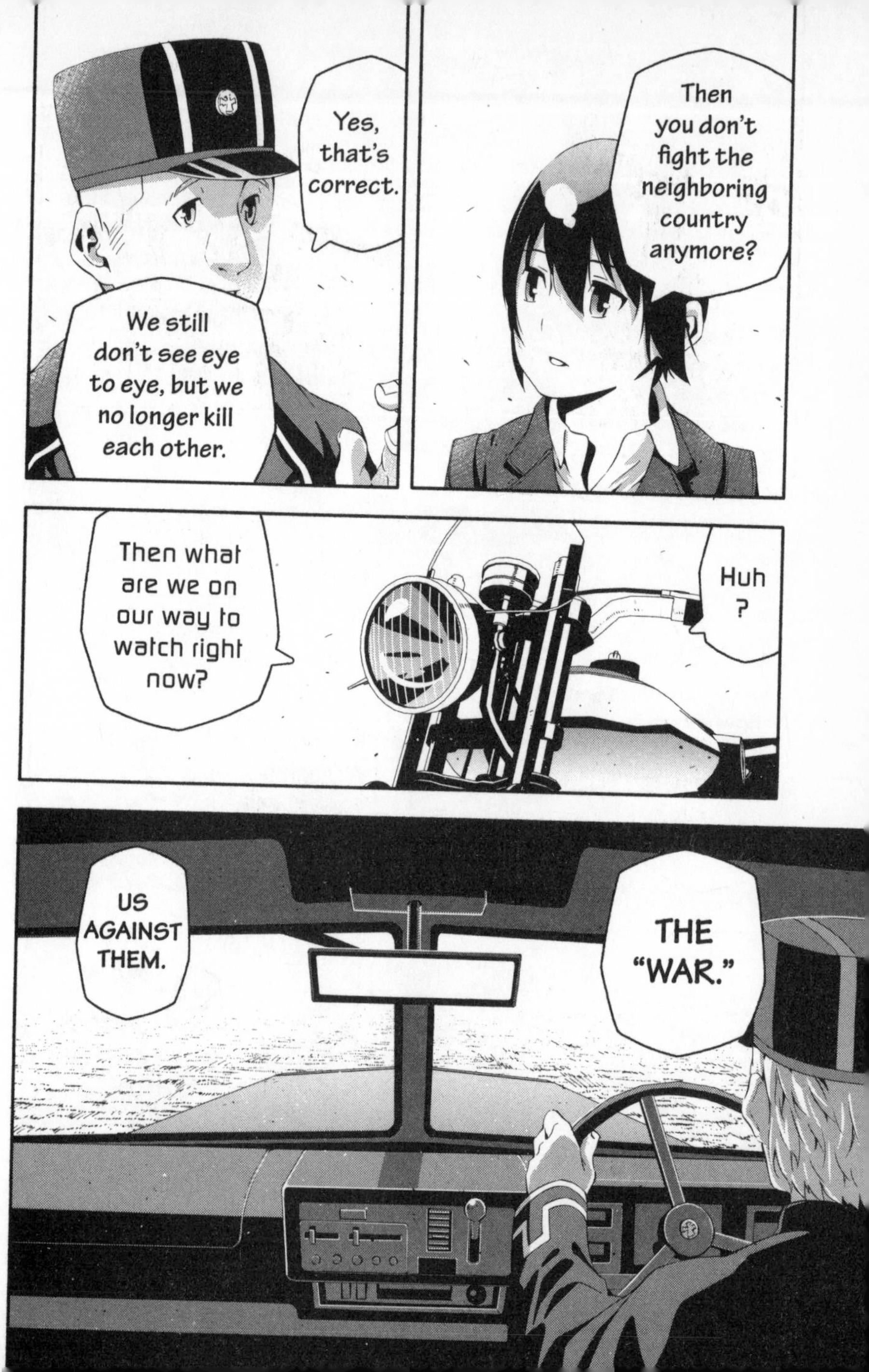
Then you don't fight the neighboring country anymore?
Yes, that's correct.
We still don't see eye to eye, but we no longer kill each other.
Huh?
Then what are we on our way to watch right now?
THE "WAR."
US AGAINST THEM.

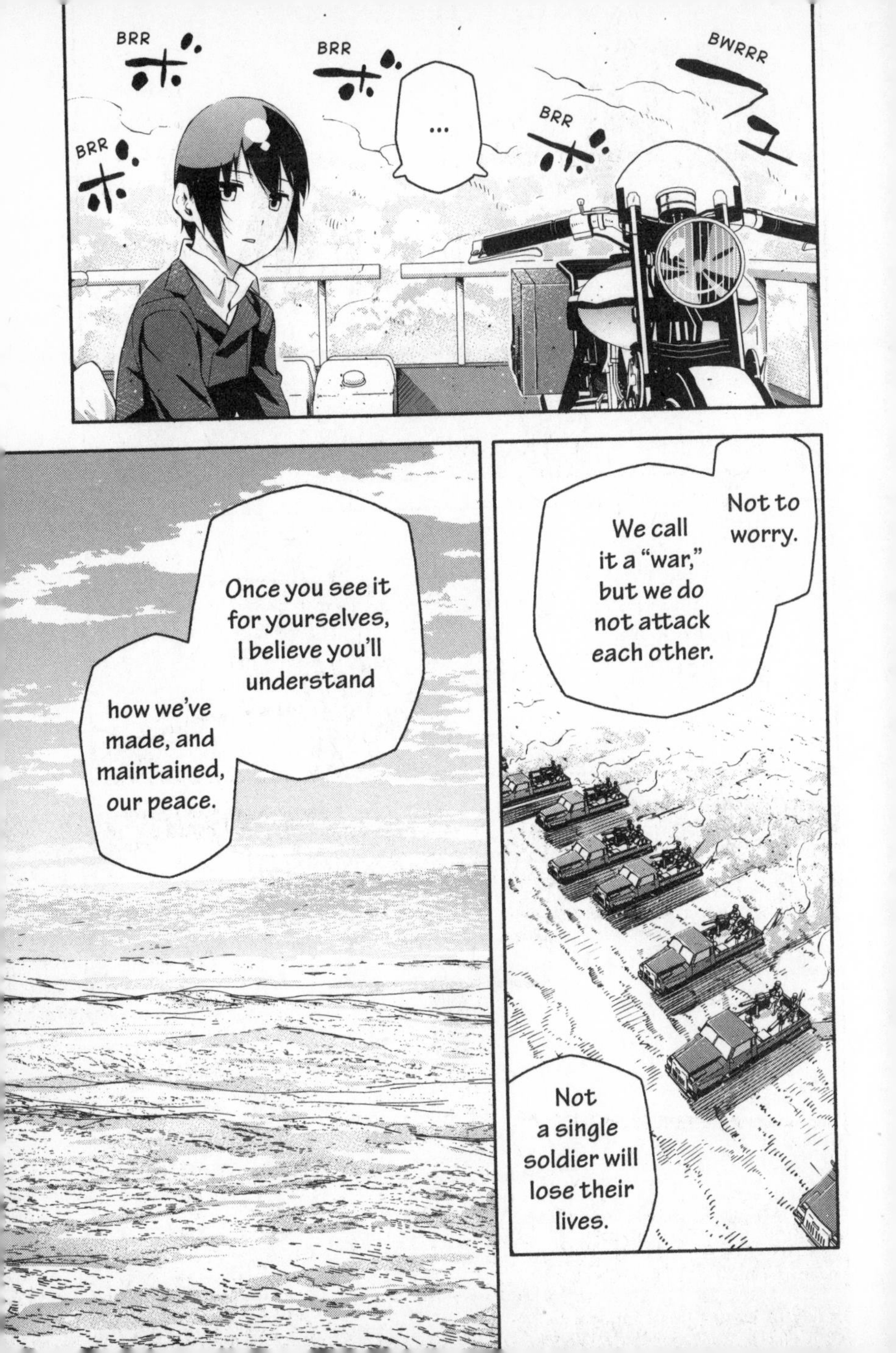
BWRRR
BRR
BRR
...
BRR
BRR
Not to worry.
We call it a "war," but we do not attack each other.
Not a single soldier will lose their lives.
Once you see it for yourselves, I believe you'll understand
how we've made, and maintained, our peace.

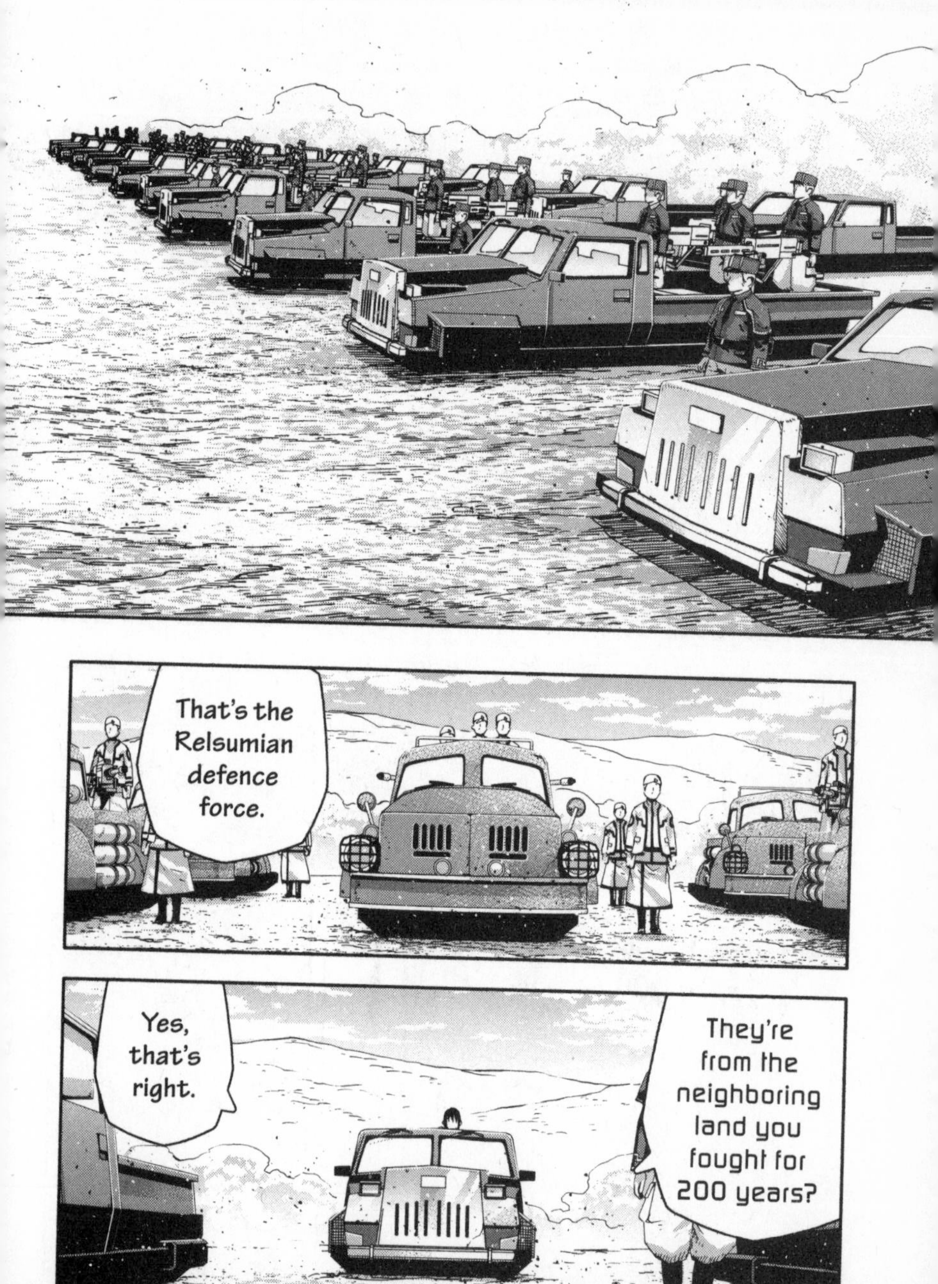
That's the Relsumian defence force.
They're from the neighboring land you fought for 200 years?
Yes, that's right.

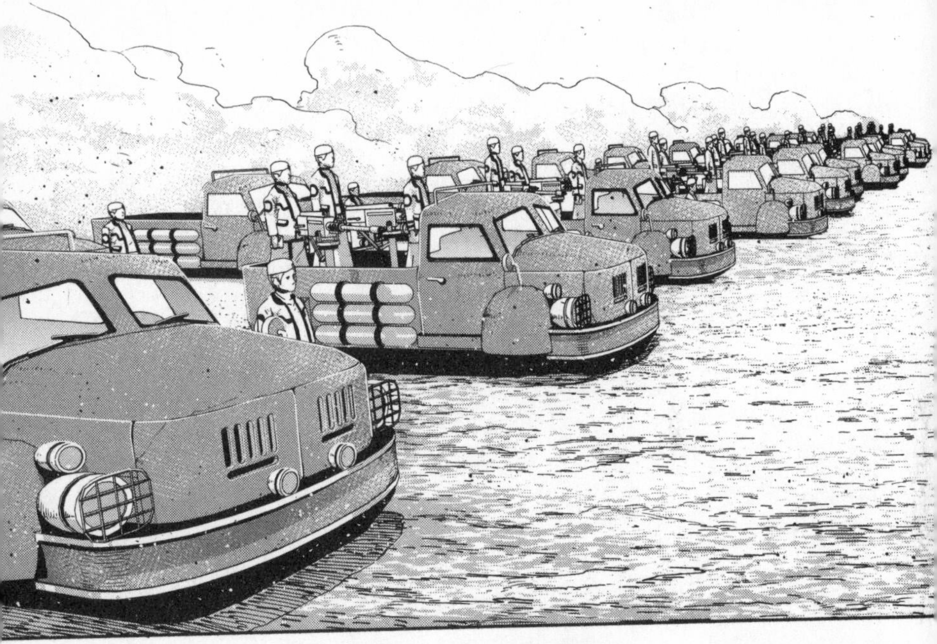

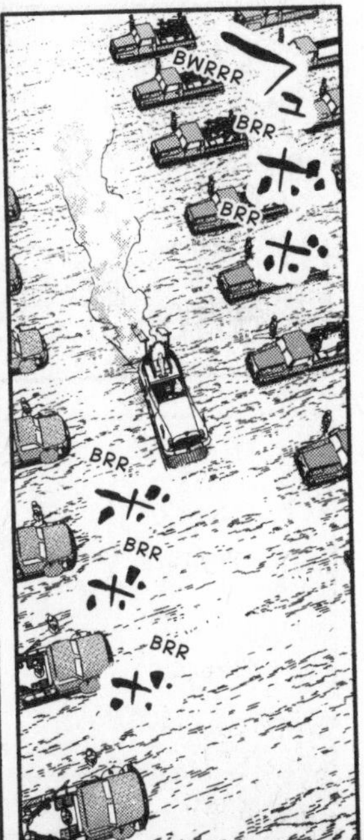
BWRRR
BRR
BRR
BRR
BRR
BRR

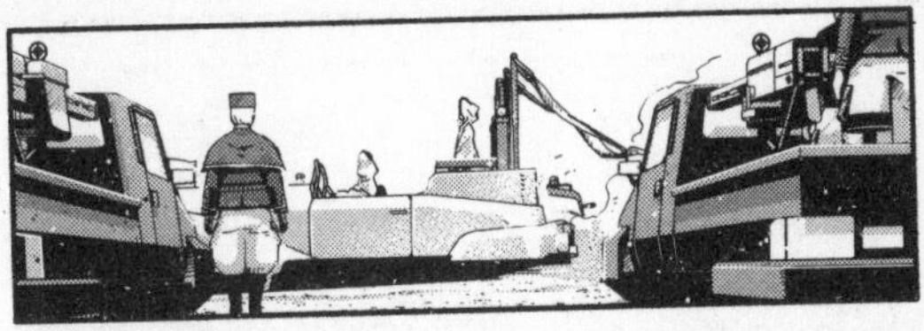

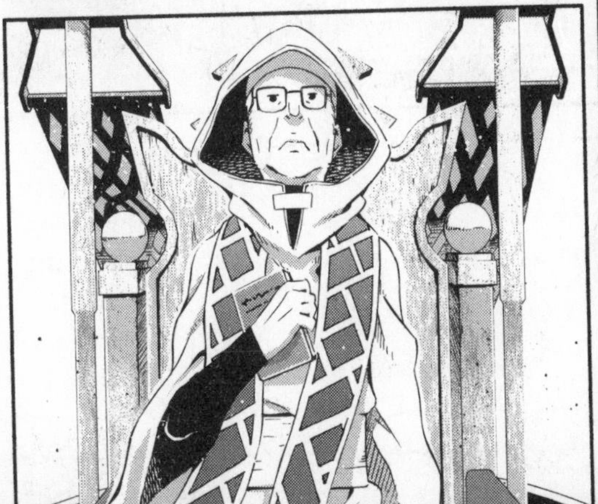

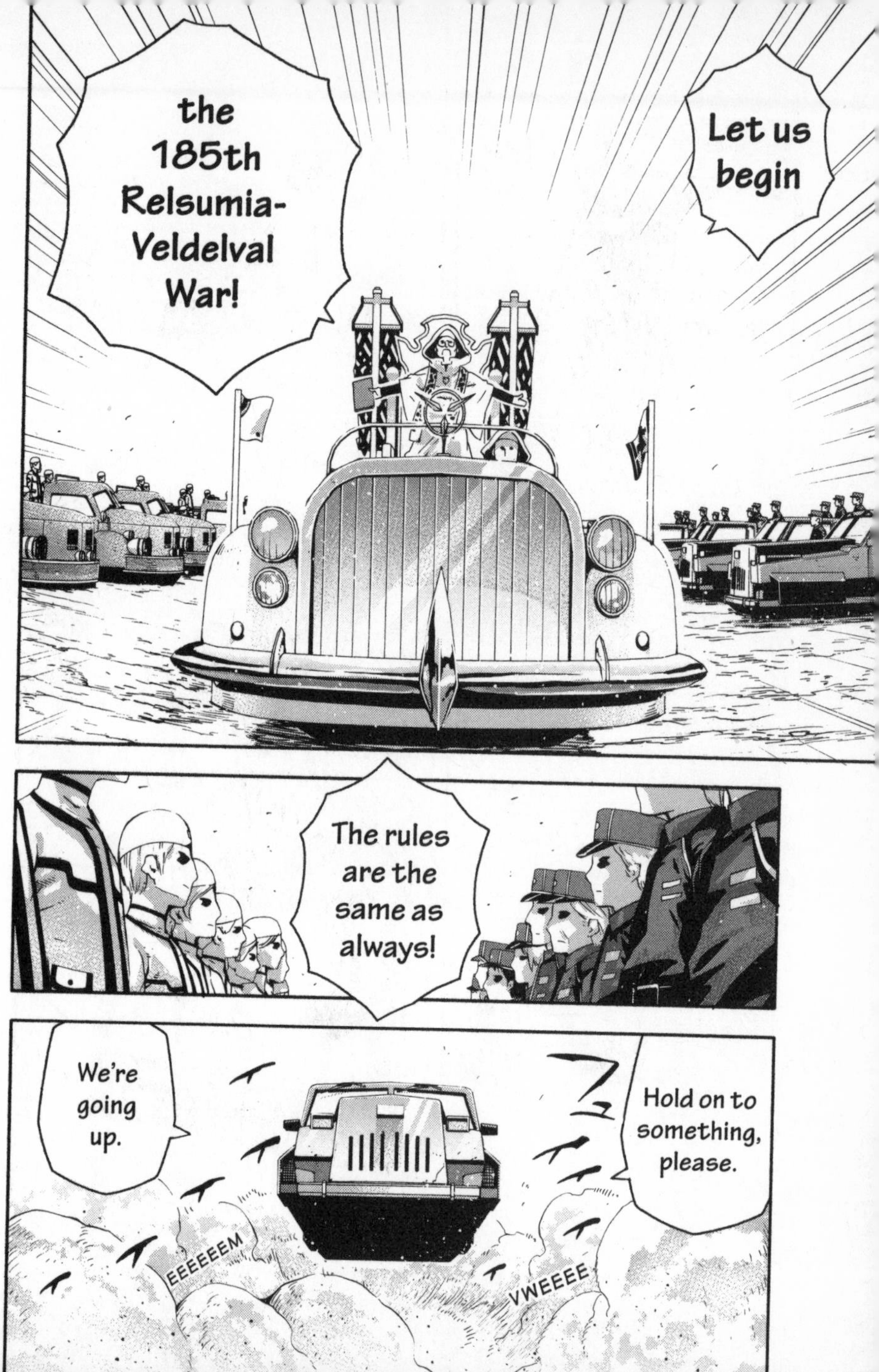
Let us begin
the 185th Relsumia-Veldelval War!
The rules are the same as always!
Hold on to something, please.
We're going up.
VWEEEE
EEEEEEM

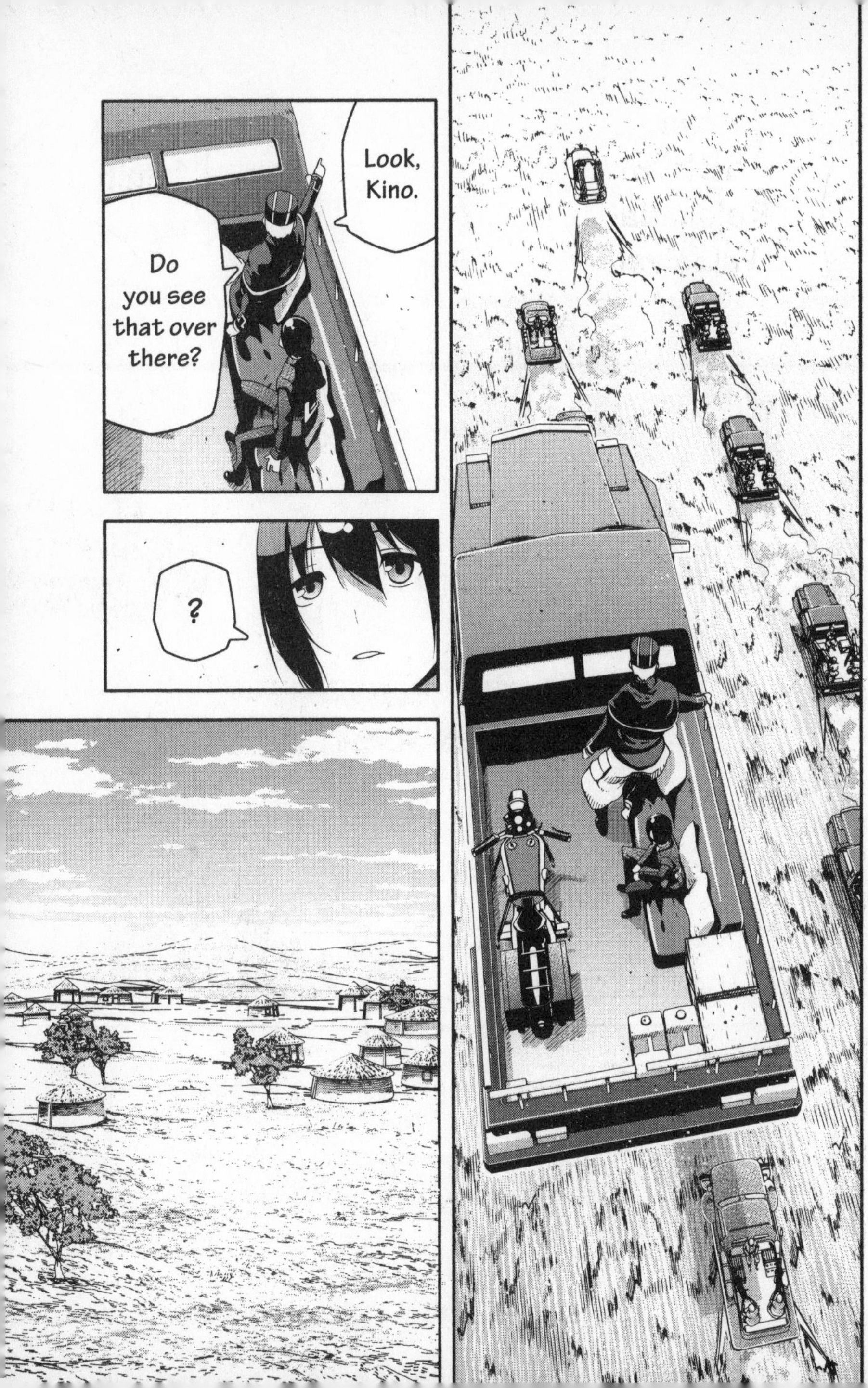
Look, Kino.
Do you see that over there?
?

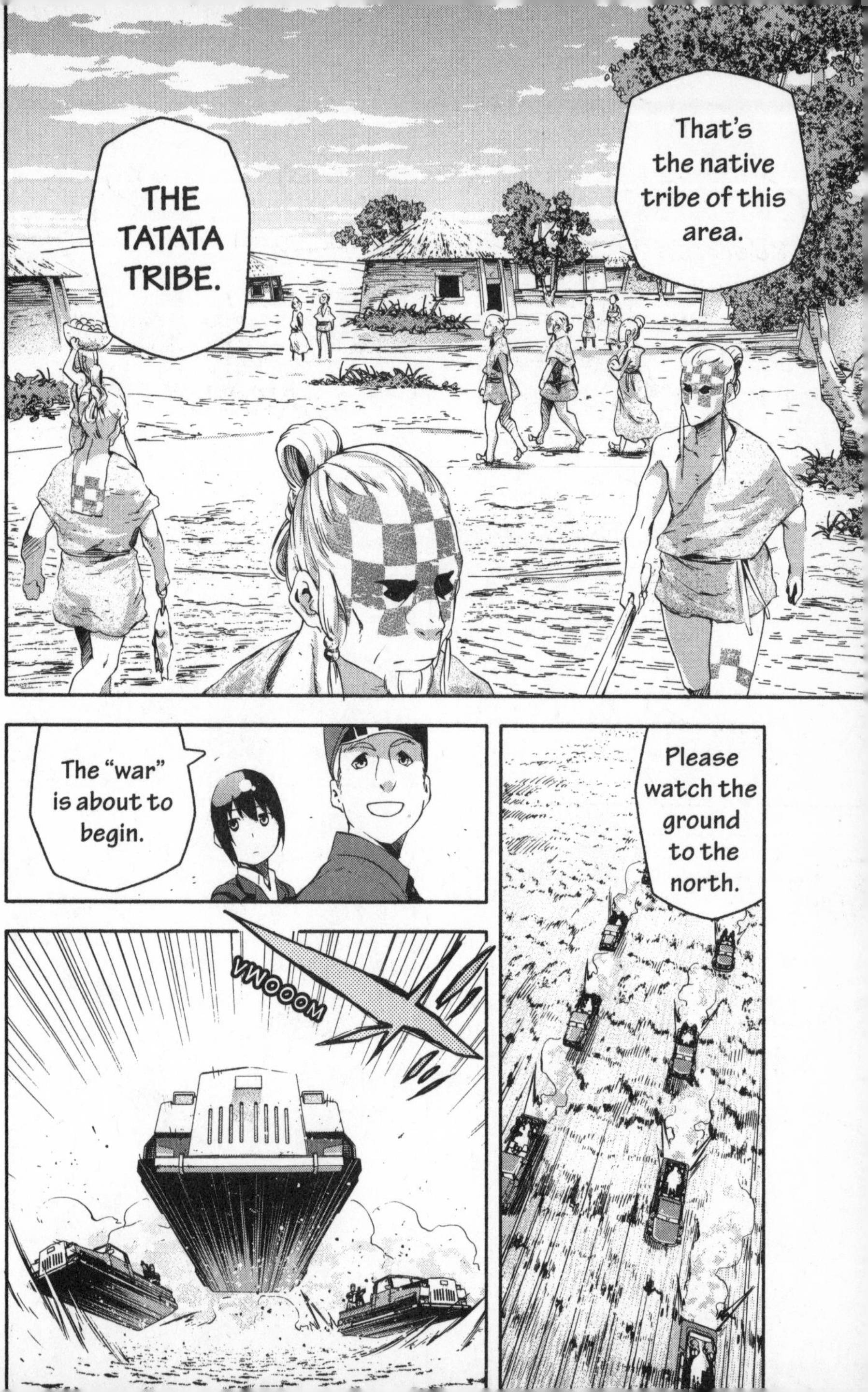
That's the native tribe of this area.
THE TATATA TRIBE.
Please watch the ground to the north.
The "war" is about to begin.
VWOOOM

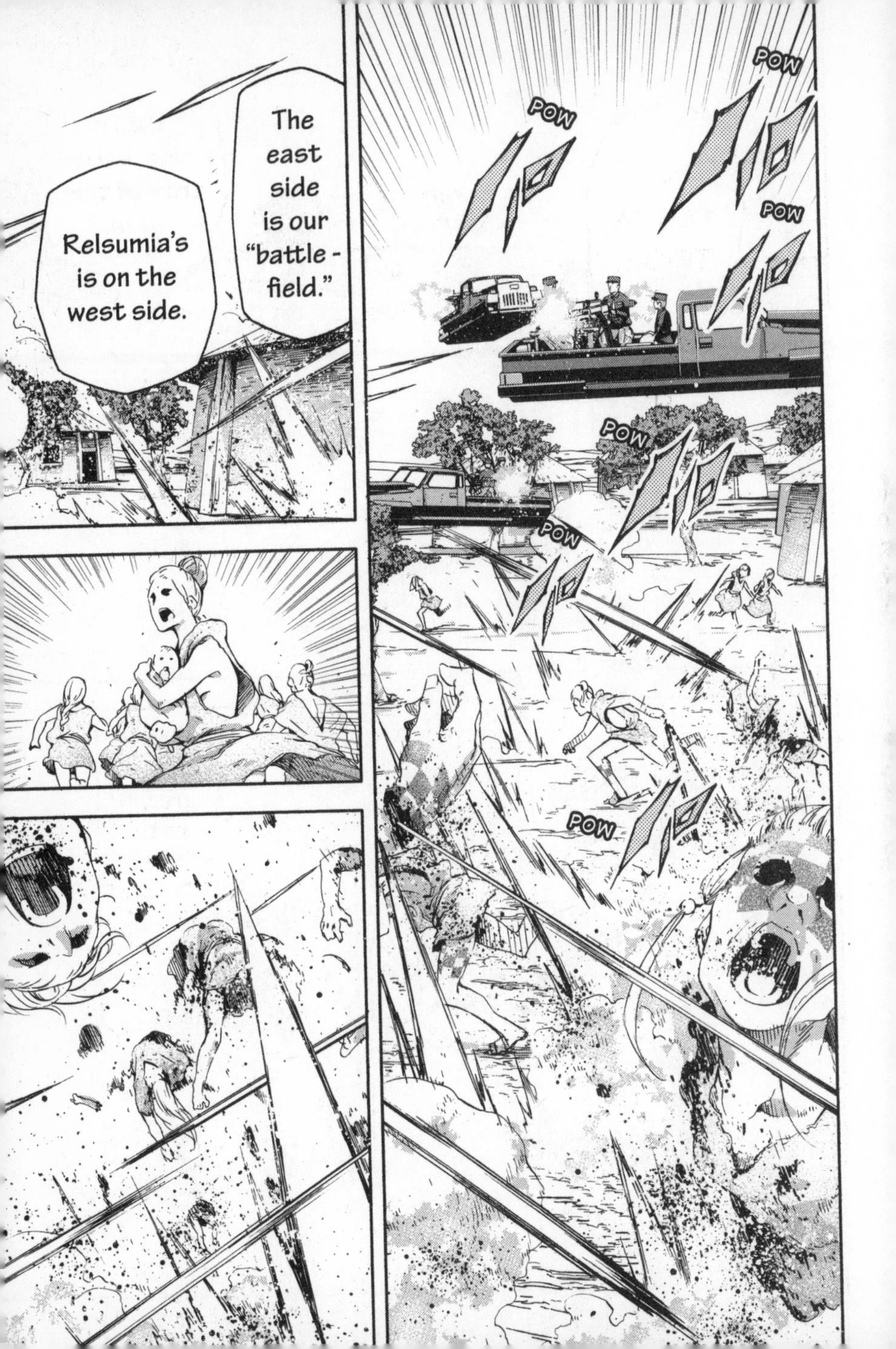
POW
POW
POW
POW
POW
POW
The east side is our "battle-field."
Relsumia's is on the west side.

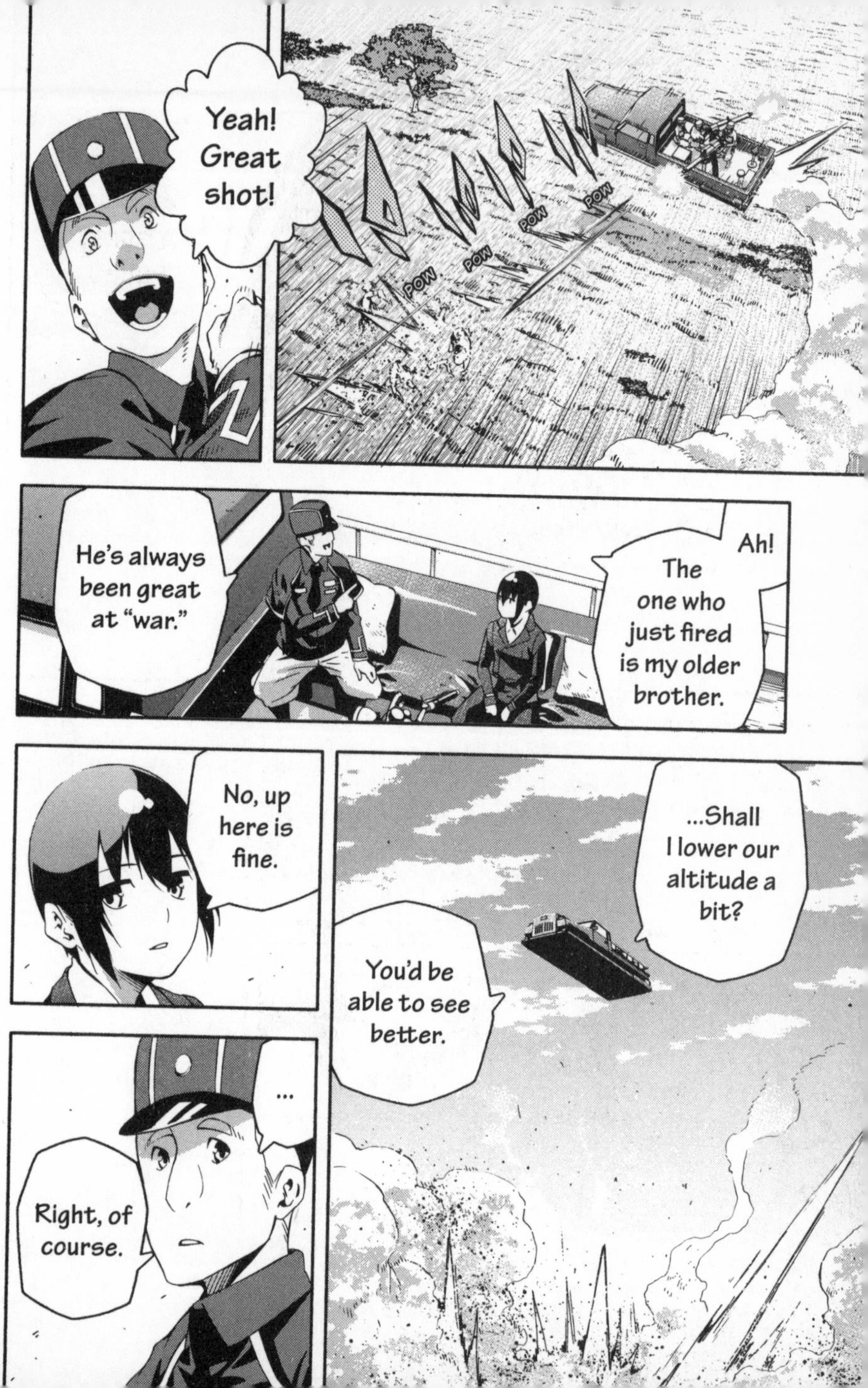
POW
POW
POW
POW
POW
Yeah! Great shot!
Ah! The one who just fired is my older brother.
He's always been great at "war."
...Shall I lower our altitude a bit?
You'd be able to see better.
No, up here is fine.
...
Right, of course.

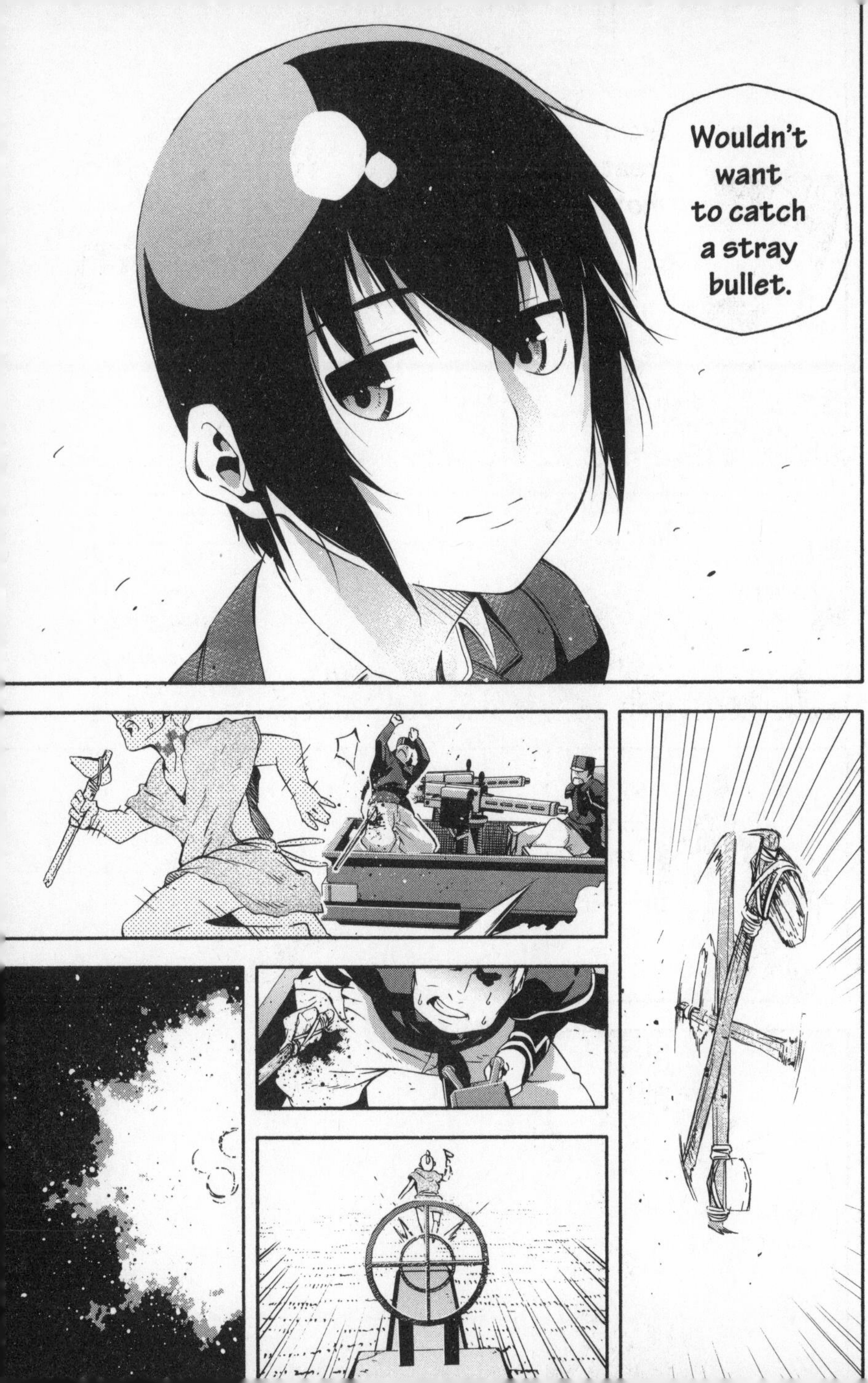
Wouldn't want to catch a stray bullet.

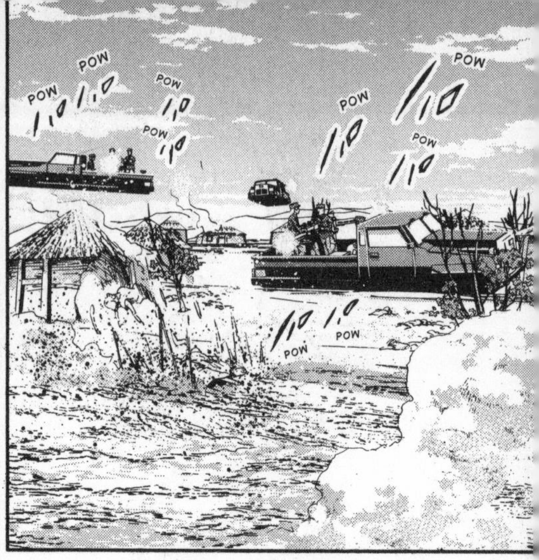
POW
POW
POW
POW
POW
POW
POW
POW
POW

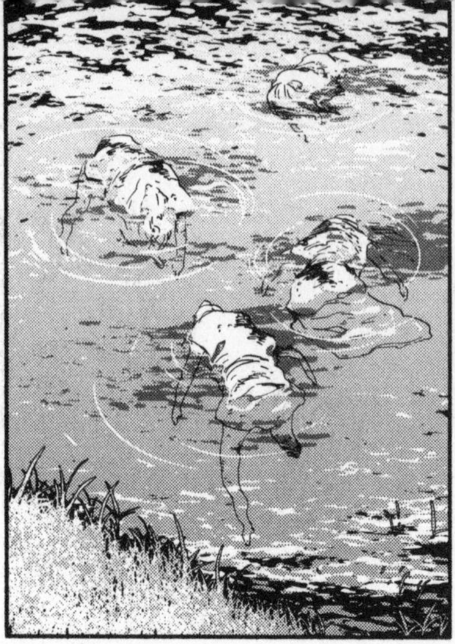

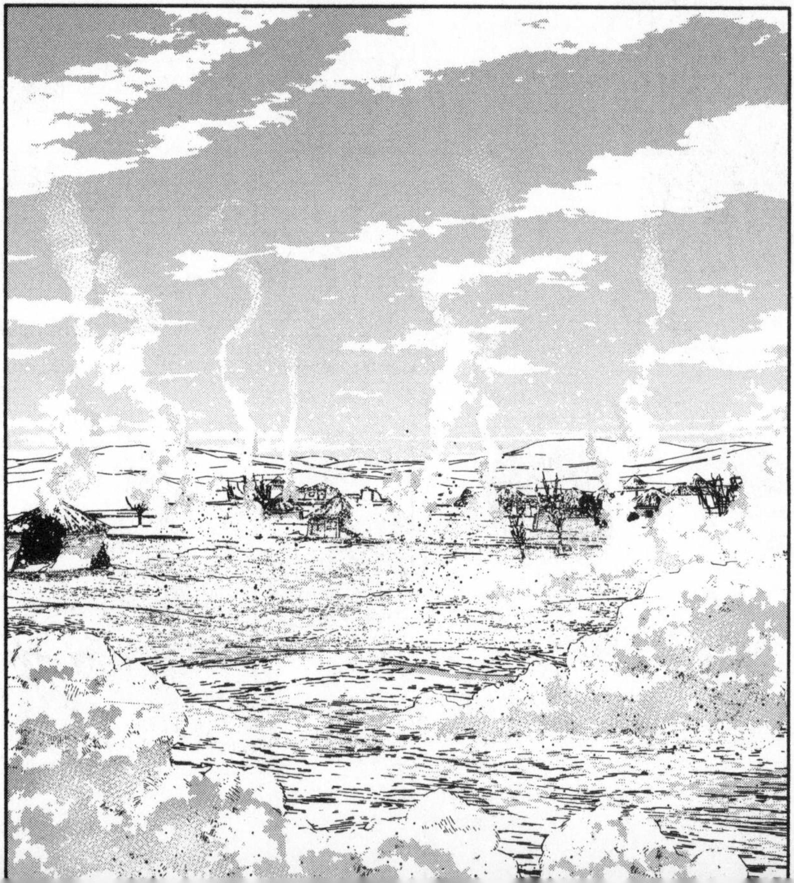

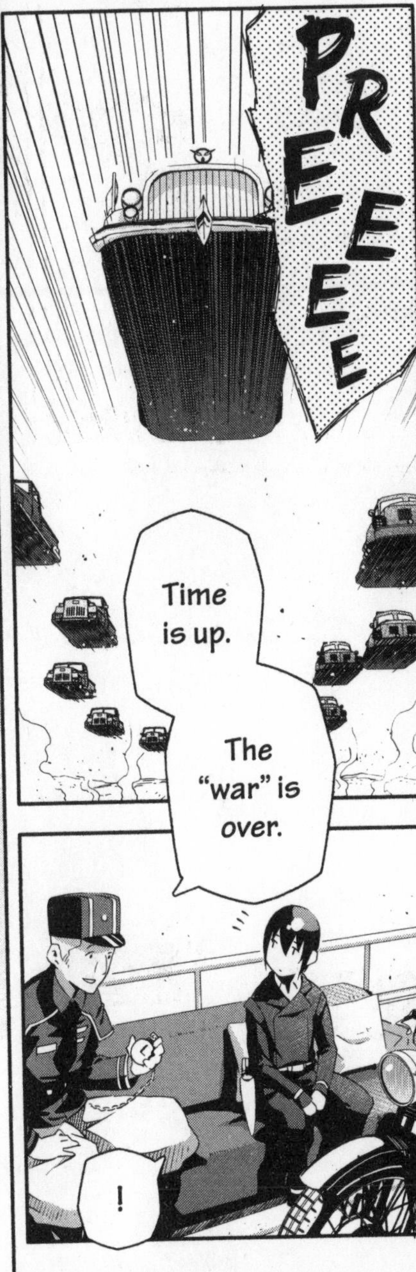
PREEEEE
Time is up.
The "war" is over.
!

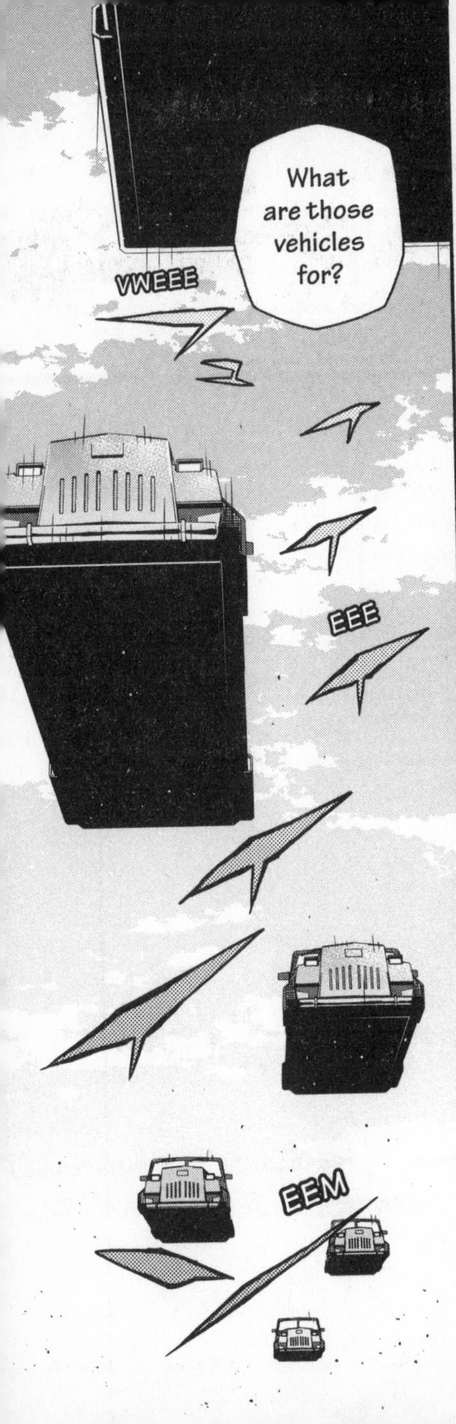
What are those vehicles for?
VWEEE
EEE
EEM

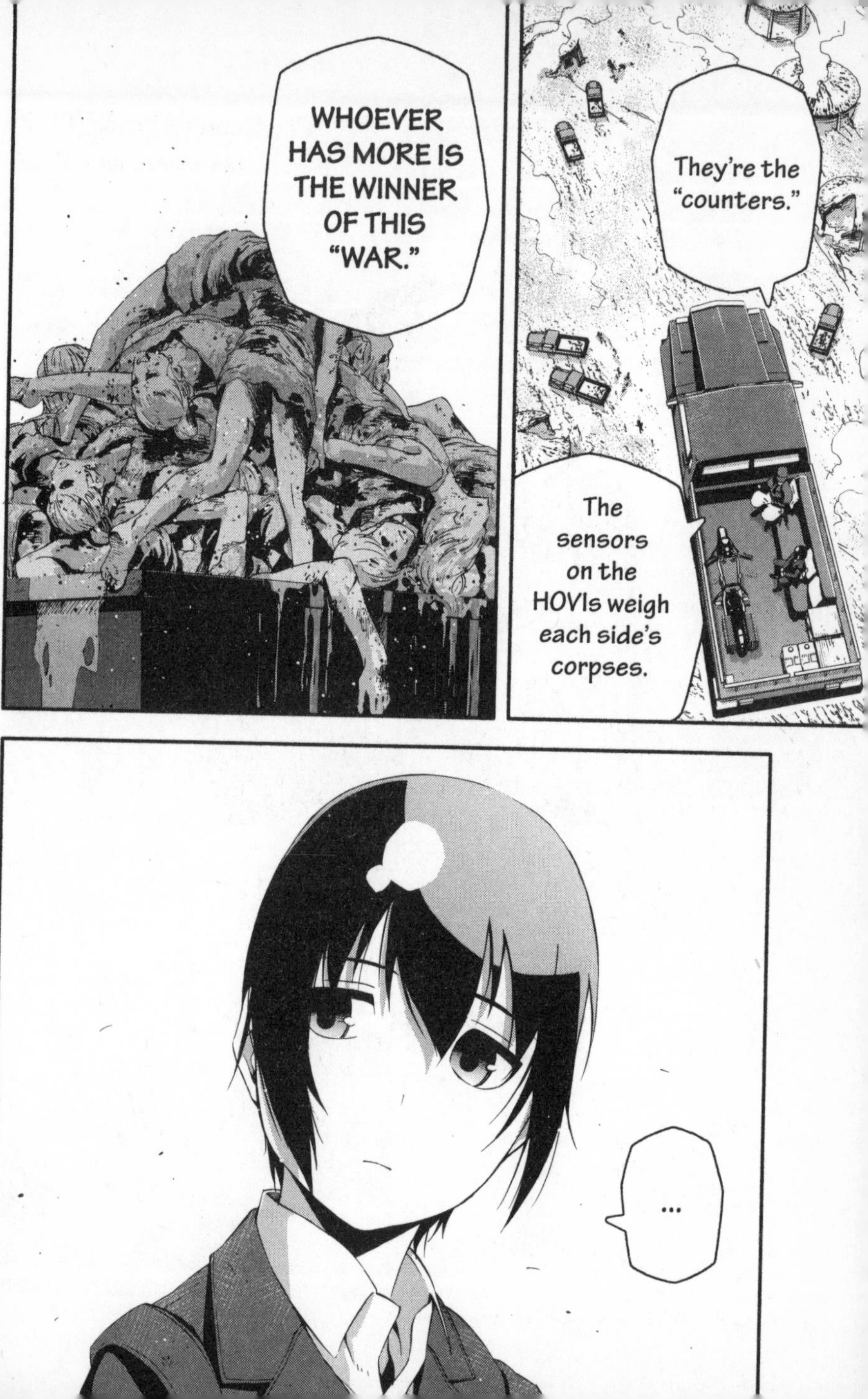
They're the "counters."
The sensors on the HOVIs weigh each side's corpses.
WHOEVER HAS MORE IS THE WINNER OF THIS "WAR."
...

Chapter 4

The Land of Peace (Pt. 2)

-Mother's Love-

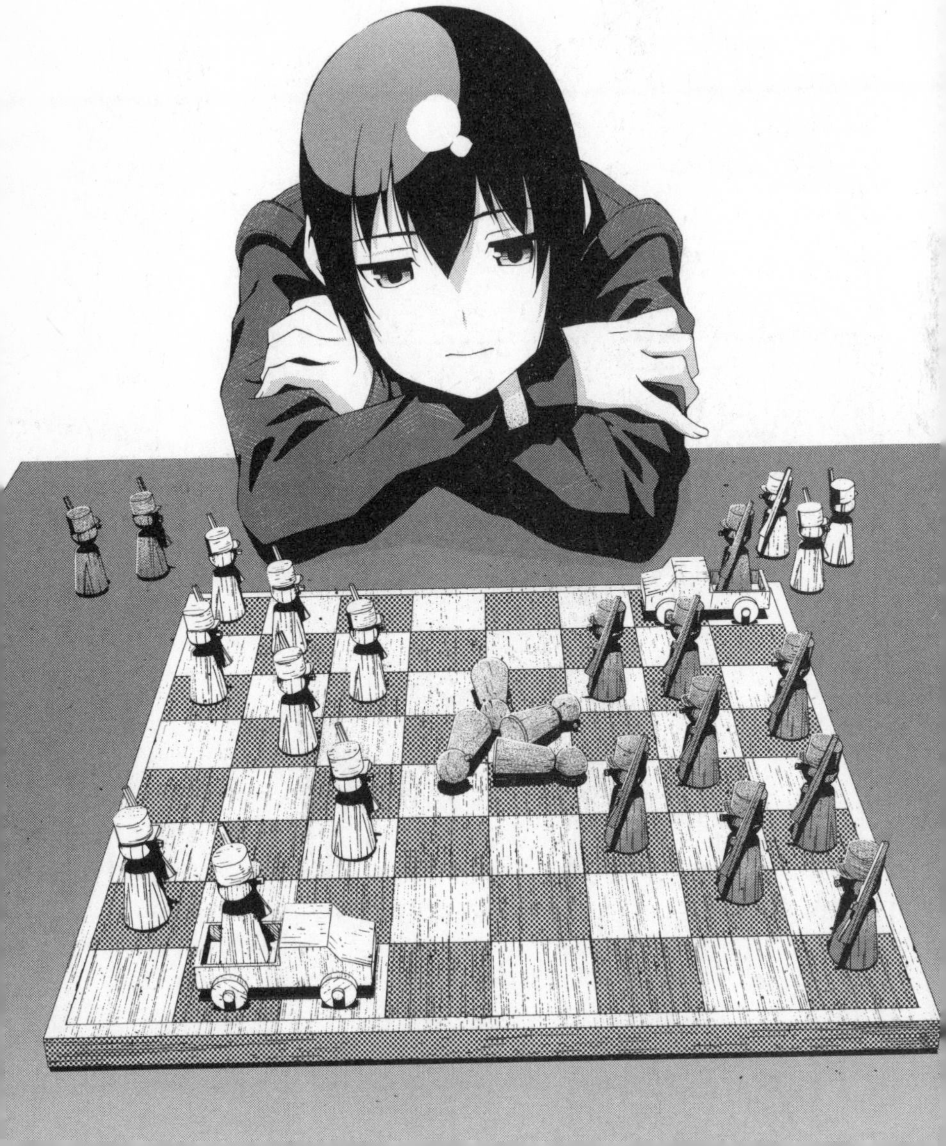

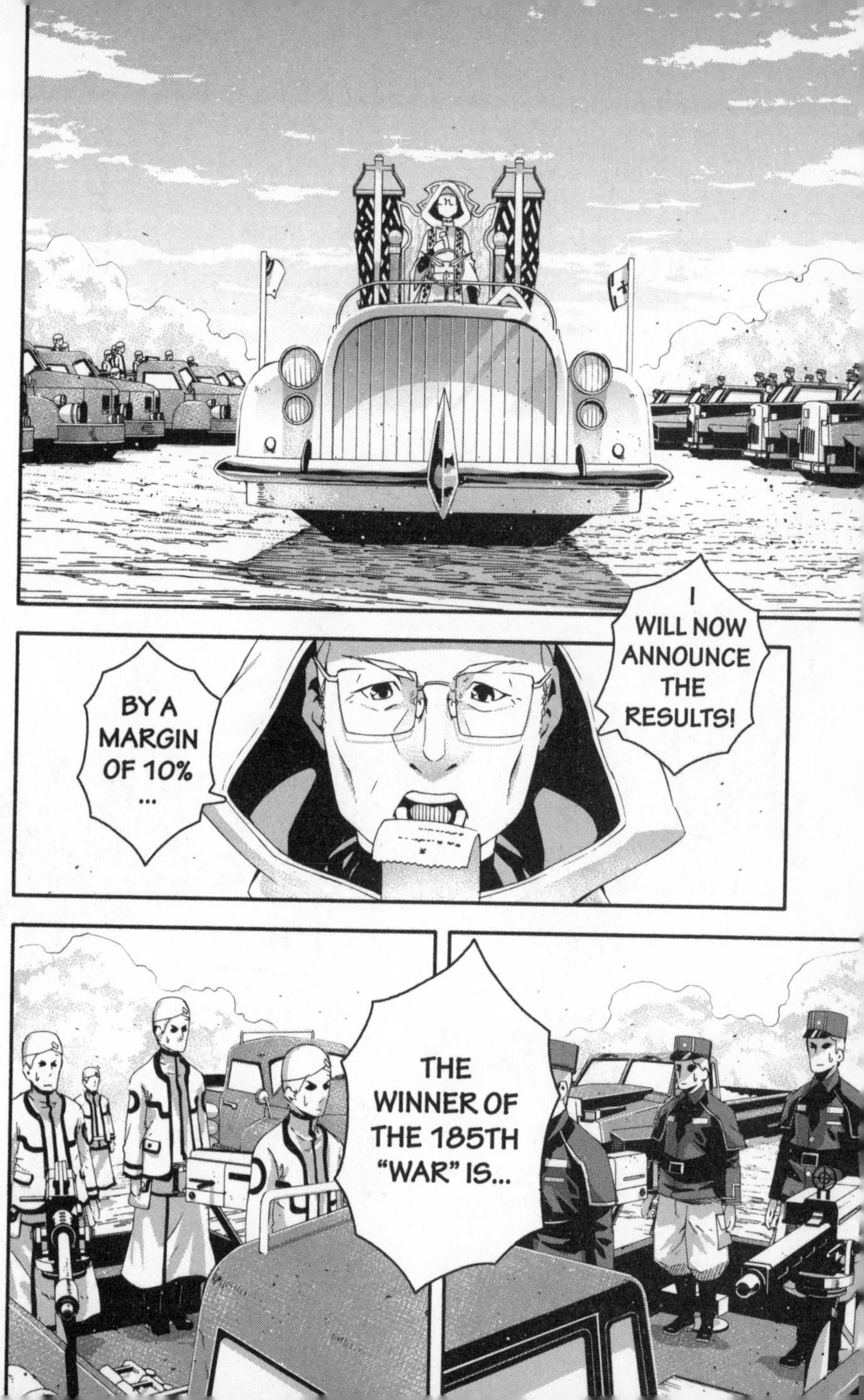
I WILL NOW ANNOUNCE THE RESULTS!
BY A MARGIN OF 10% ...
THE WINNER OF THE 185TH "WAR" IS...

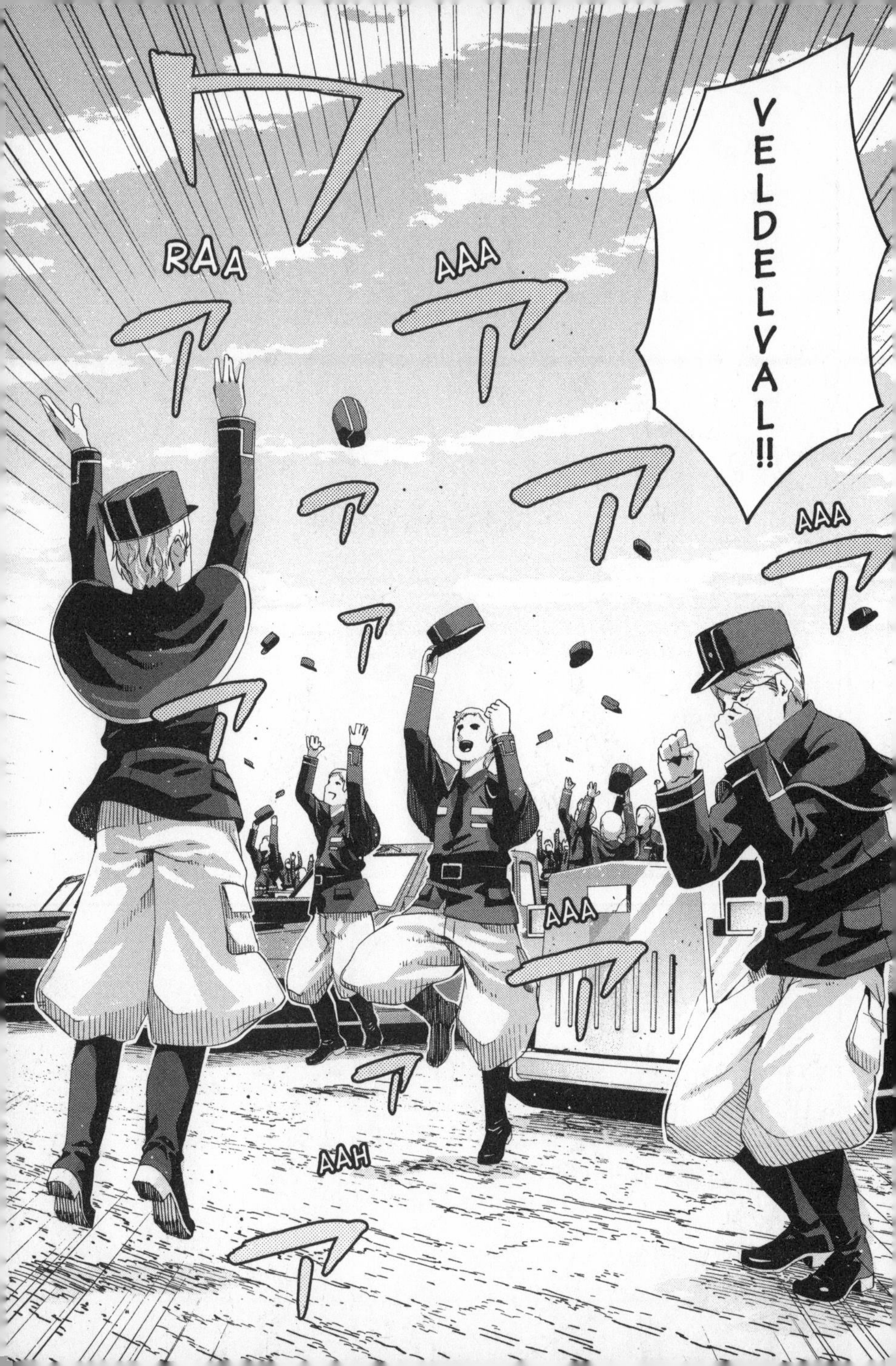
VELDELVAL!!
AAA
RAA
AAA
AAA
AAH

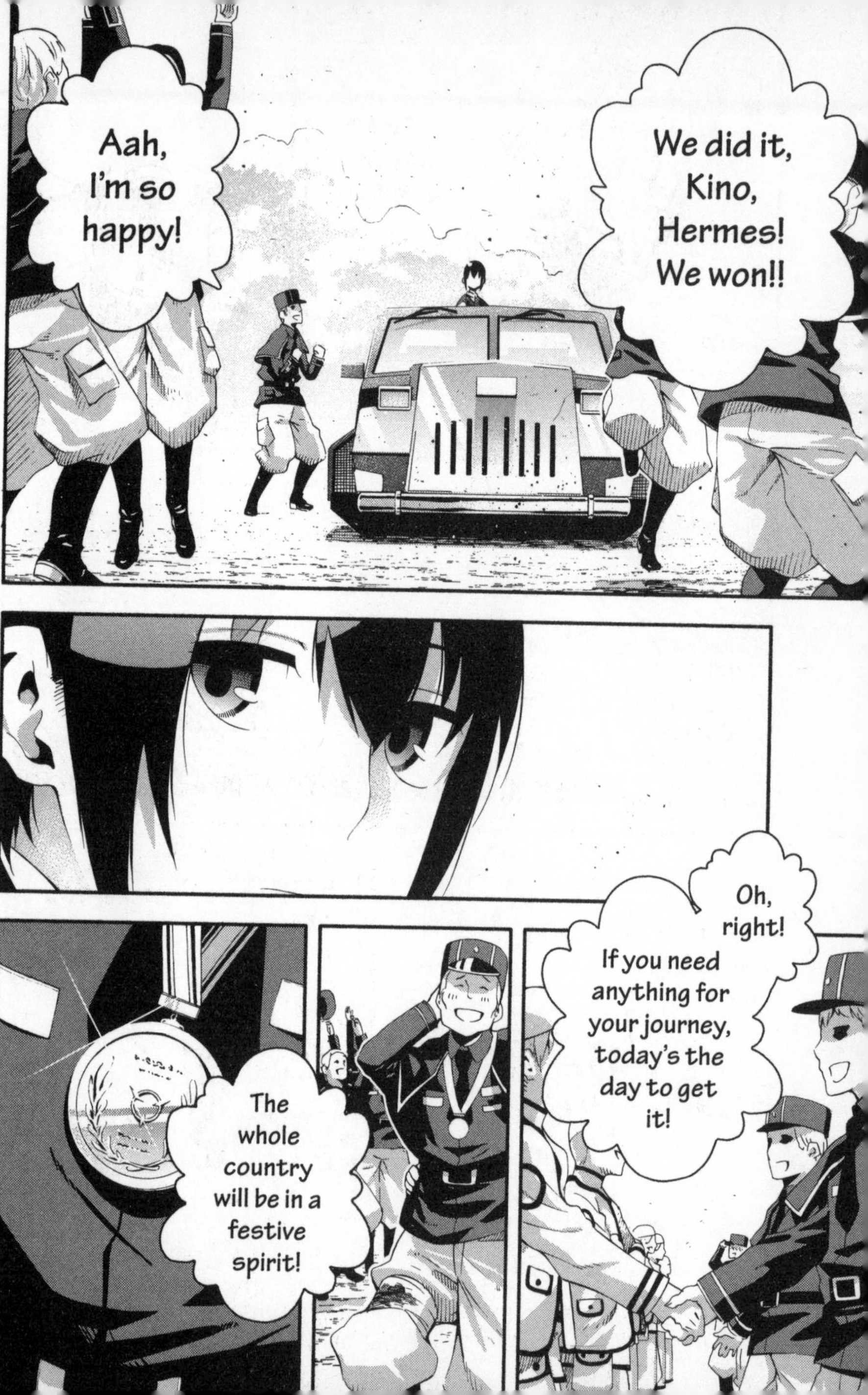

We did it, Kino, Hermes! We won!!
Aah, I'm so happy!
Oh, right!
If you need anything for your journey, today's the day to get it!
The whole country will be in a festive spirit!

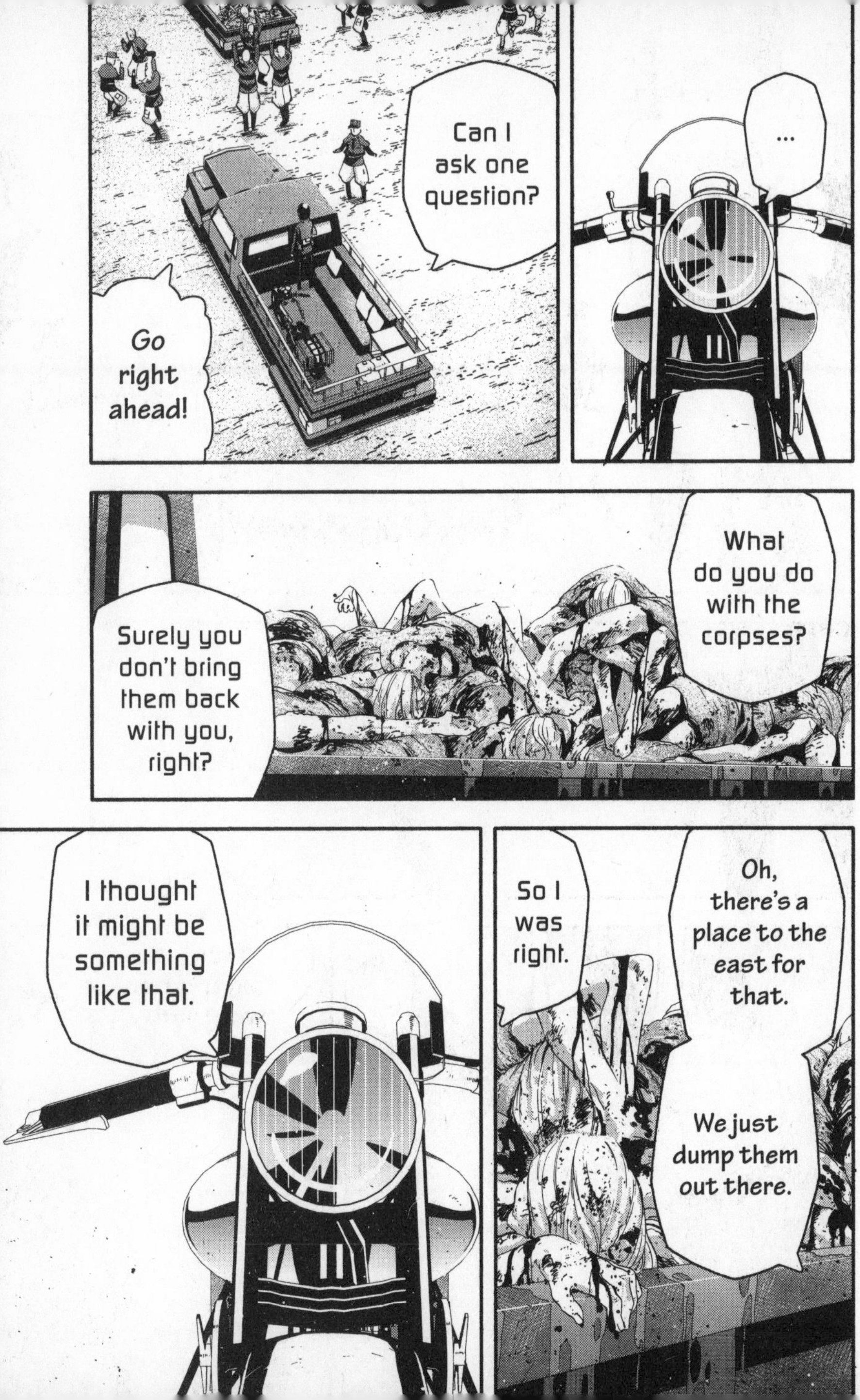
...
Can I ask one question?
Go right ahead!
What do you do with the corpses?
Surely you don't bring them back with you, right?
Oh, there's a place to the east for that.
We just dump them out there.
So I was right.
I thought it might be something like that.

Day Three

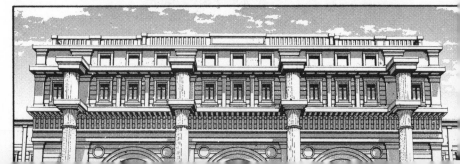

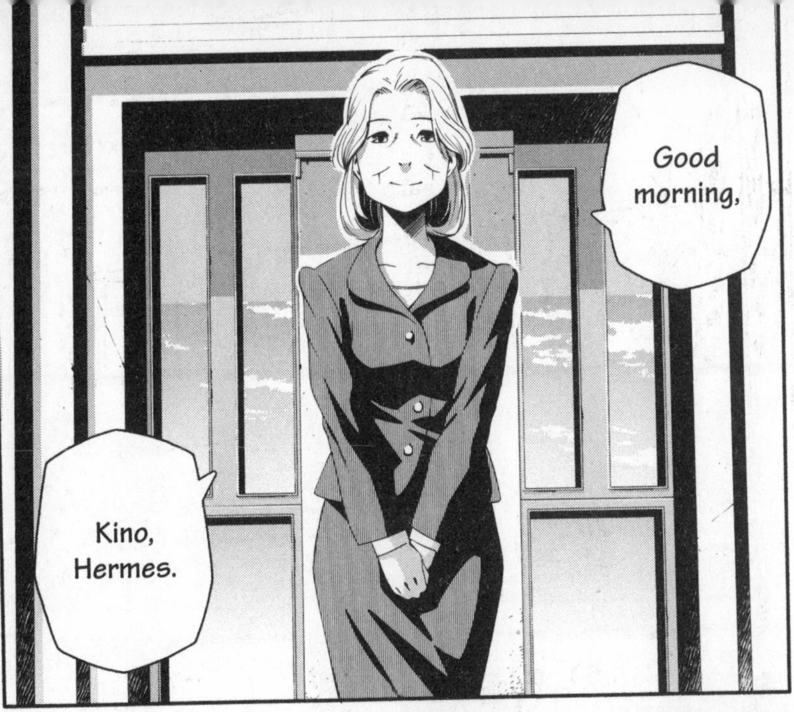
Good morning,
Kino, Hermes.
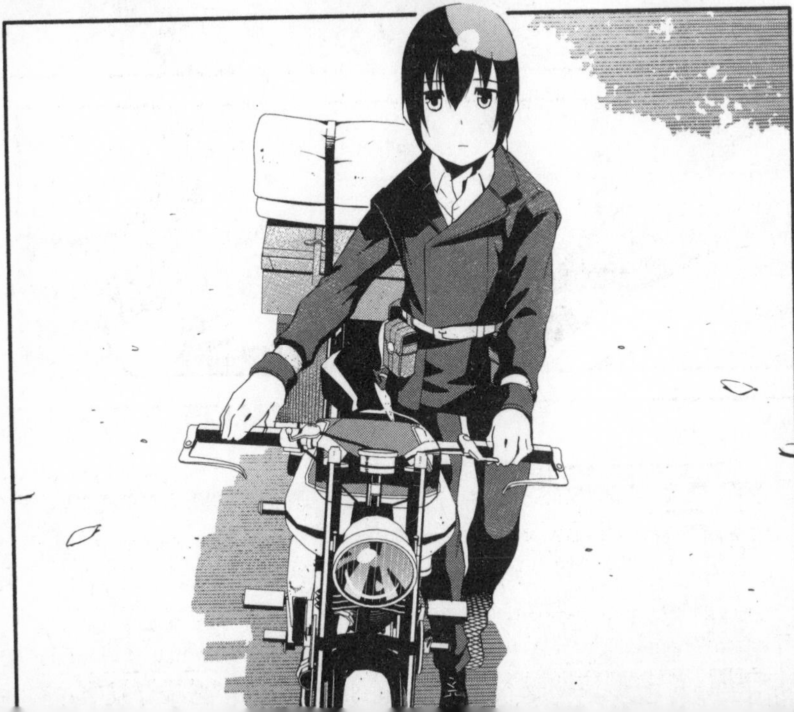

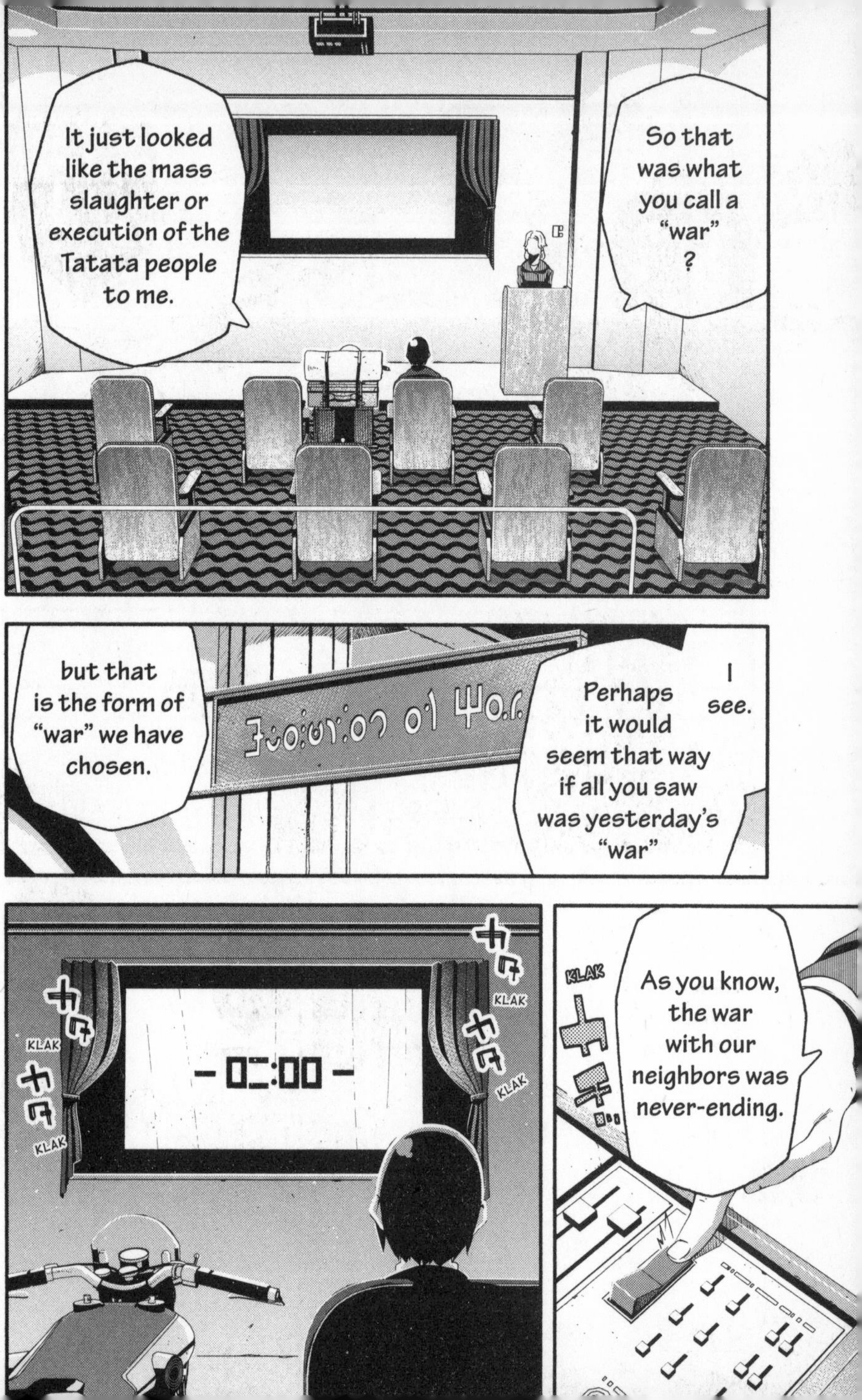
So that was what you call a "war"?
It just looked like the mass slaughter or execution of the Tatata people to me.
I see.
Perhaps it would seem that way if all you saw was yesterday's "war"
but that is the form of "war" we have chosen.
KLAK
As you know, the war with our neighbors was never-ending.
KLAK
KLAK
KLAK
KLAK
– 02:00 –

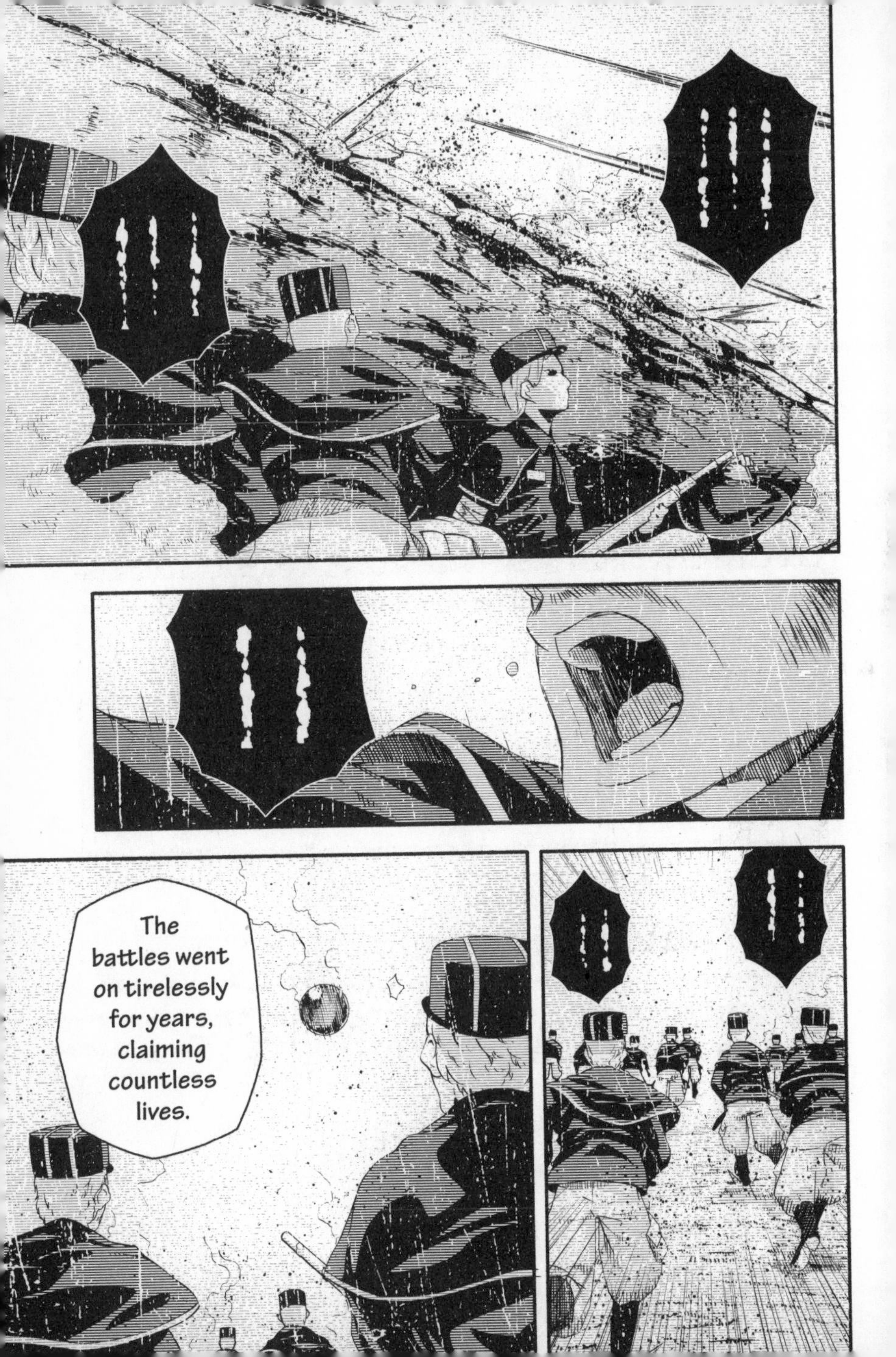
The battles went on tirelessly for years, claiming countless lives.

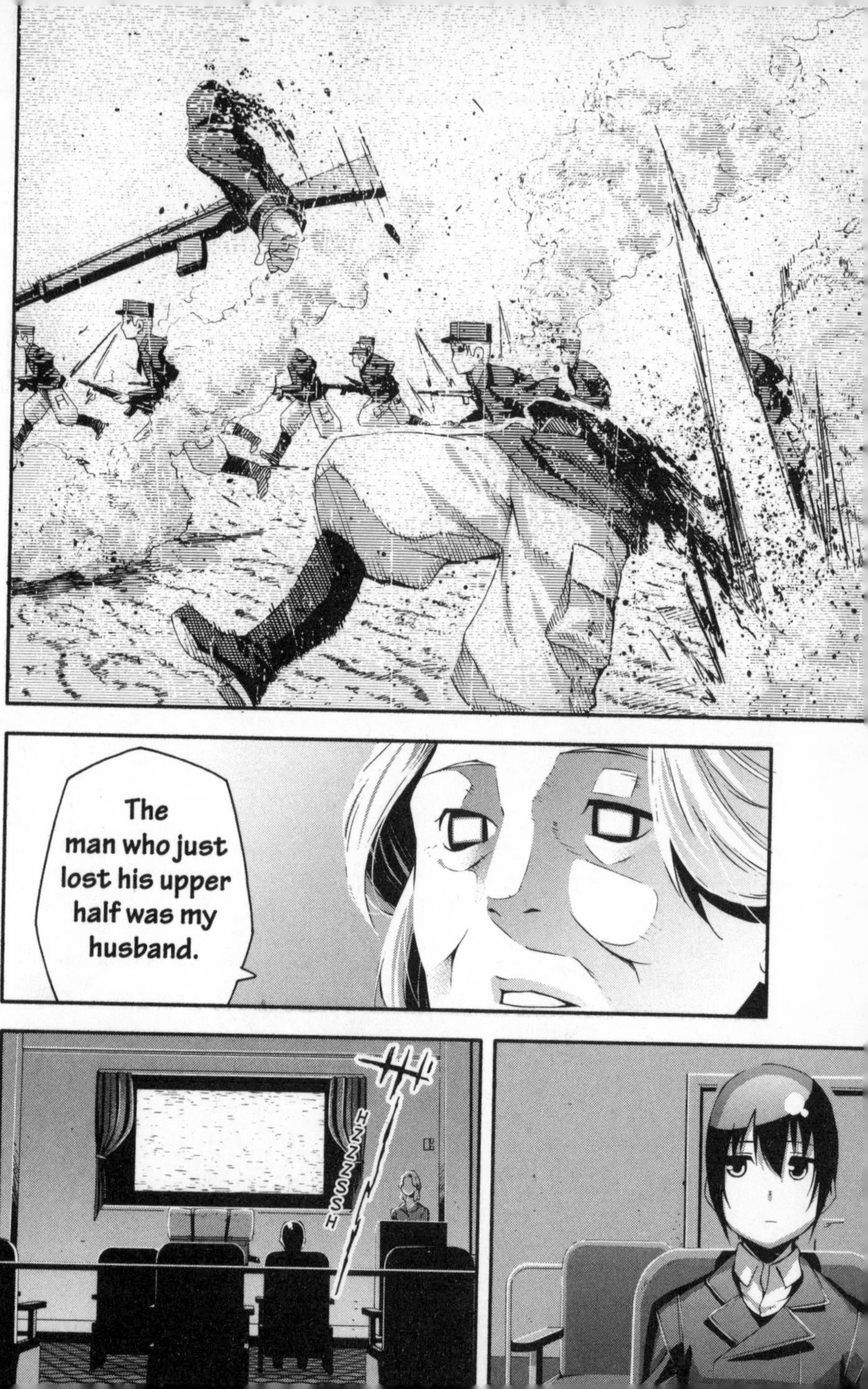
The man who just lost his upper half was my husband.
HZZZSSH

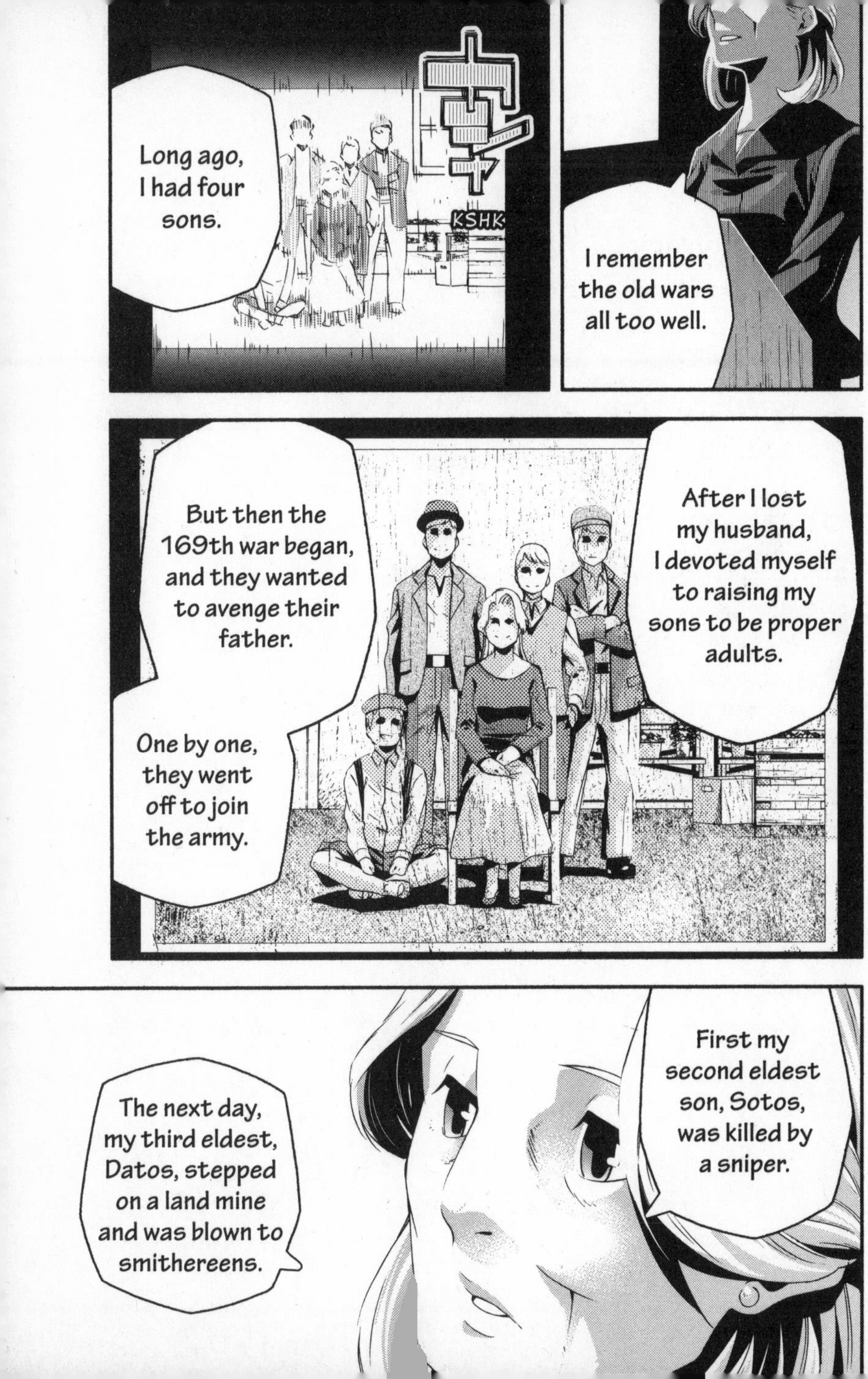
I remember the old wars all too well.
Long ago, I had four sons.
KSHK
After I lost my husband, I devoted myself to raising my sons to be proper adults.
But then the 169th war began, and they wanted to avenge their father.
One by one, they went off to join the army.
First my second eldest son, Sotos, was killed by a sniper.
The next day, my third eldest, Datos, stepped on a land mine and was blown to smithereens.

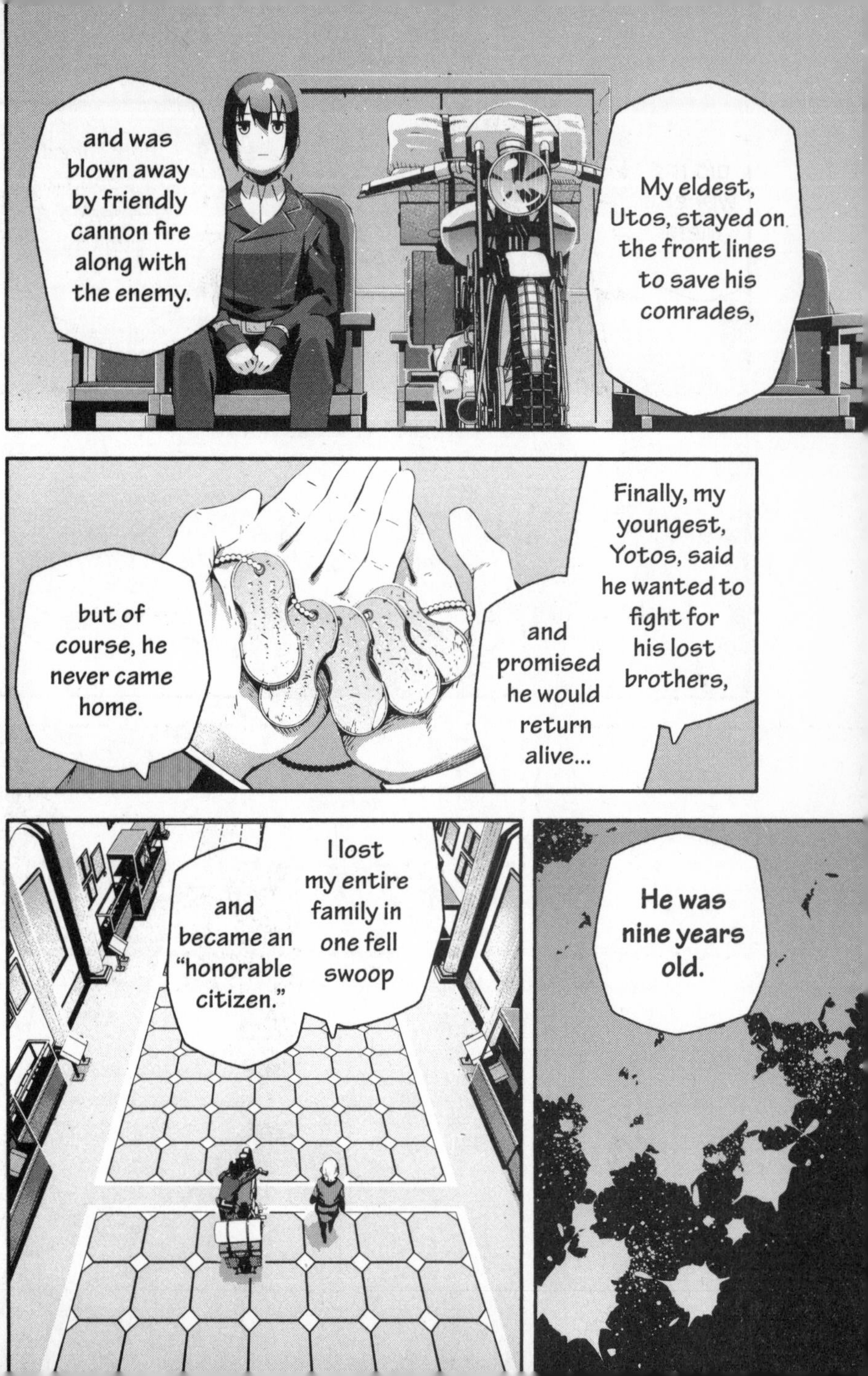
My eldest, Utos, stayed on the front lines to save his comrades,
and was blown away by friendly cannon fire along with the enemy.
Finally, my youngest, Yotos, said he wanted to fight for his lost brothers,
and promised he would return alive...
but of course, he never came home.
He was nine years old.
I lost my entire family in one fell swoop
and became an "honorable citizen."

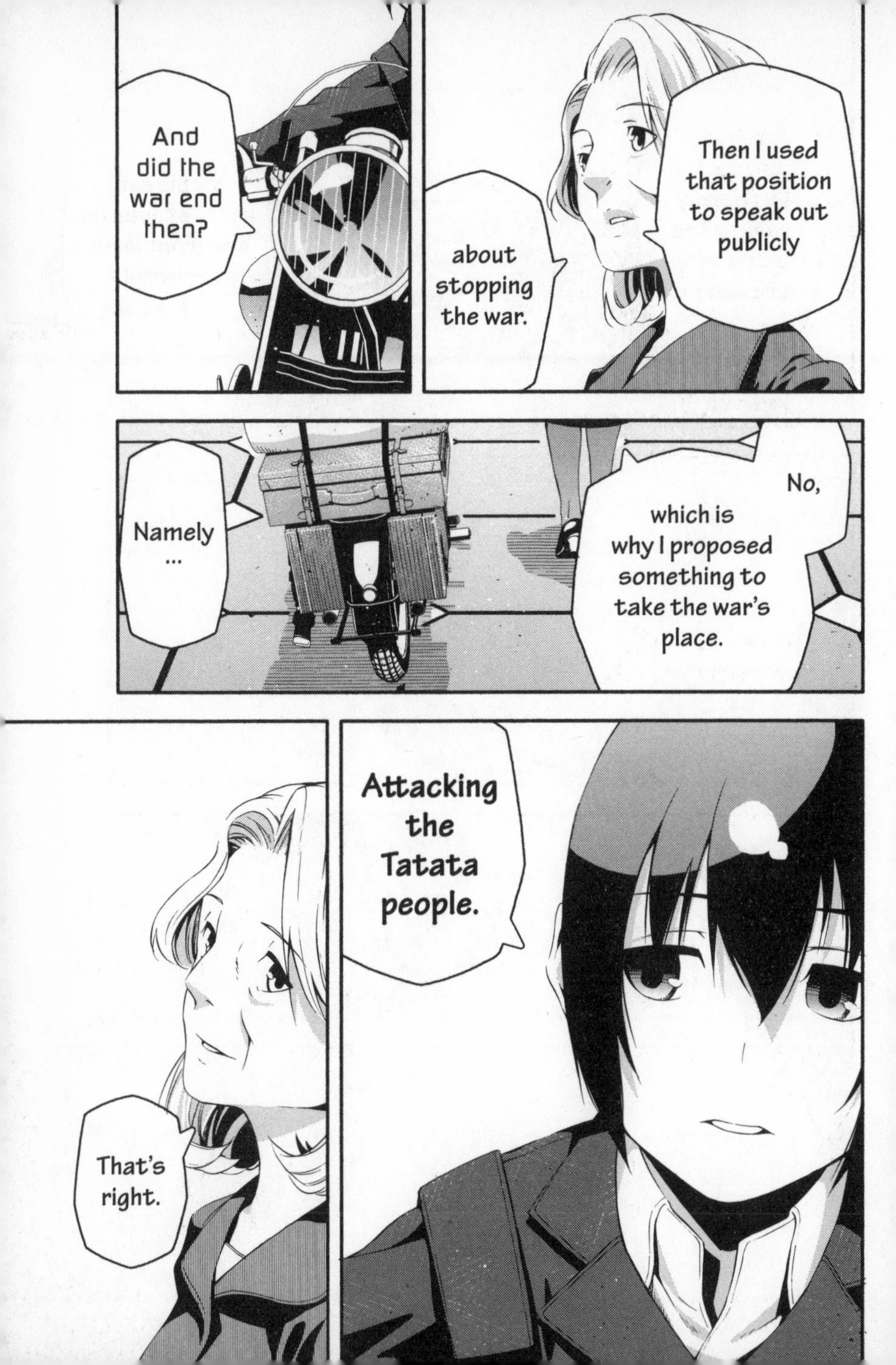
Then I used that position to speak out publicly
about stopping the war.
And did the war end then?
No, which is why I proposed something to take the war's place.
Namely ...
Attacking the Tatata people.
That's right.

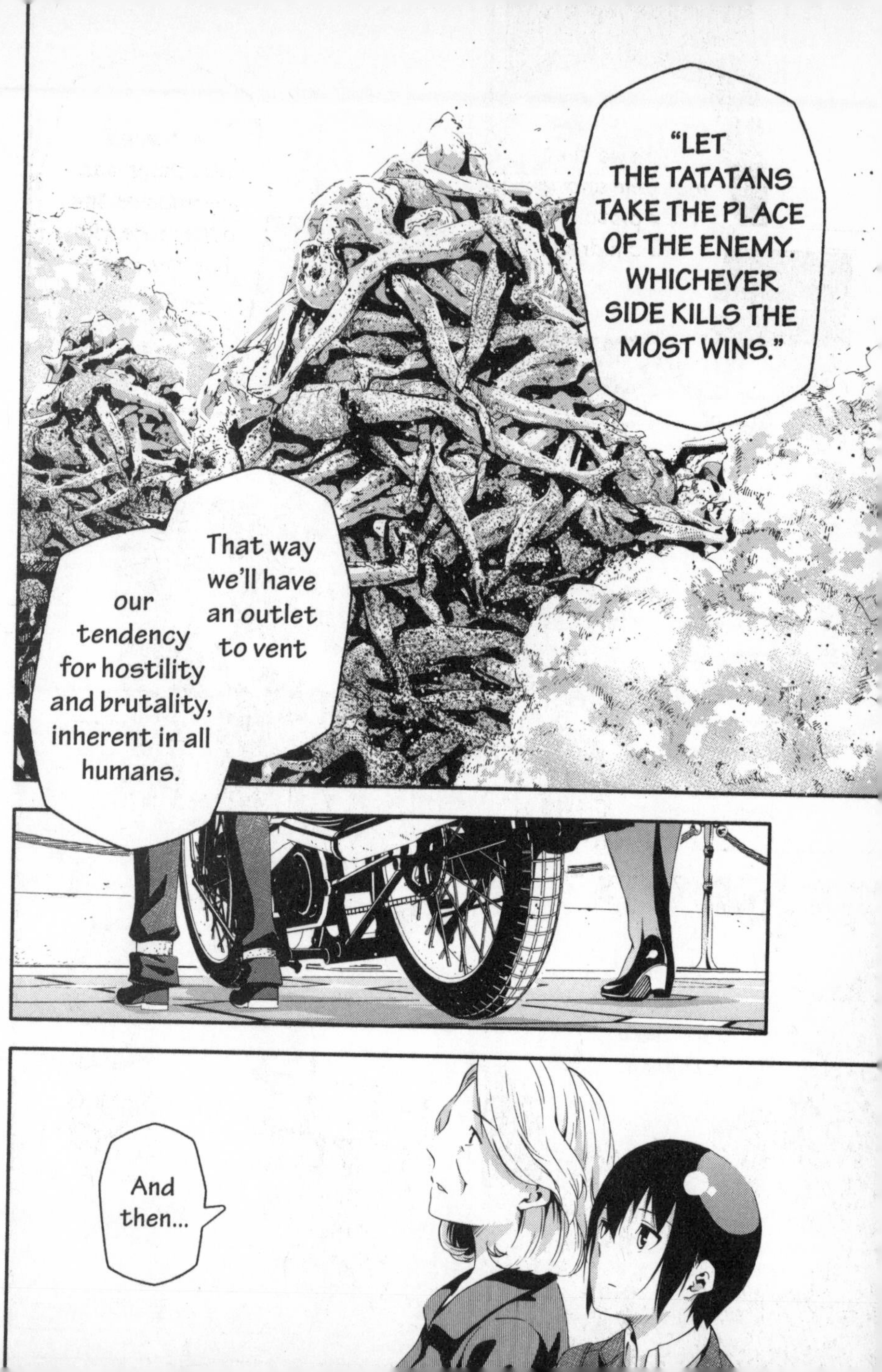
"LET THE TATATANS TAKE THE PLACE OF THE ENEMY. WHICHEVER SIDE KILLS THE MOST WINS."
That way we'll have an outlet to vent our tendency for hostility and brutality, inherent in all humans.
And then...

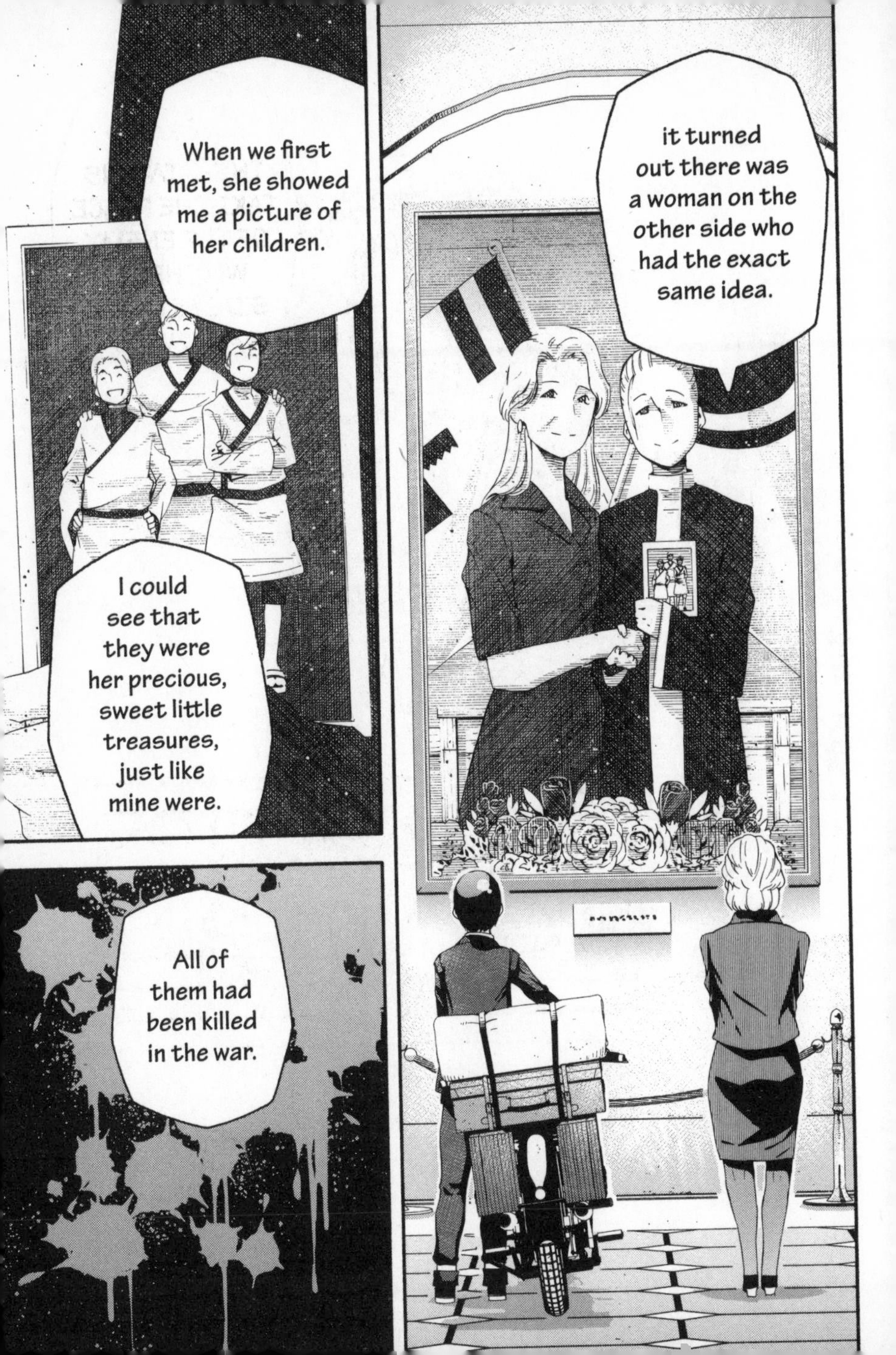
it turned out there was a woman on the other side who had the exact same idea.
When we first met, she showed me a picture of her children.
I could see that they were her precious, sweet little treasures, just like mine were.
All of them had been killed in the war.

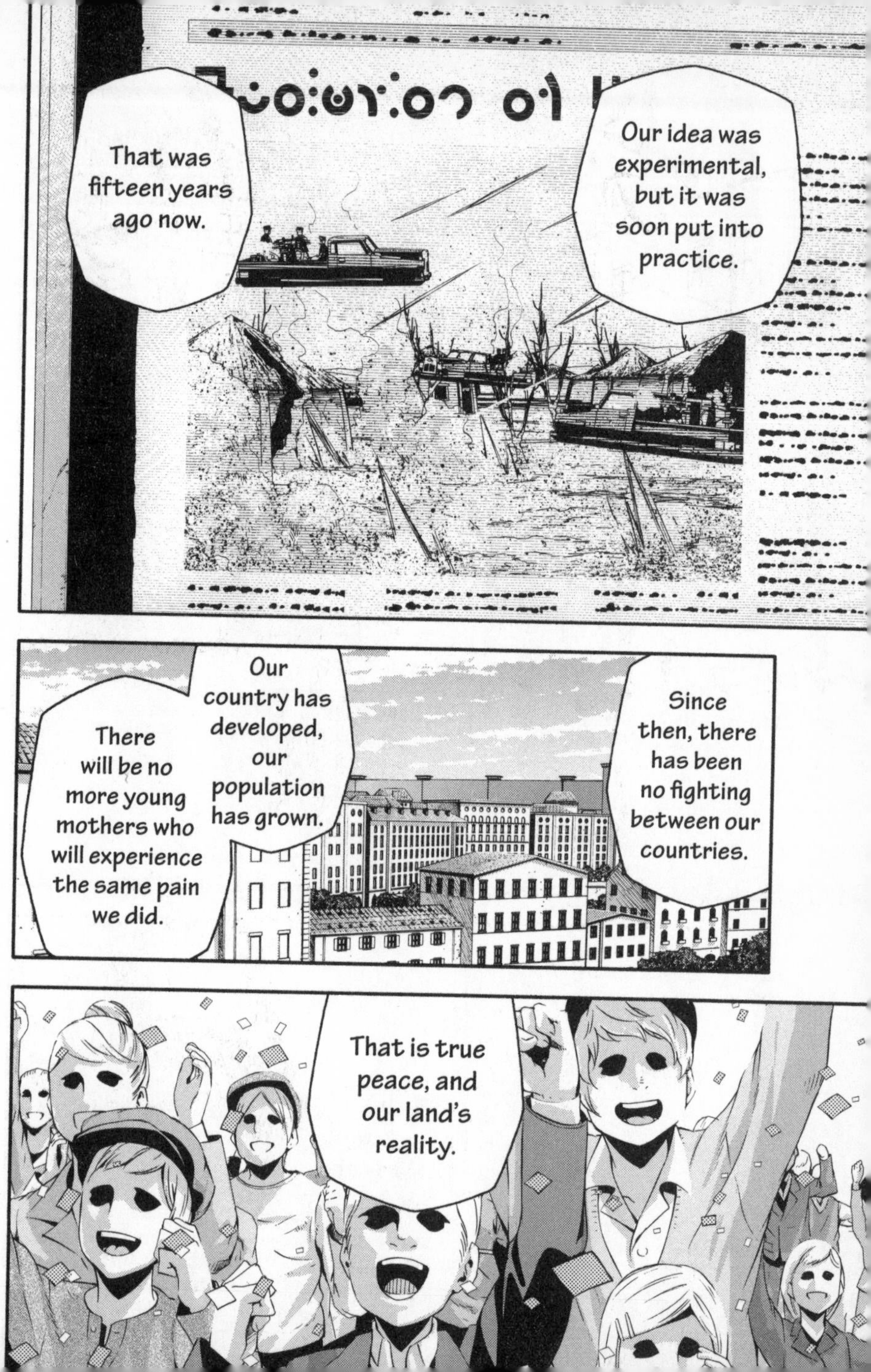
Our idea was experimental, but it was soon put into practice.
That was fifteen years ago now.
Since then, there has been no fighting between our countries.
Our country has developed, our population has grown.
There will be no more young mothers who will experience the same pain we did.
That is true peace, and our land's reality.

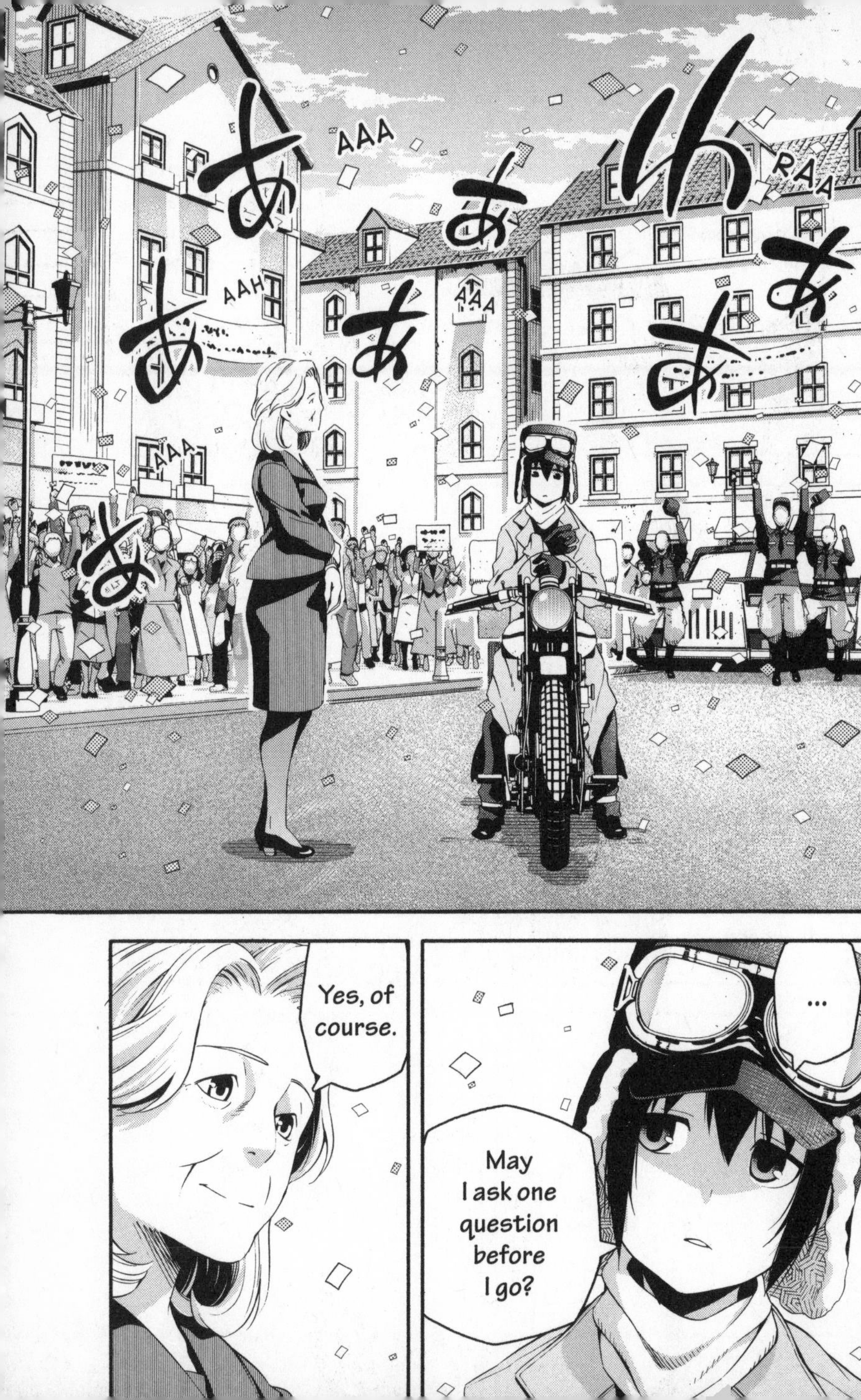
RAA
AAA
AAA
AAH
AAA
...
May I ask one question before I go?
Yes, of course.

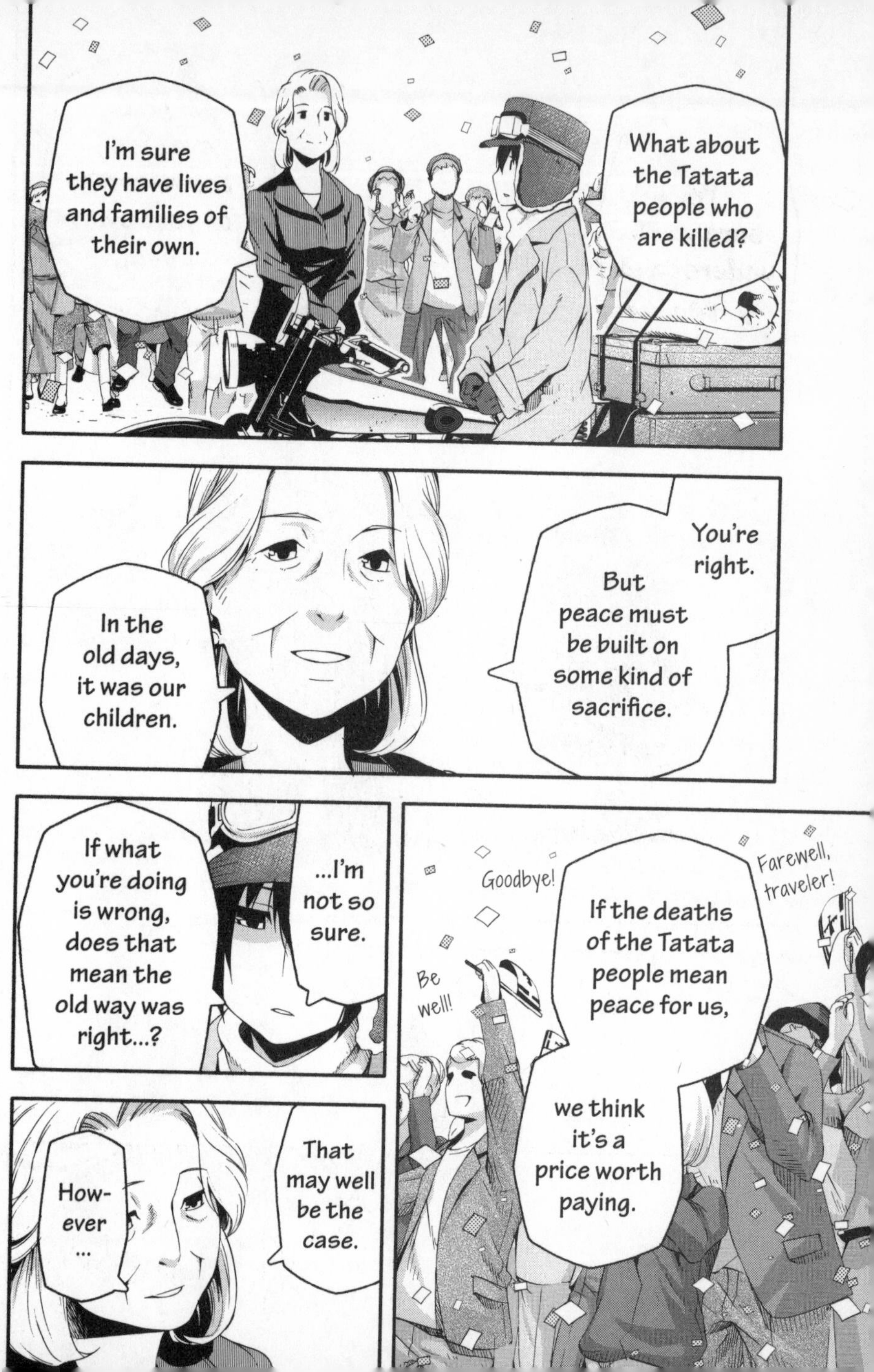
What about the Tatata people who are killed?
I'm sure they have lives and families of their own.
You're right.
But peace must be built on some kind of sacrifice.
In the old days, it was our children.
Farewell, traveler!
Goodbye!
If the deaths of the Tatata people mean peace for us,
Be well!
we think it's a price worth paying.
...I'm not so sure.
If what you're doing is wrong, does that mean the old way was right...?
That may well be the case.
How-ever...

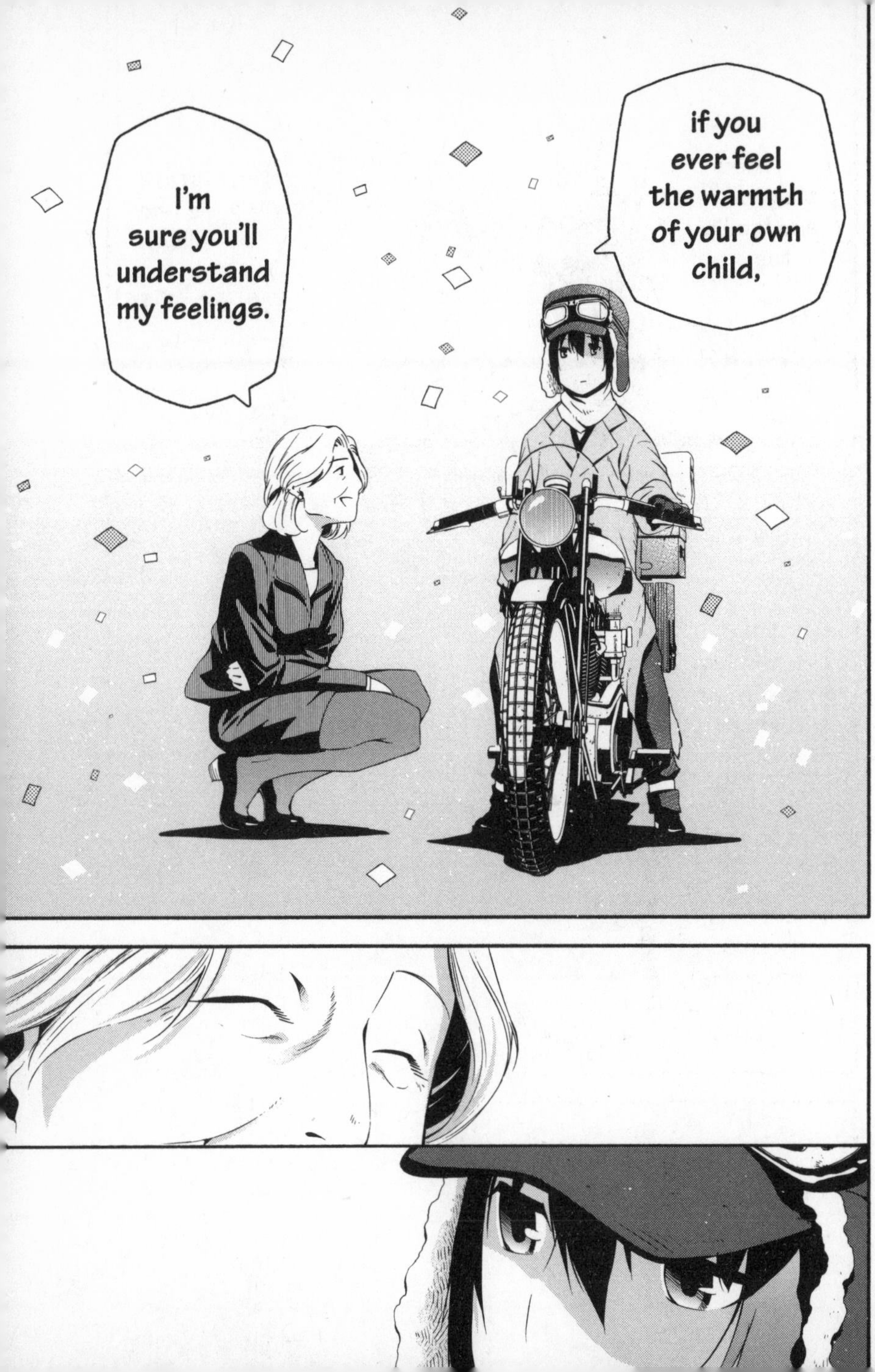
if you ever feel the warmth of your own child,
I'm sure you'll understand my feelings.

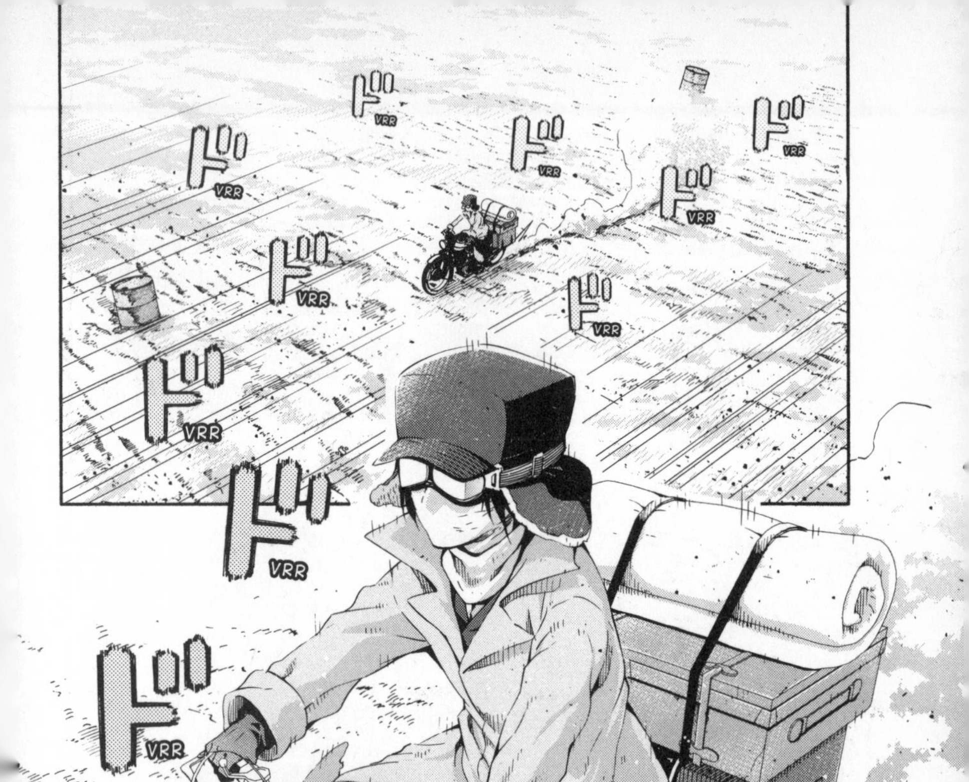

ド VRR
ド VRR
ド VRR
ド VRR
ド VRR
ド VRR
ド VRR
ド VRR
ド VRR
ド VRR

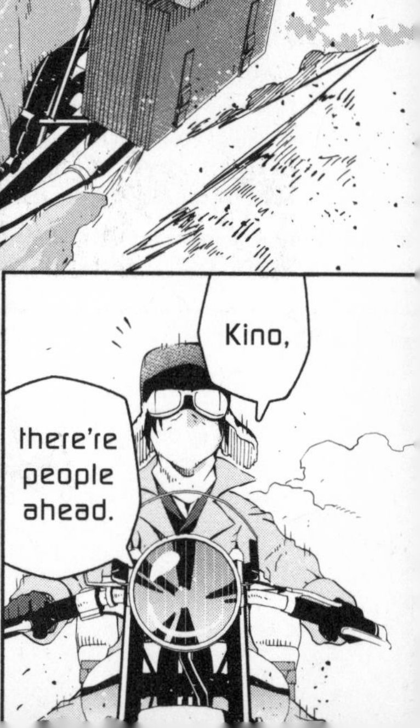

Kino,
there're people ahead.

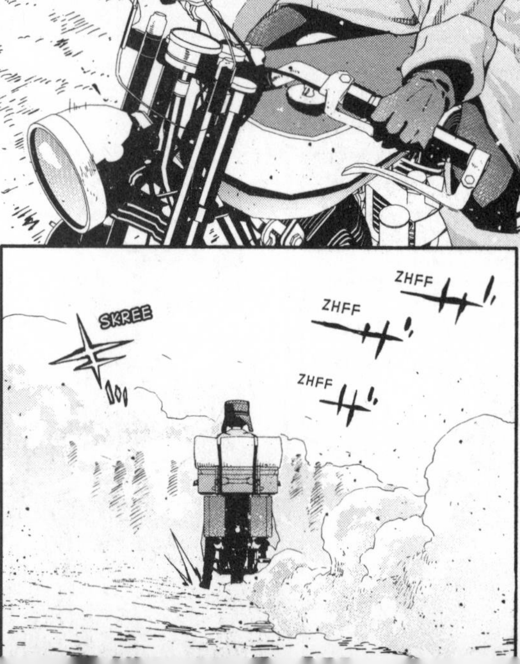

ZHFF
ZHFF
ZHFF
SKREE

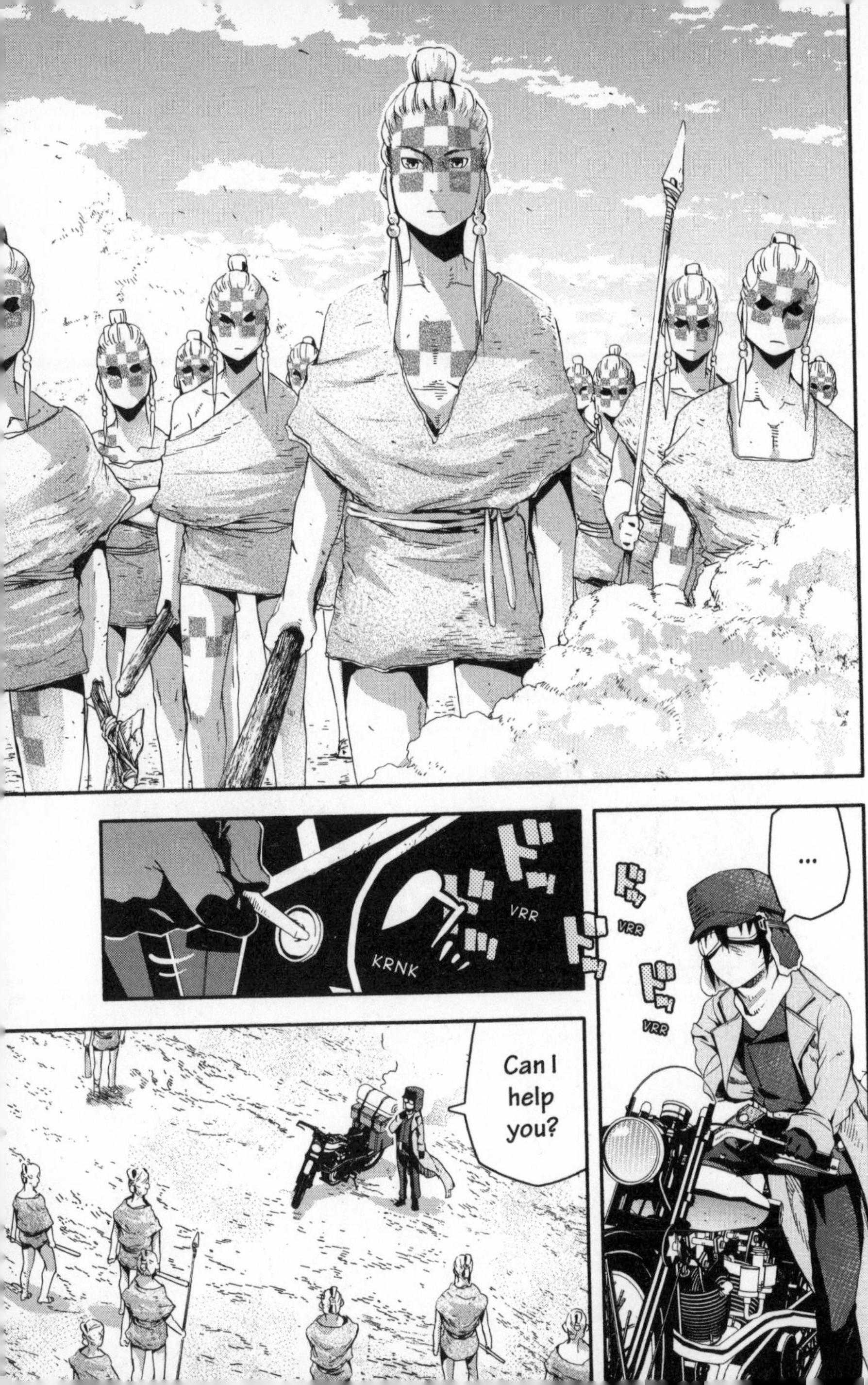
...
VRR
VRR
VRR
KRNK
Can I help you?

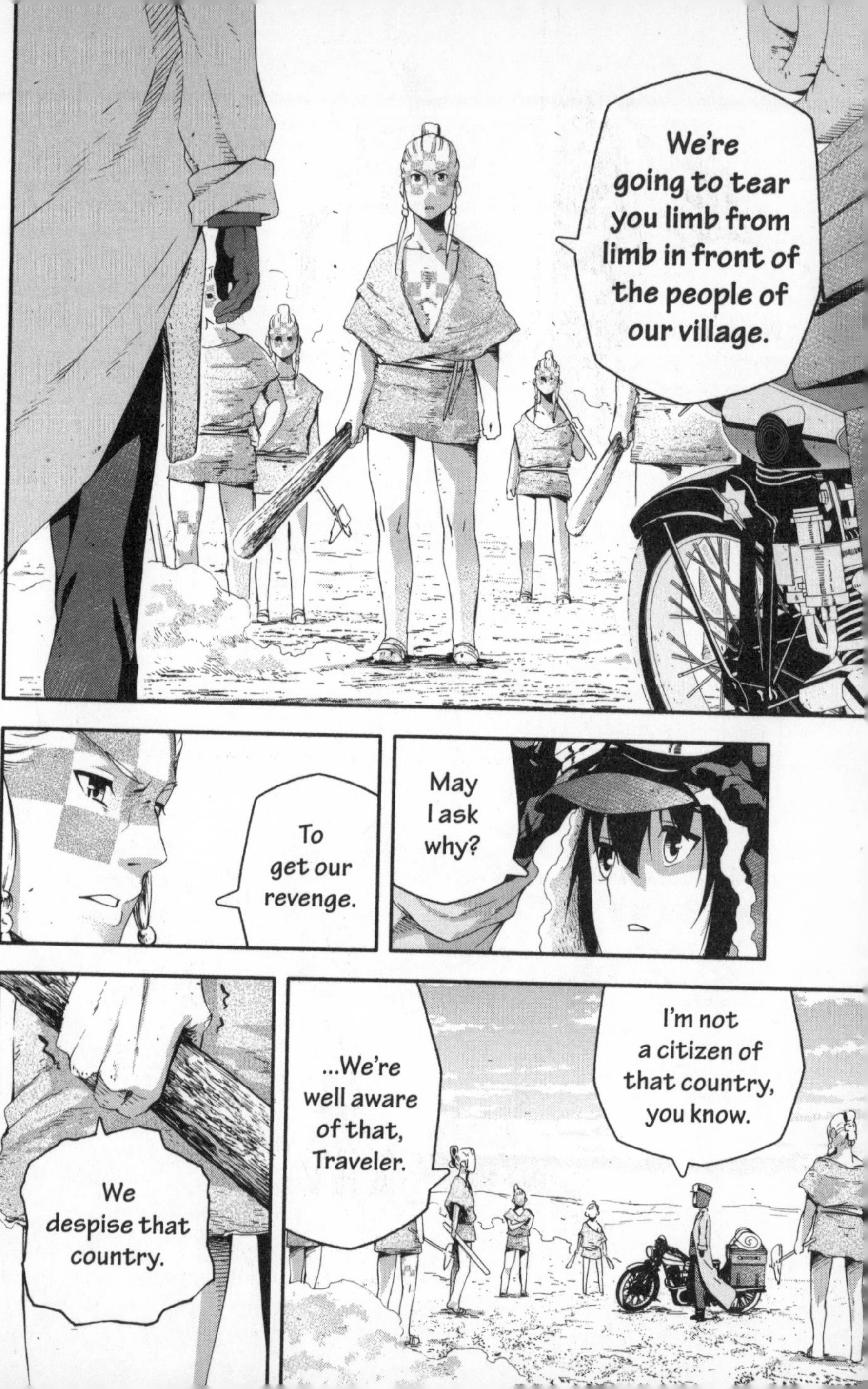
We're going to tear you limb from limb in front of the people of our village.
May I ask why?
To get our revenge.
I'm not a citizen of that country, you know.
...We're well aware of that, Traveler.
We despise that country.

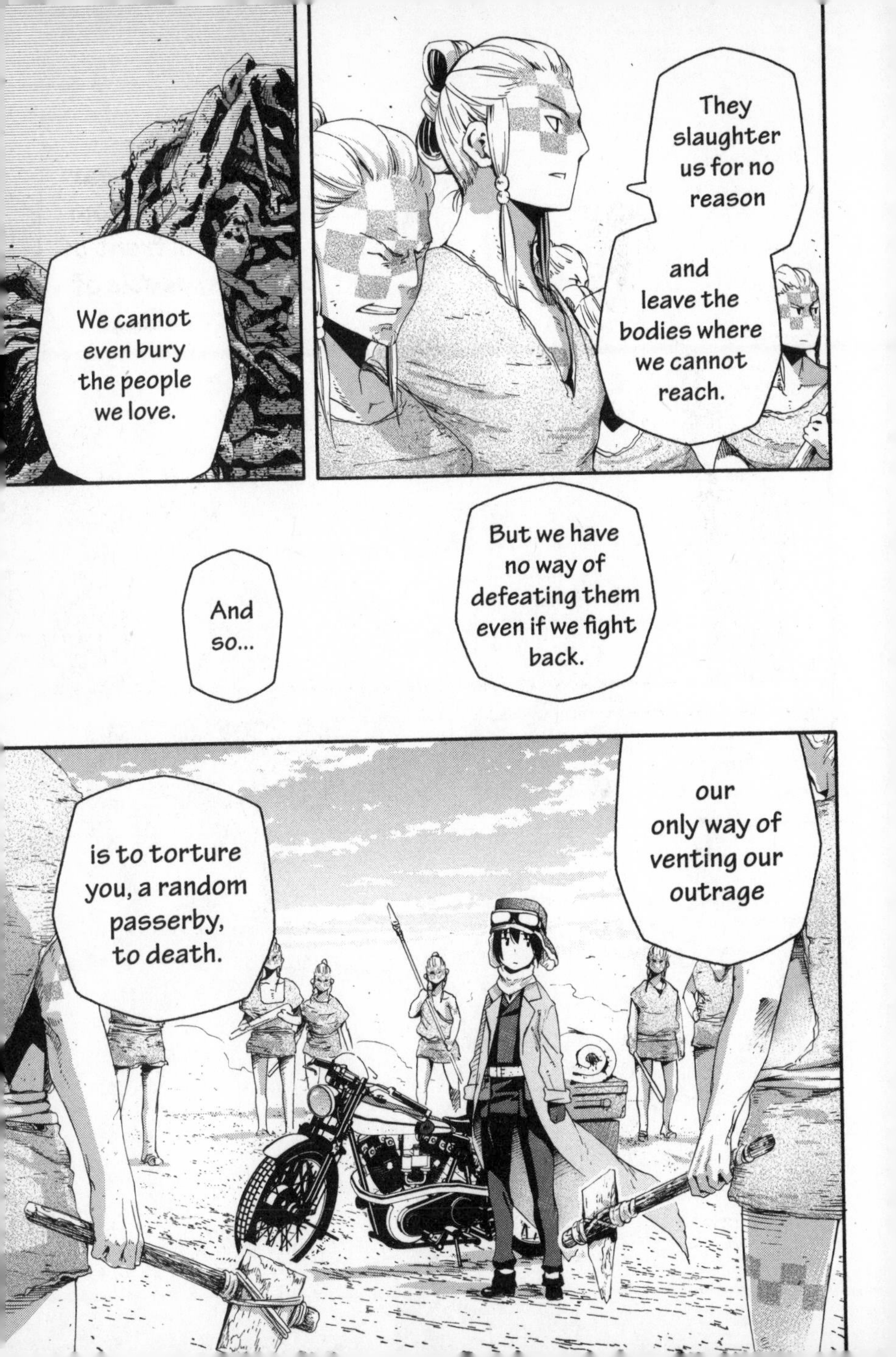
They slaughter us for no reason
and leave the bodies where we cannot reach.
We cannot even bury the people we love.
But we have no way of defeating them even if we fight back.
And so...
our only way of venting our outrage
is to torture you, a random passerby, to death.

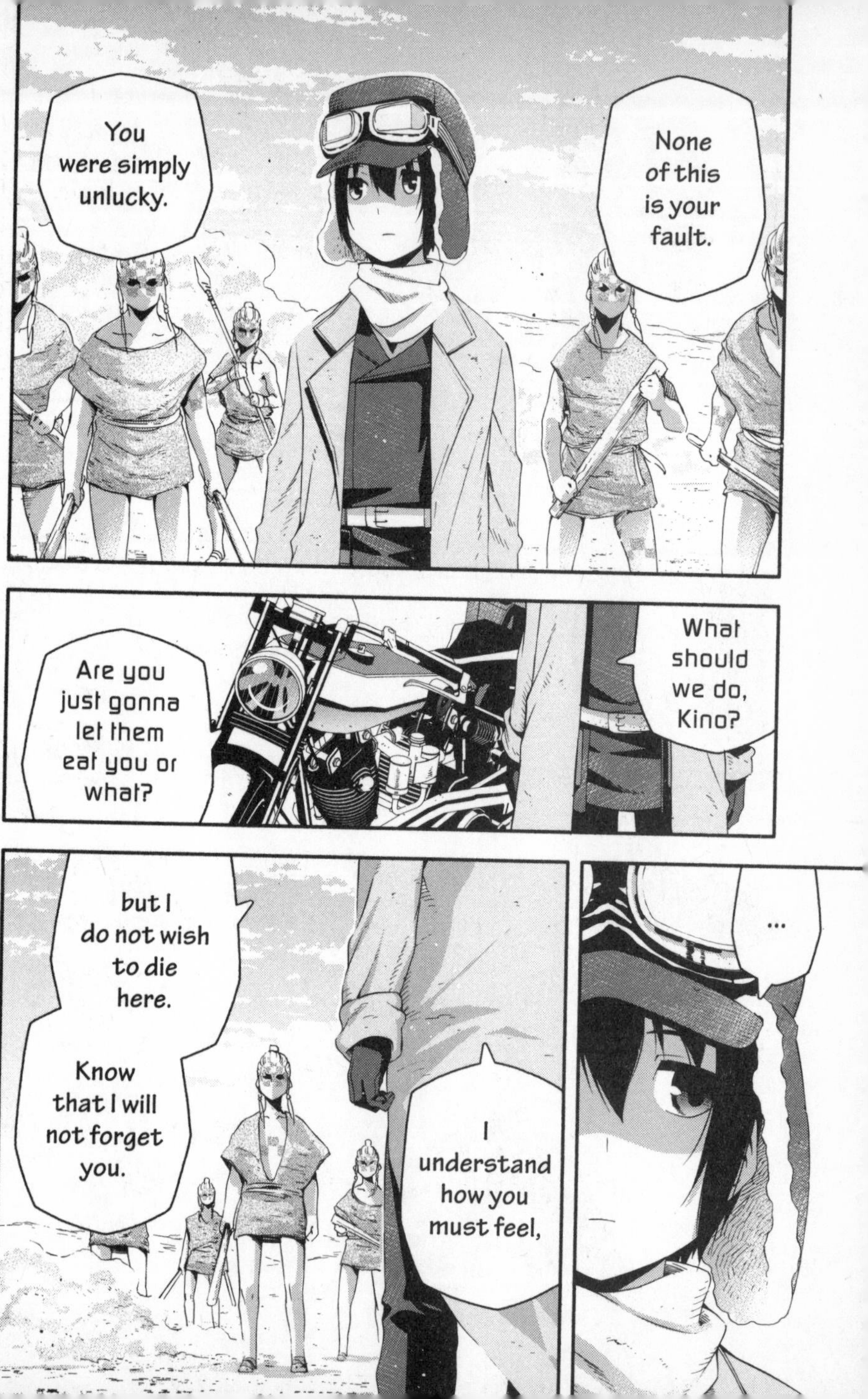
None of this is your fault.
You were simply unlucky.
What should we do, Kino?
Are you just gonna let them eat you or what?
...
I understand how you must feel,
but I do not wish to die here.
Know that I will not forget you.

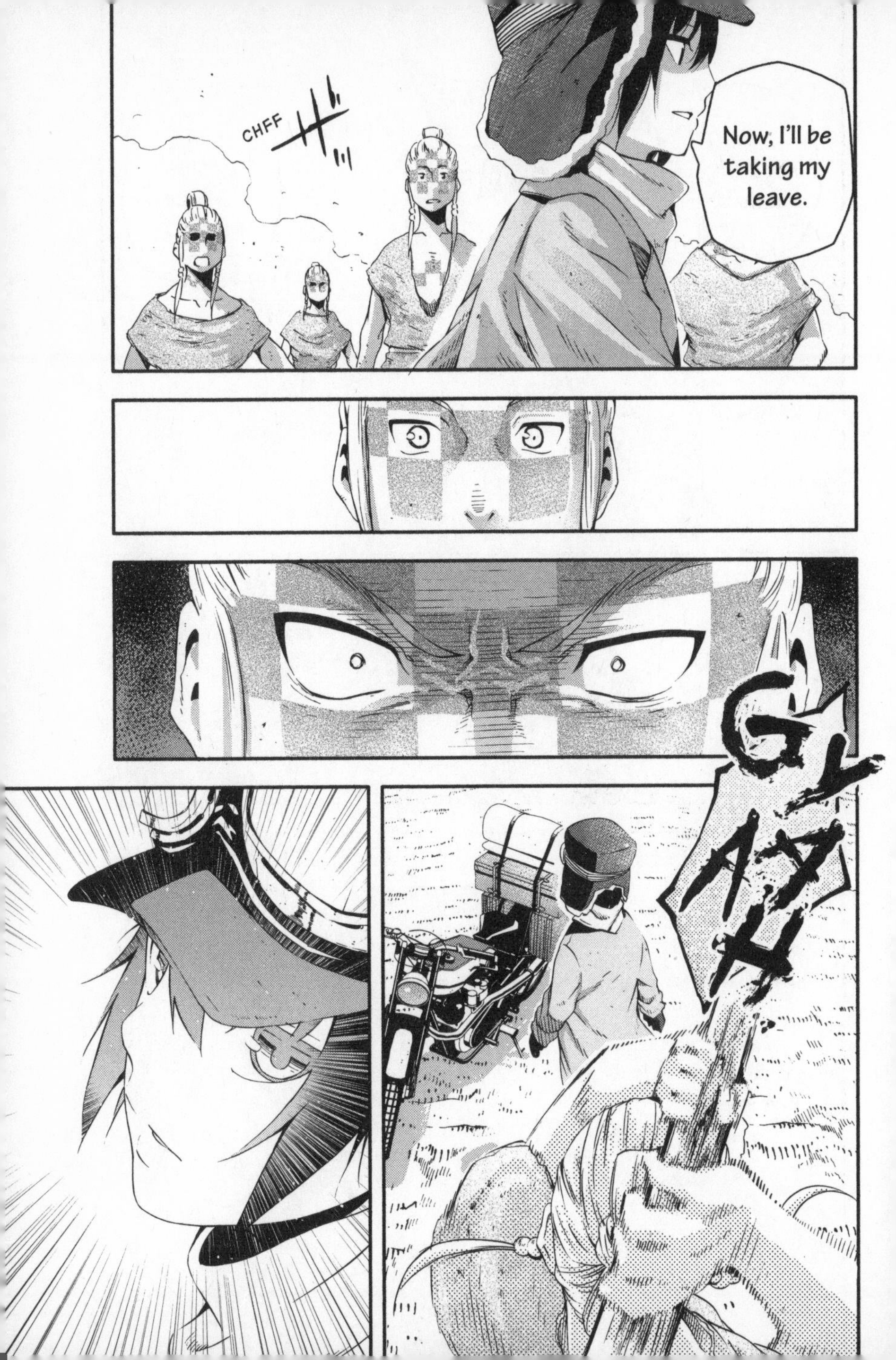
Now, I'll be taking my leave.
CHFF
GYAAH

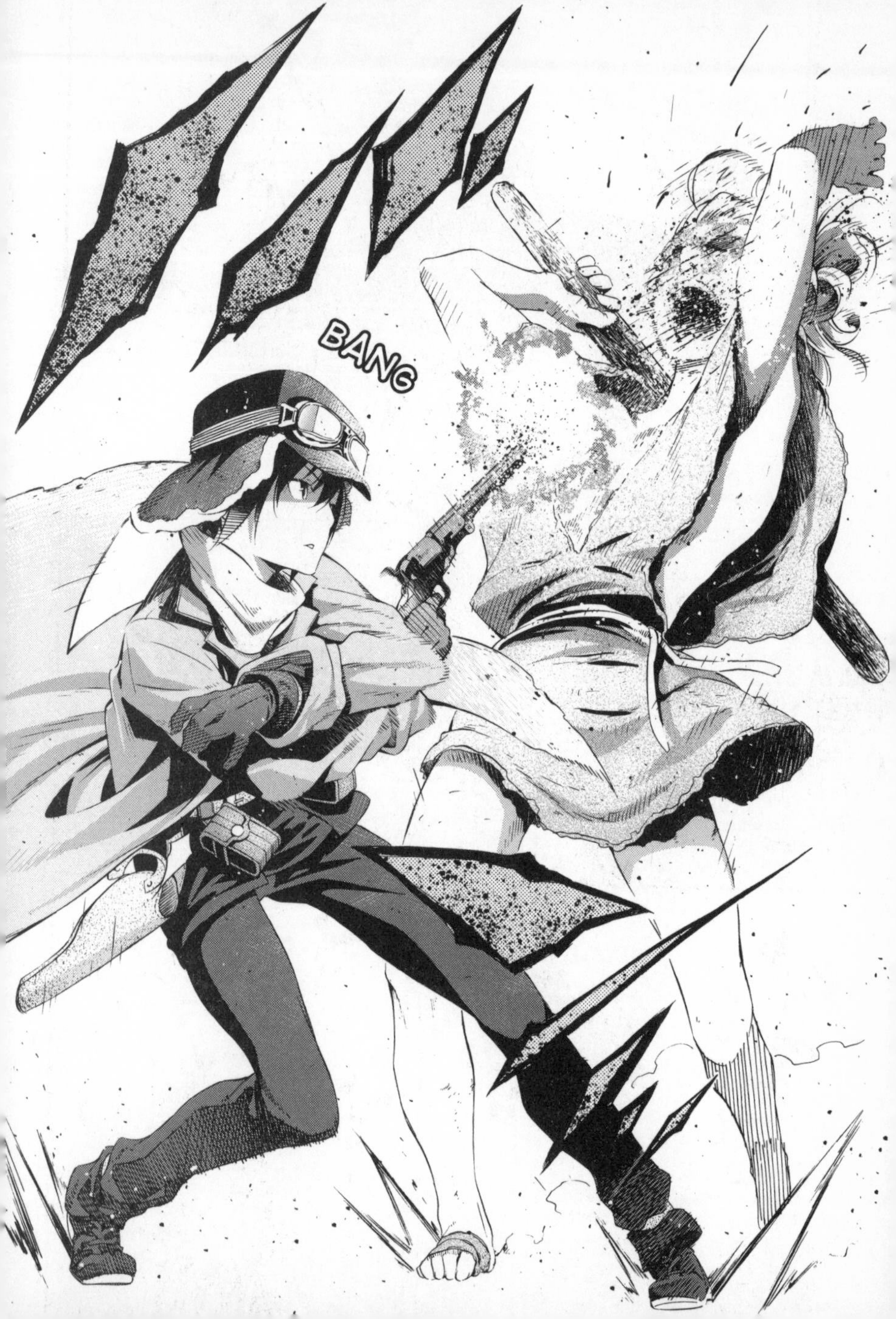
BANG

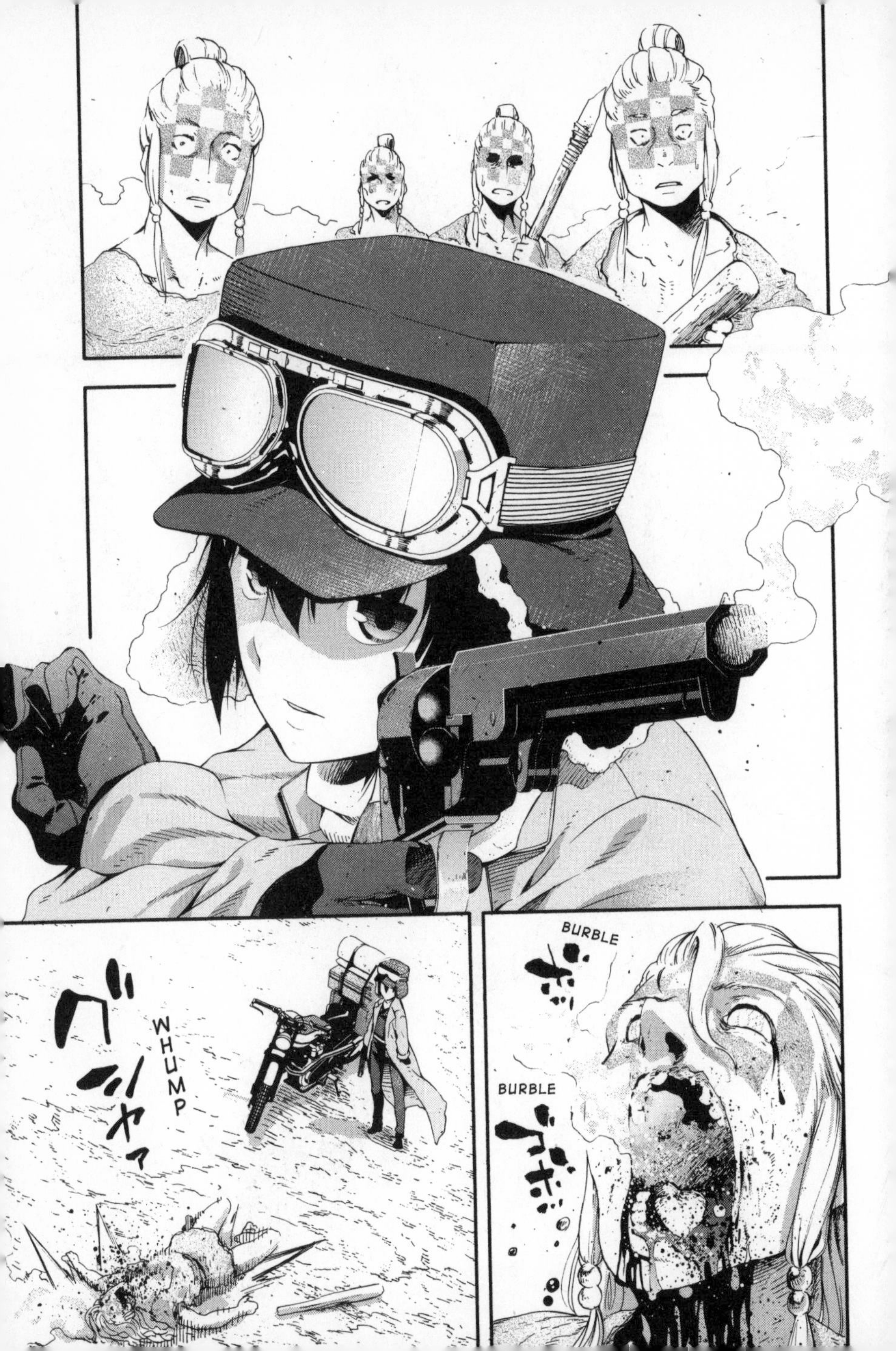
BURBLE
BURBLE
WHUMP

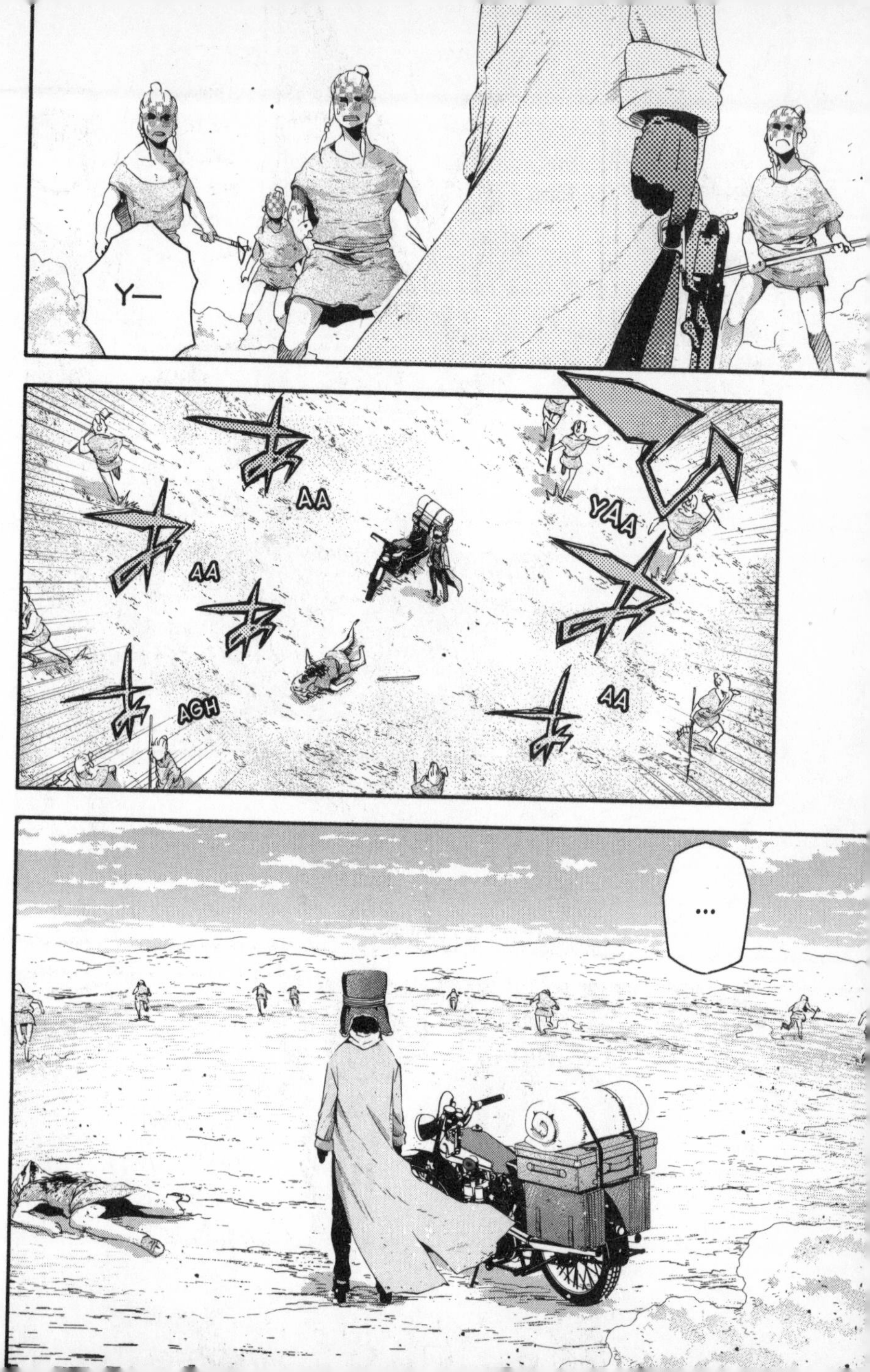
Y—
YAA
AA
AA
AA
AGH
AA
...

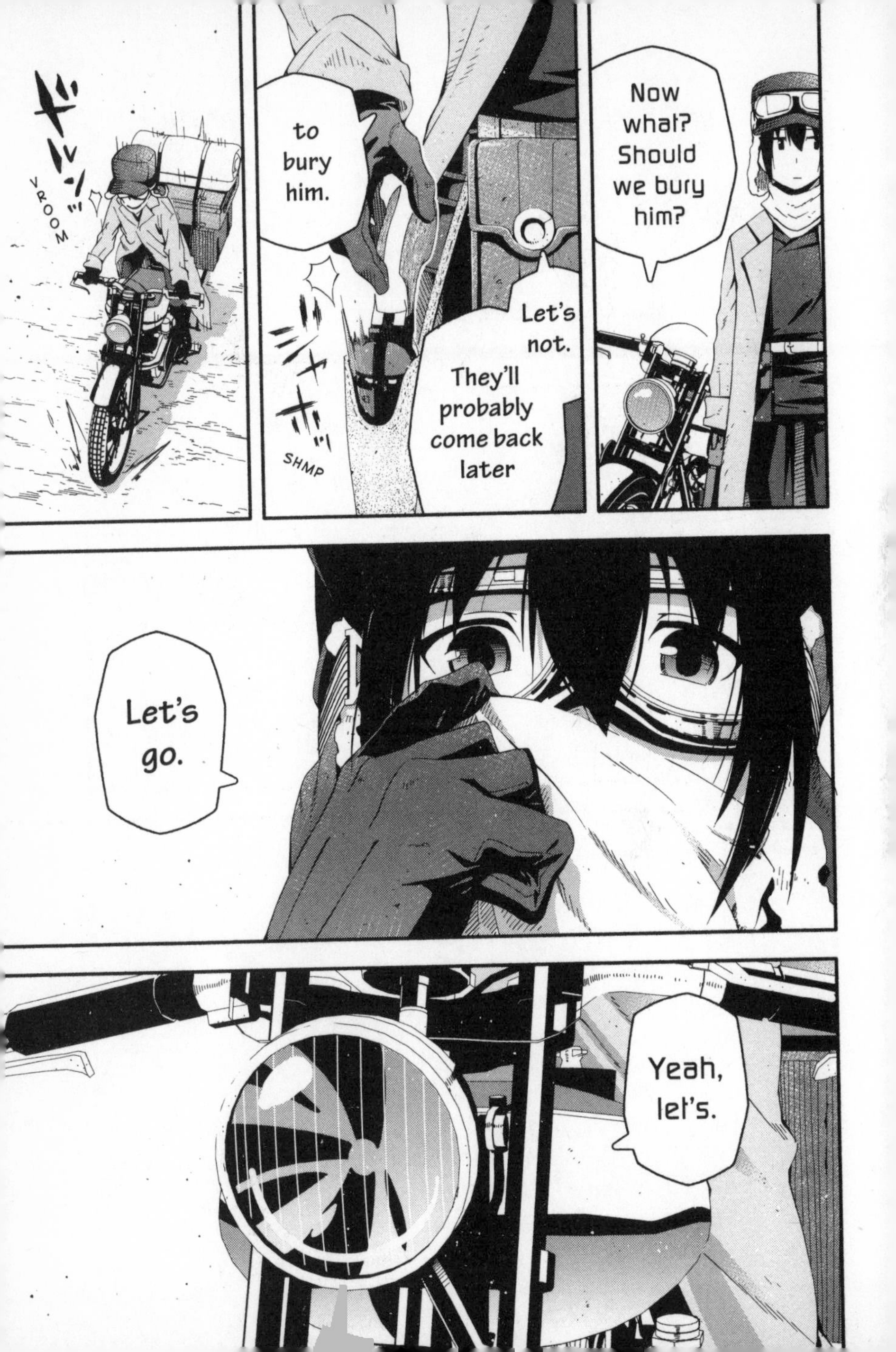
Now what? Should we bury him?
Let's not. They'll probably come back later
to bury him.
SHMP
VROOM
Let's go.
Yeah, let's.

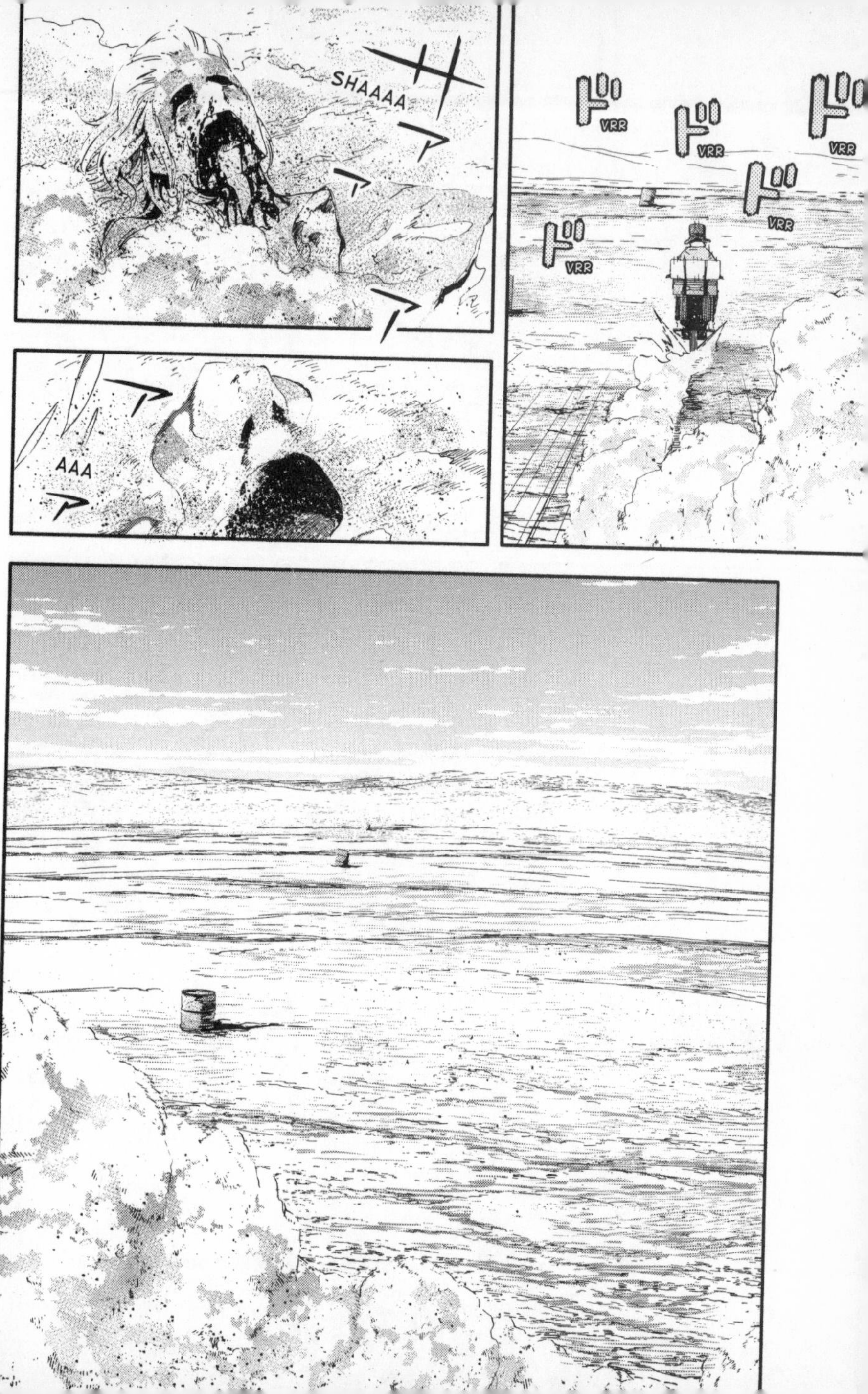

ドッ VRR
ドッ VRR
ドッ VRR
ドッ VRR
ドッ VRR
SHAAAA
ア
ア
ア
AAA
ア
ア

Kino's Journey

—→ The Beautiful World ←—

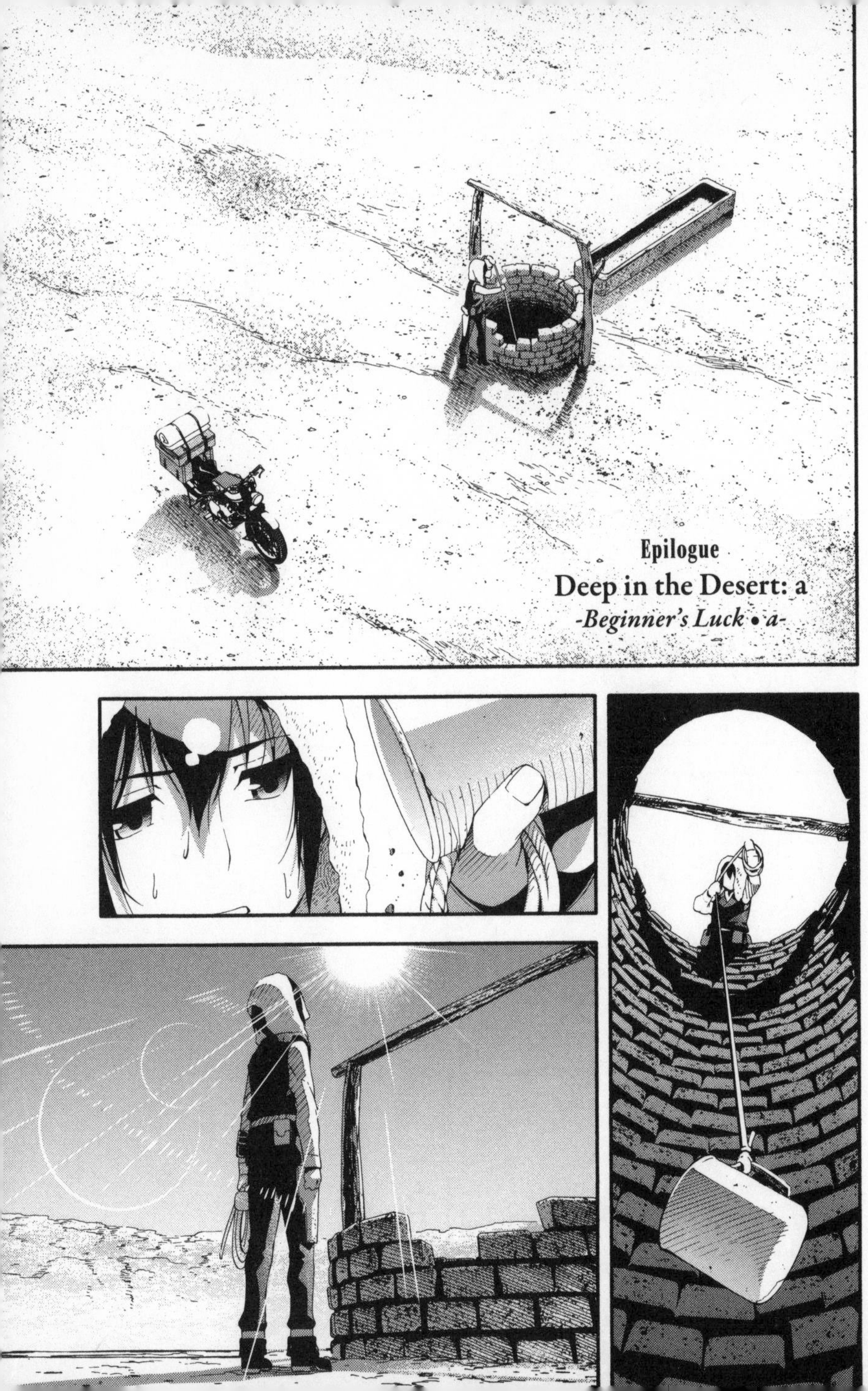
Epilogue
Deep in the Desert: a
-Beginner's Luck • a-

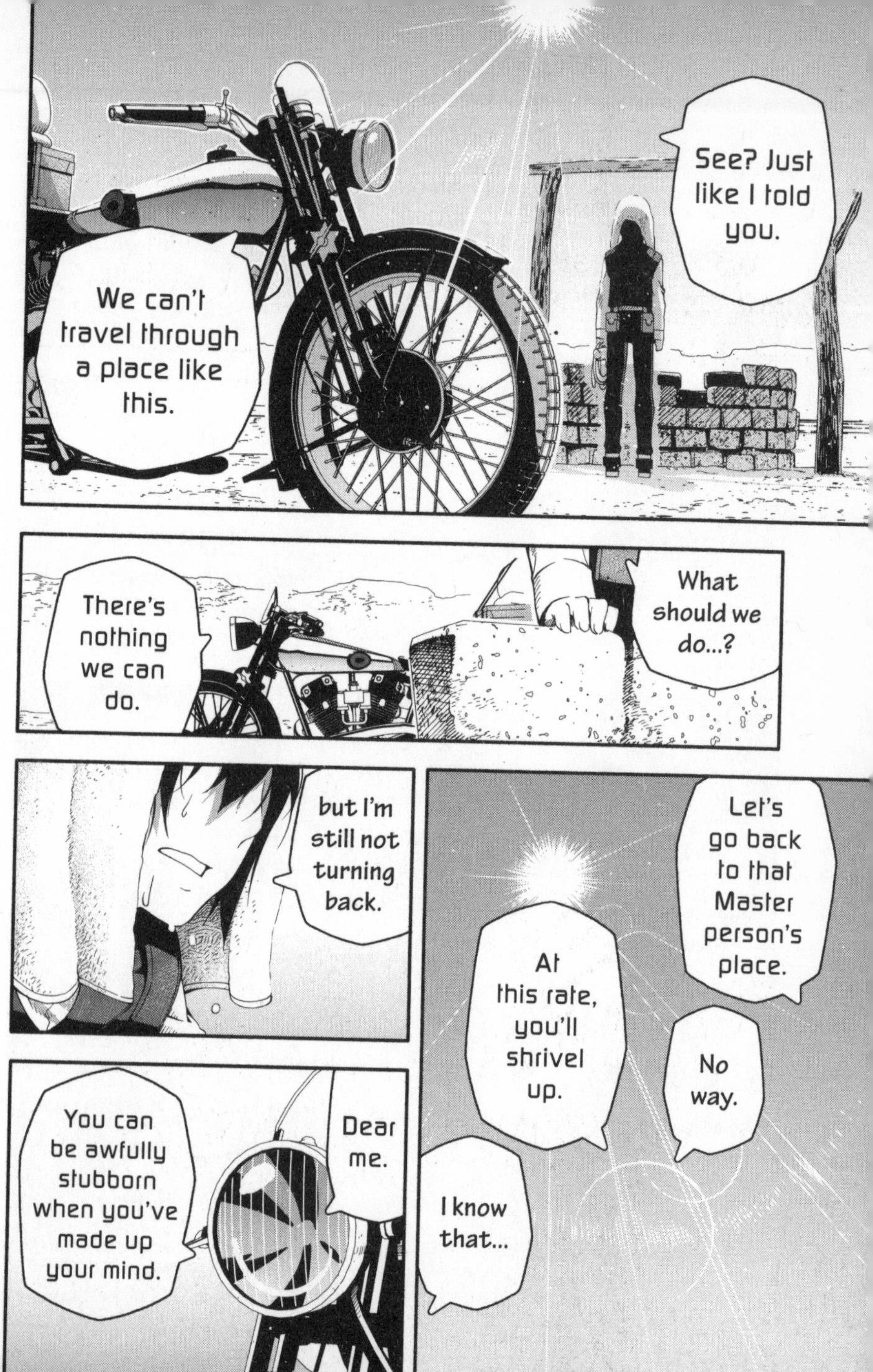

See? Just like I told you.
We can't travel through a place like this.
What should we do...?
There's nothing we can do.
Let's go back to that Master person's place.
No way.
At this rate, you'll shrivel up.
I know that...
but I'm still not turning back.
Dear me.
You can be awfully stubborn when you've made up your mind.

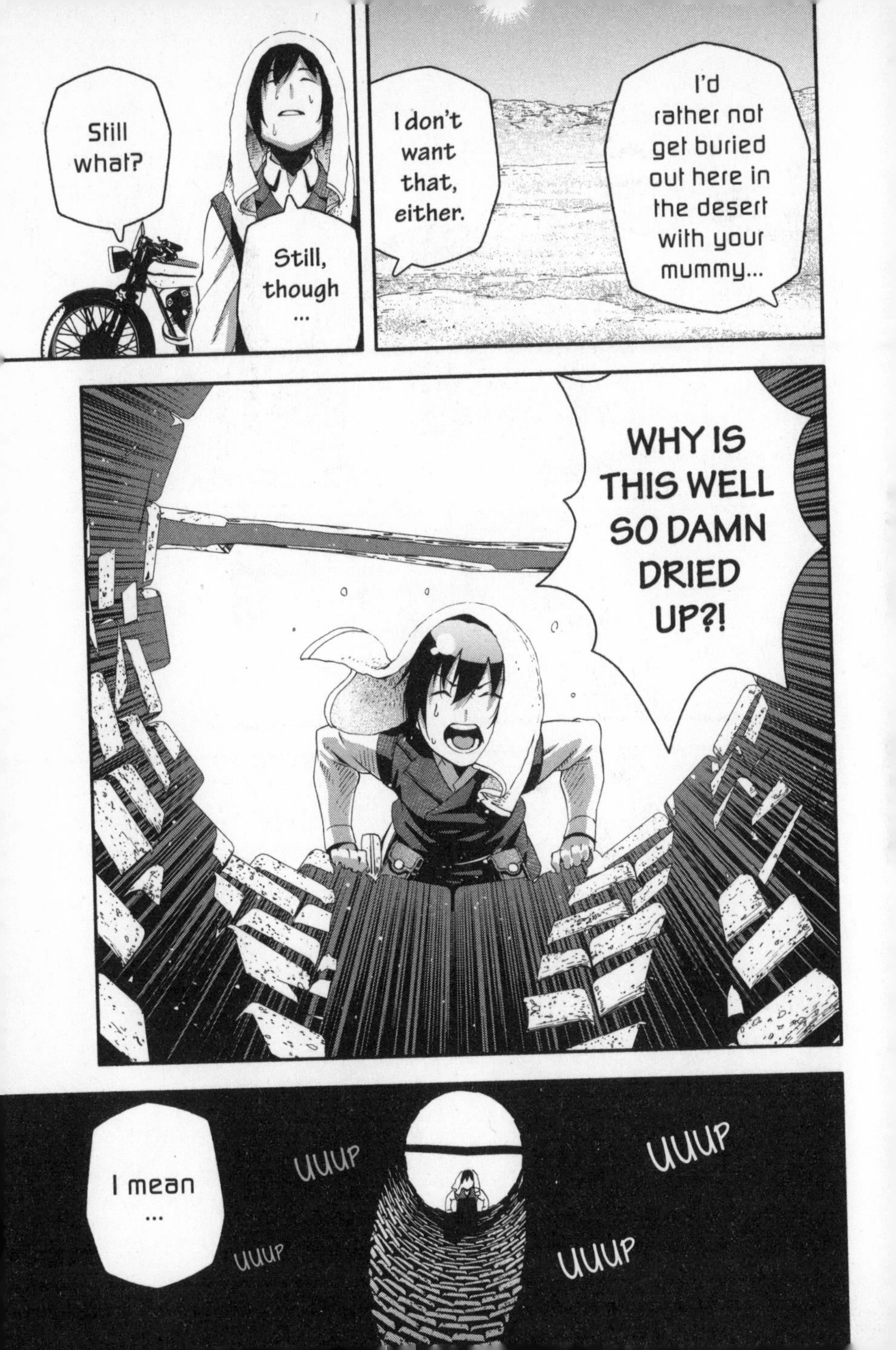
I'd rather not get buried out here in the desert with your mummy...
I don't want that, either.
Still, though ...
Still what?
WHY IS THIS WELL SO DAMN DRIED UP?!
UUUP
UUUP
UUUP
UUUP
I mean ...

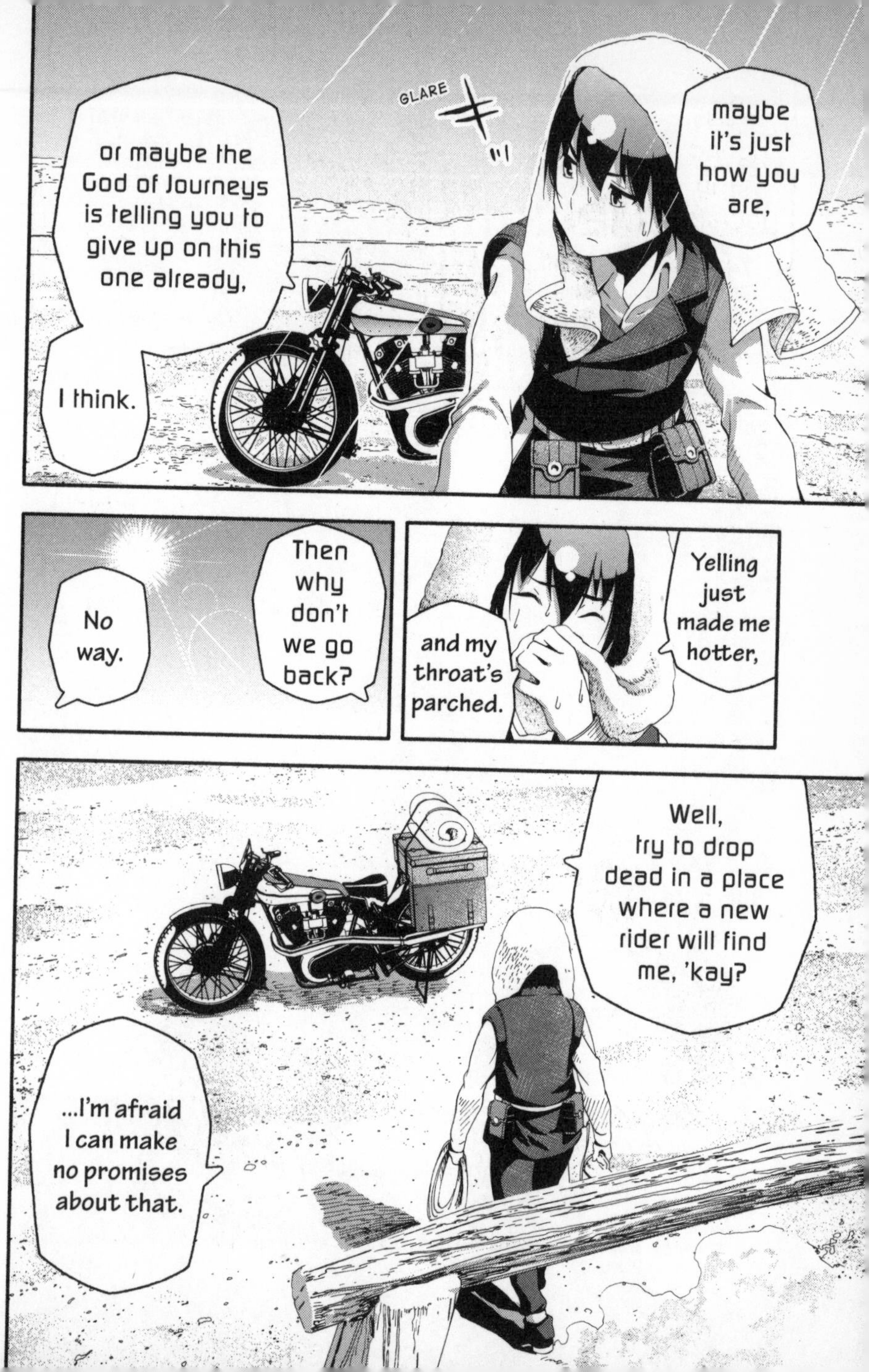
maybe it's just how you are,
GLARE
or maybe the God of Journeys is telling you to give up on this one already,
I think.
Yelling just made me hotter,
and my throat's parched.
Then why don't we go back?
No way.
Well, try to drop dead in a place where a new rider will find me, 'kay?
...I'm afraid I can make no promises about that.

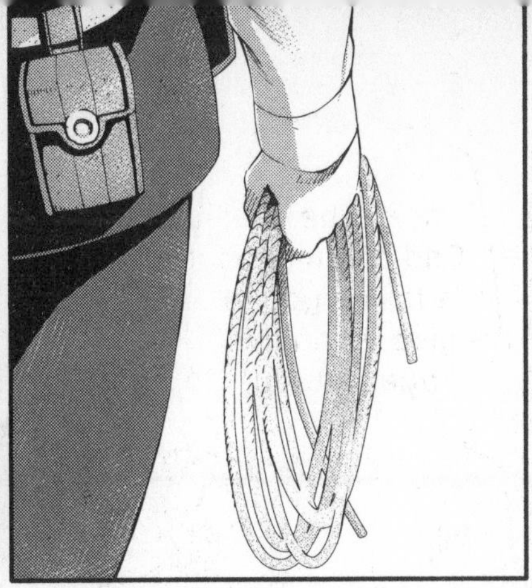

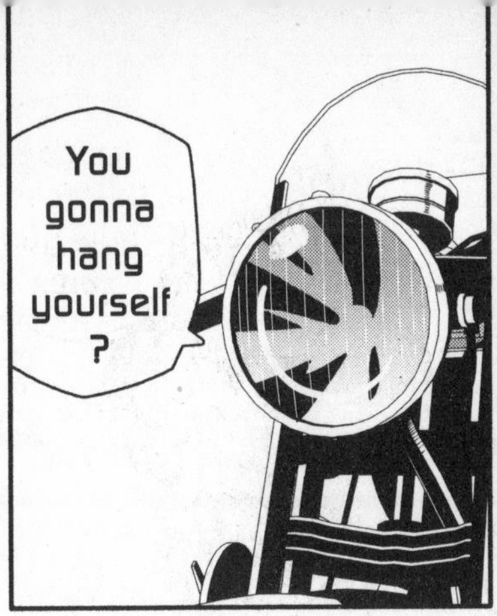
You gonna hang yourself?

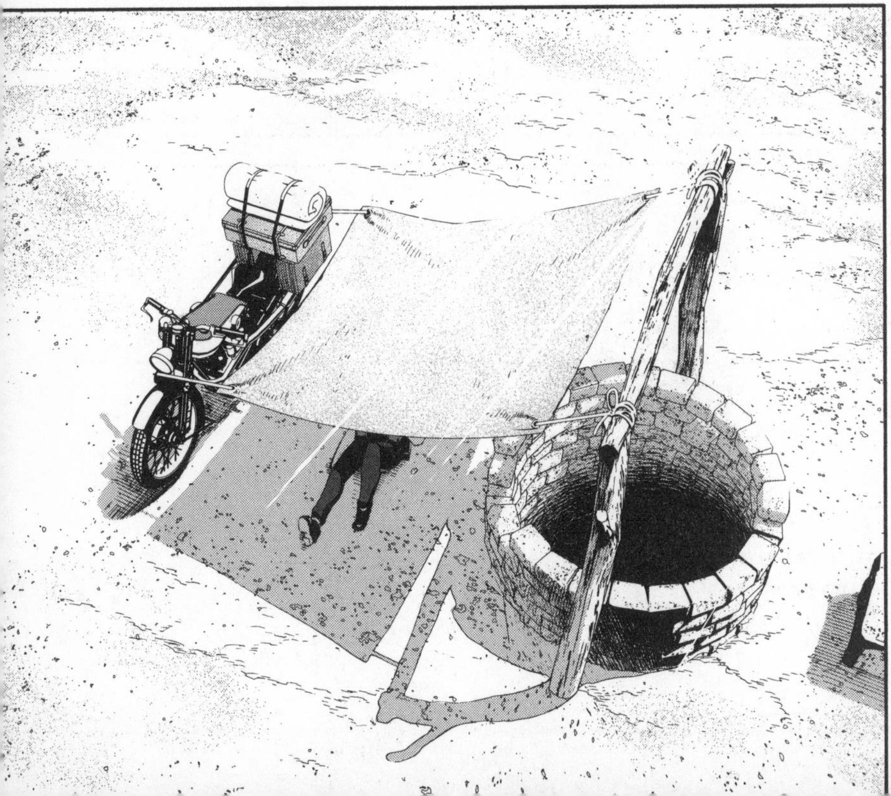

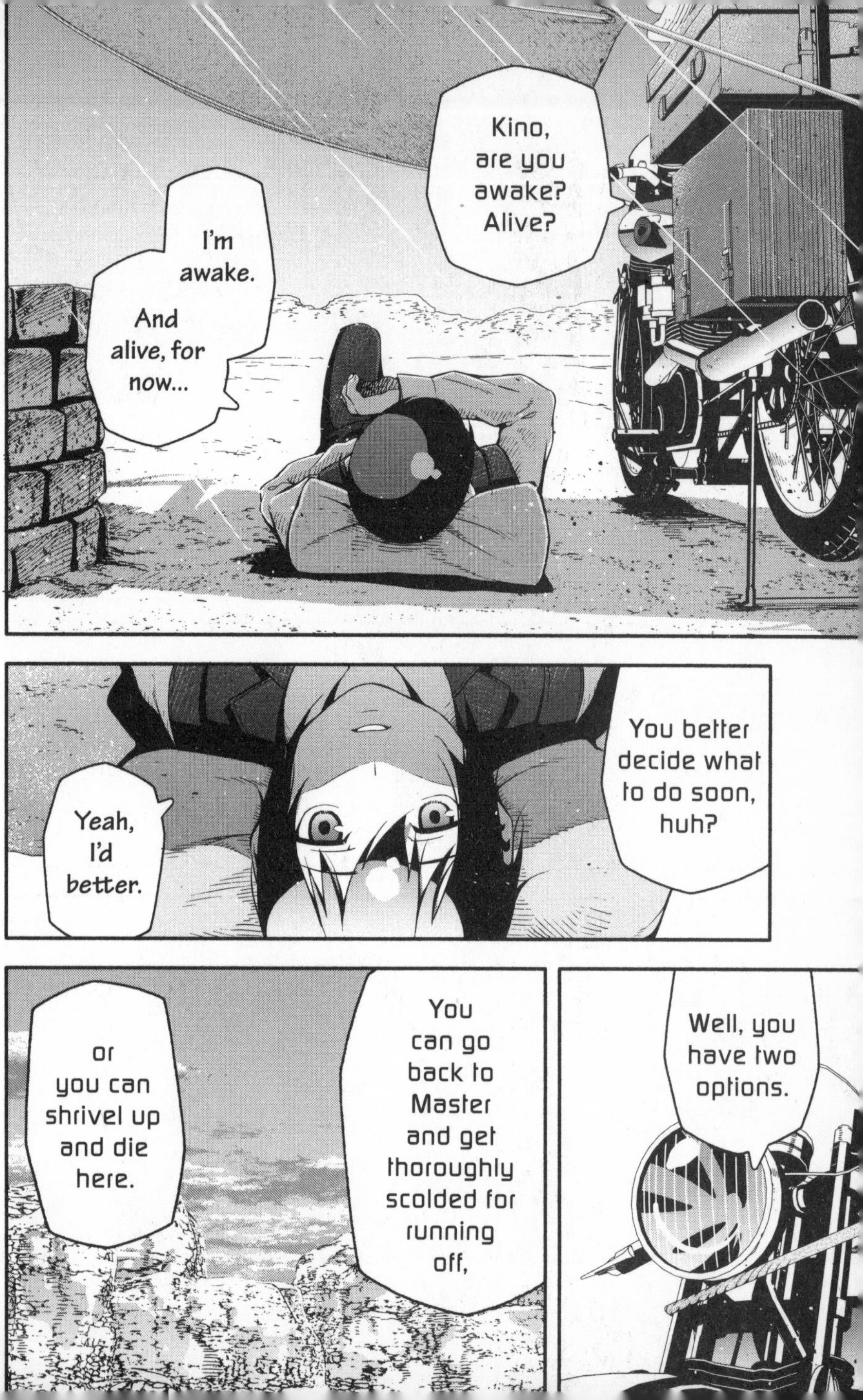
Kino, are you awake? Alive?
I'm awake.
And alive, for now...
You better decide what to do soon, huh?
Yeah, I'd better.
Well, you have two options.
You can go back to Master and get thoroughly scolded for running off,
or you can shrivel up and die here.

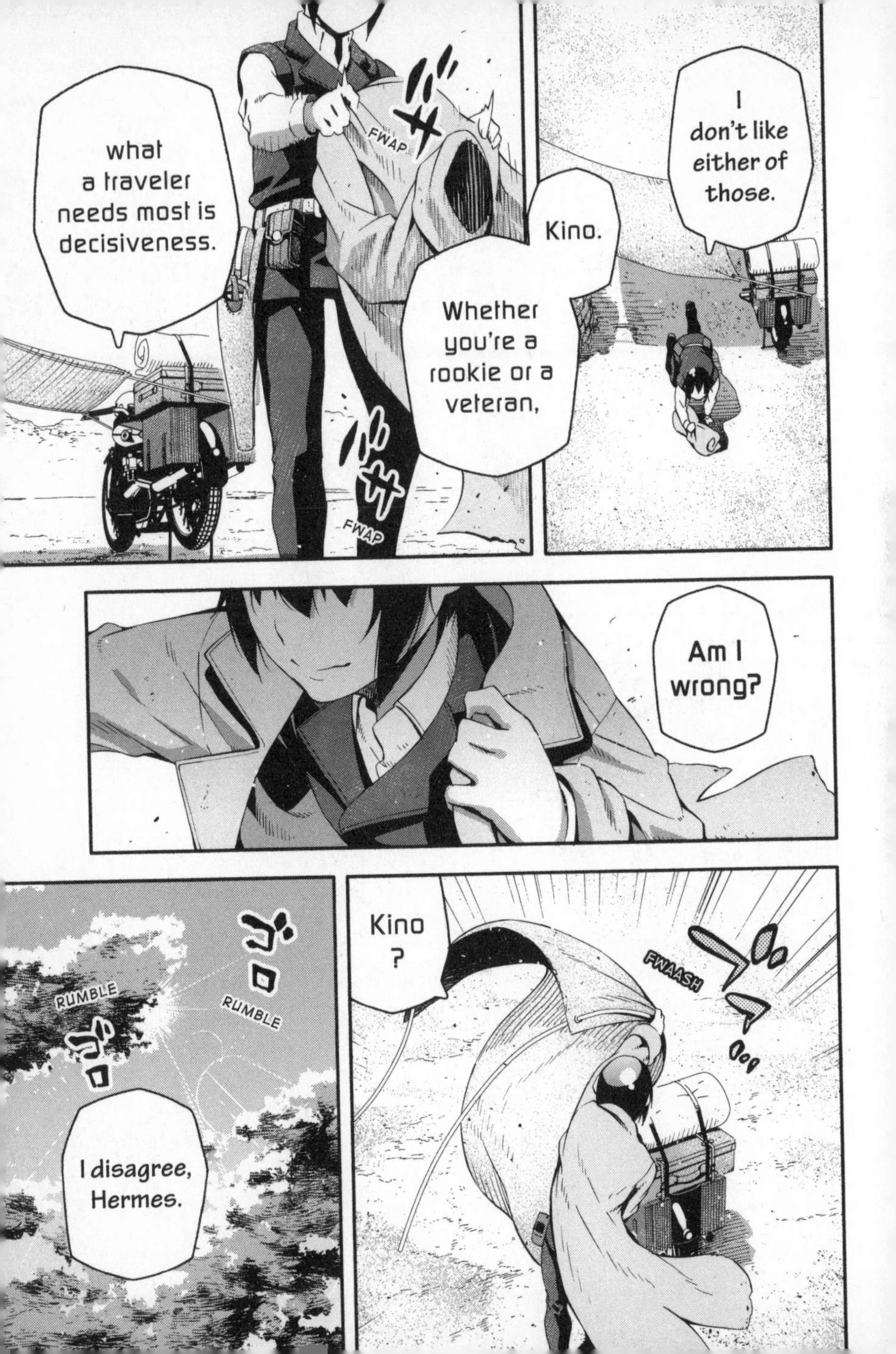
I don't like either of those.
Kino.
FWAP
Whether you're a rookie or a veteran,
what a traveler needs most is decisiveness.
FWAP
Am I wrong?
Kino ?
FWAASH
RUMBLE
RUMBLE
I disagree, Hermes.

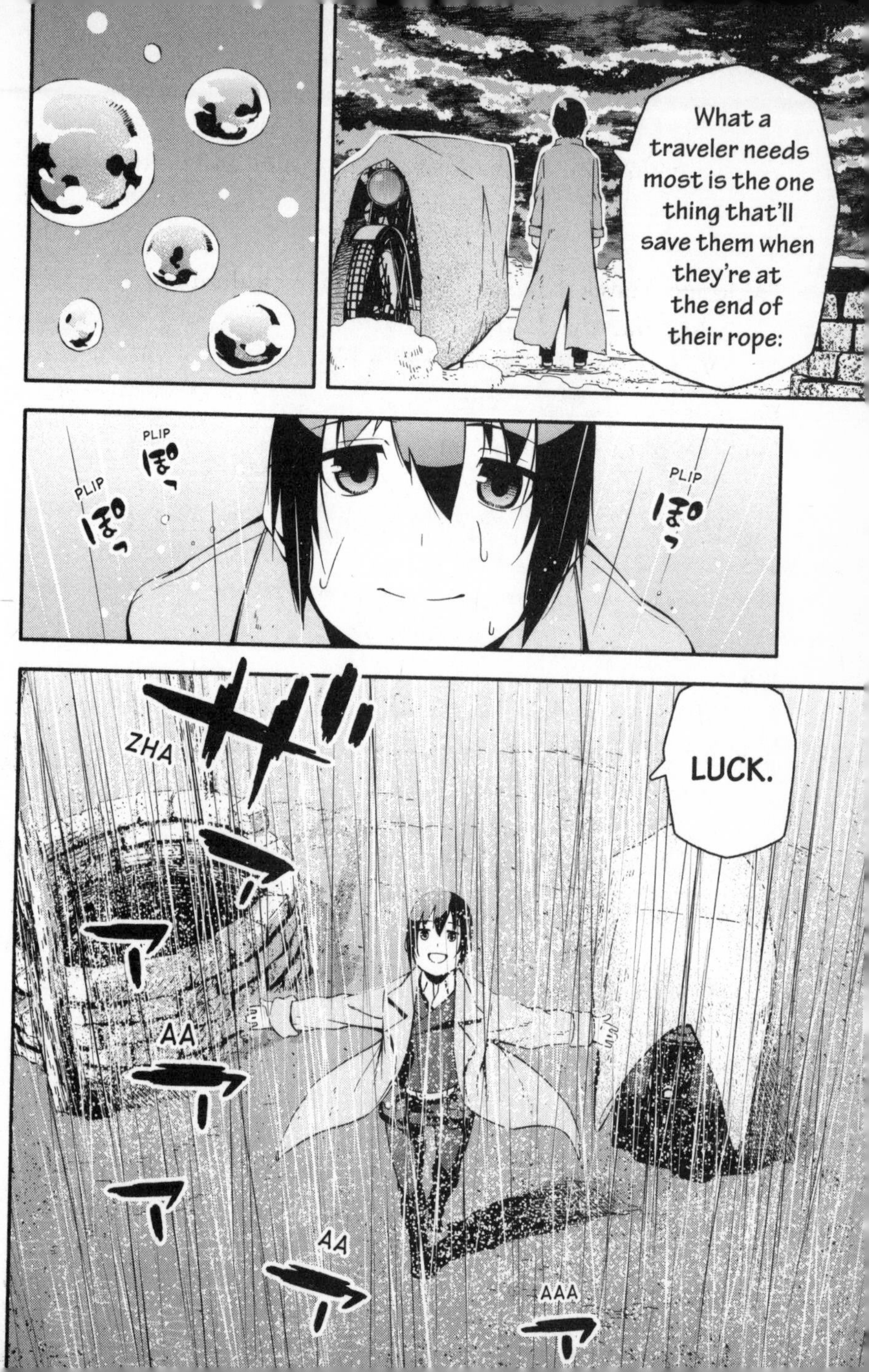
What a traveler needs most is the one thing that'll save them when they're at the end of their rope:
PLIP
ぽっ
PLIP
ぽっ
PLIP
ぽっ
LUCK.
ZHA
AA
AA
AAA

Afterword Special Short Story:
"The Land of Comicalization –You Can Do It!–"

"Welcome, Traveler! This is the 'Land of Comicalization'!"

"Uhm, and what is that, exactly...?"

"Whaaat? You don't know, Kino? If you come here, they'll turn you into a comic! It's also known as 'The Land of Manga Adaptations.' I've always wanted to come here..."

"I didn't know you could look so ecstatic, Hermes."

"Of course I can! Motorrads* have limitless potential, you know!"

"I wasn't aware of that...By the way, Mr. Immigration Officer?"

"Yes. My name is Yoshida. It's a pleasure to make your acquaintance."

"Mr. Yoshida, then. I'm told that if we enter this land, Hermes and I will become a comic. But what does that mean, exactly?"

"Whaaaat! You don't know, Kino?"

"Enough, Hermes."

"Allow me to explain. First, one of our land's talented comic artists will be assigned to you. I, the immigrations officer, have the duty of selecting this artist."

"And then?"

"Then, this person will create beautiful art to represent you travelers. All of your actions will be drawn as pictures, and then, using a technique called 'panels,' separated in a way that makes the movements easy to understand. Your words will be represented in frames called 'speech bubbles' which make it clear who is speaking."

---

* A two-wheeled vehicle. Refers only to vehicles that do not fly.

"I see... That's quite a different method than the world of novels that I normally live in."

"You know, the history behind the comics in this land—"

"Hermes, keep quiet for a bit, would you? Now then, Mr. Yoshida, please continue."

"Certainly. The 'comicalization' process makes the story more approachable for many readers, such as those who don't enjoy reading novels or simply don't have the time. These 'comics' are also quite easy to recommend and share with others. And there's the additional advantage of bringing scenes to life that were not illustrated in the novels!"

"I see... However, I only stay in each place I visit for three days. What will happen after those three days? Will I return to novel form, or..."

"The only way to find out is to enter and see. Some travelers take a liking to comics and decide to stay, while others depart surprisingly quickly."

"...That's... a little scary..."

"Come on, Kino, it'll be fine. Let's go in already!"

"You're being awfully pushy about this, Hermes. I guess that's no different from usual, though..."

"If you end up liking this place, we can always just split into two and continue both the novels and the comic."

"Sorry?"

"Yes, that is an option, too."

"Huh? Wait, what?"

"All right, Kino, I'll teach you the easiest way to do it. First..."

Probably not to be continued...

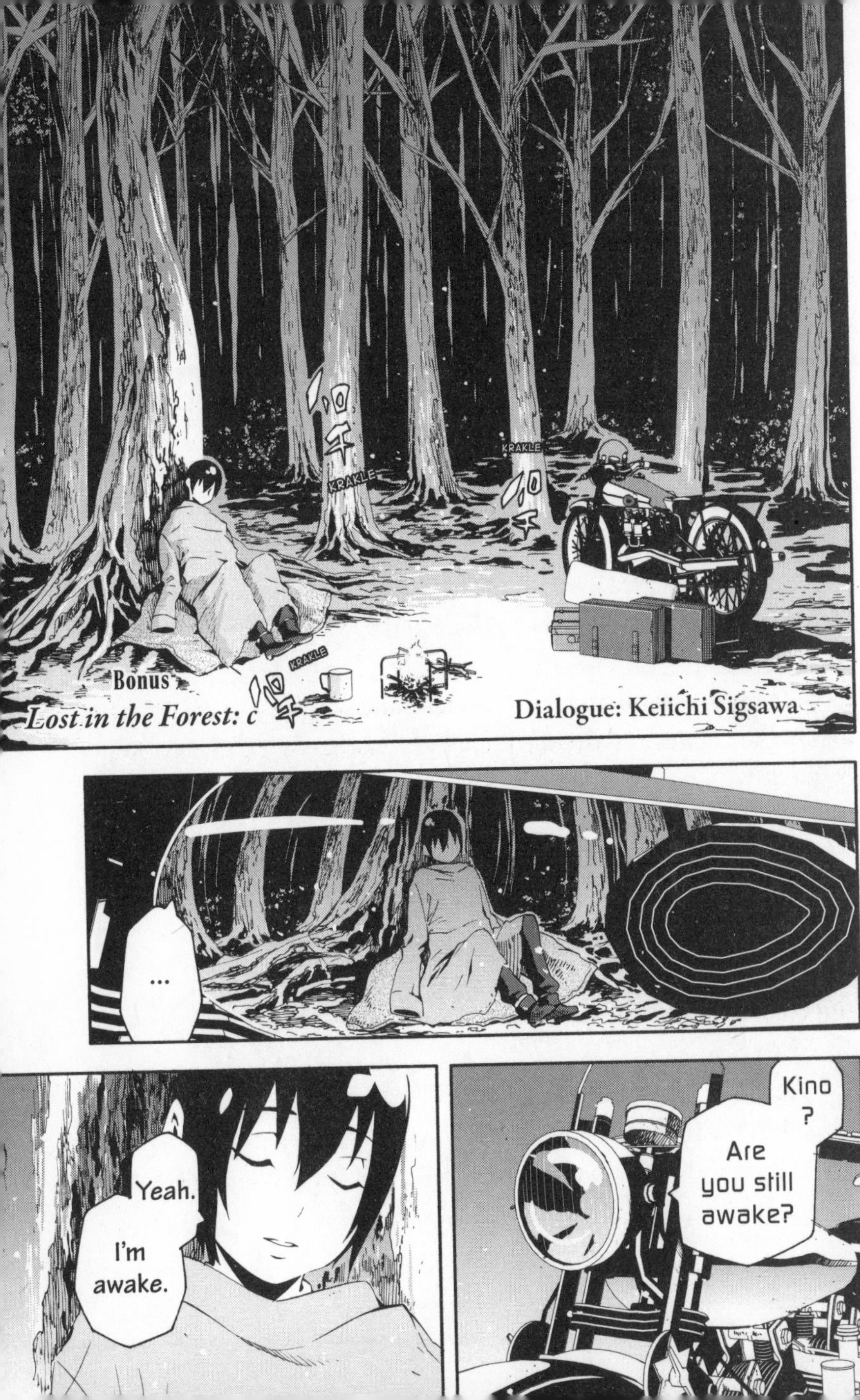

KRAKLE
KRAKLE
KRAKLE
Dialogue: Keiichi Sigsawa
Bonus
Lost in the Forest: c
...
Kino?
Are you still awake?
Yeah.
I'm awake.

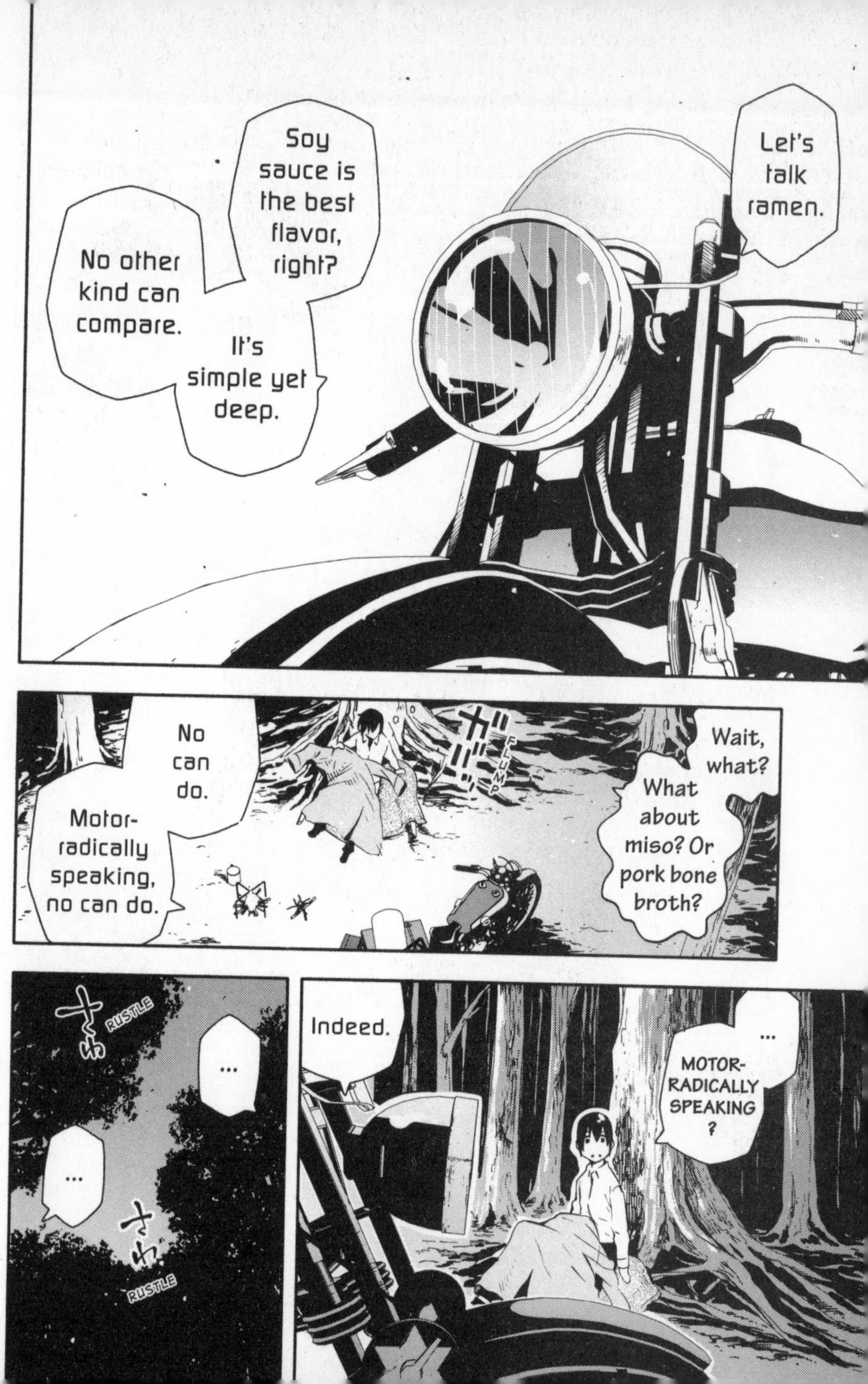

Let's talk ramen.
Soy sauce is the best flavor, right?
No other kind can compare.
It's simple yet deep.
Wait, what? What about miso? Or pork bone broth?
FLUMP
No can do.
Motor-radically speaking, no can do.
...
MOTOR-RADICALLY SPEAKING?
Indeed.
RUSTLE
...
...
RUSTLE

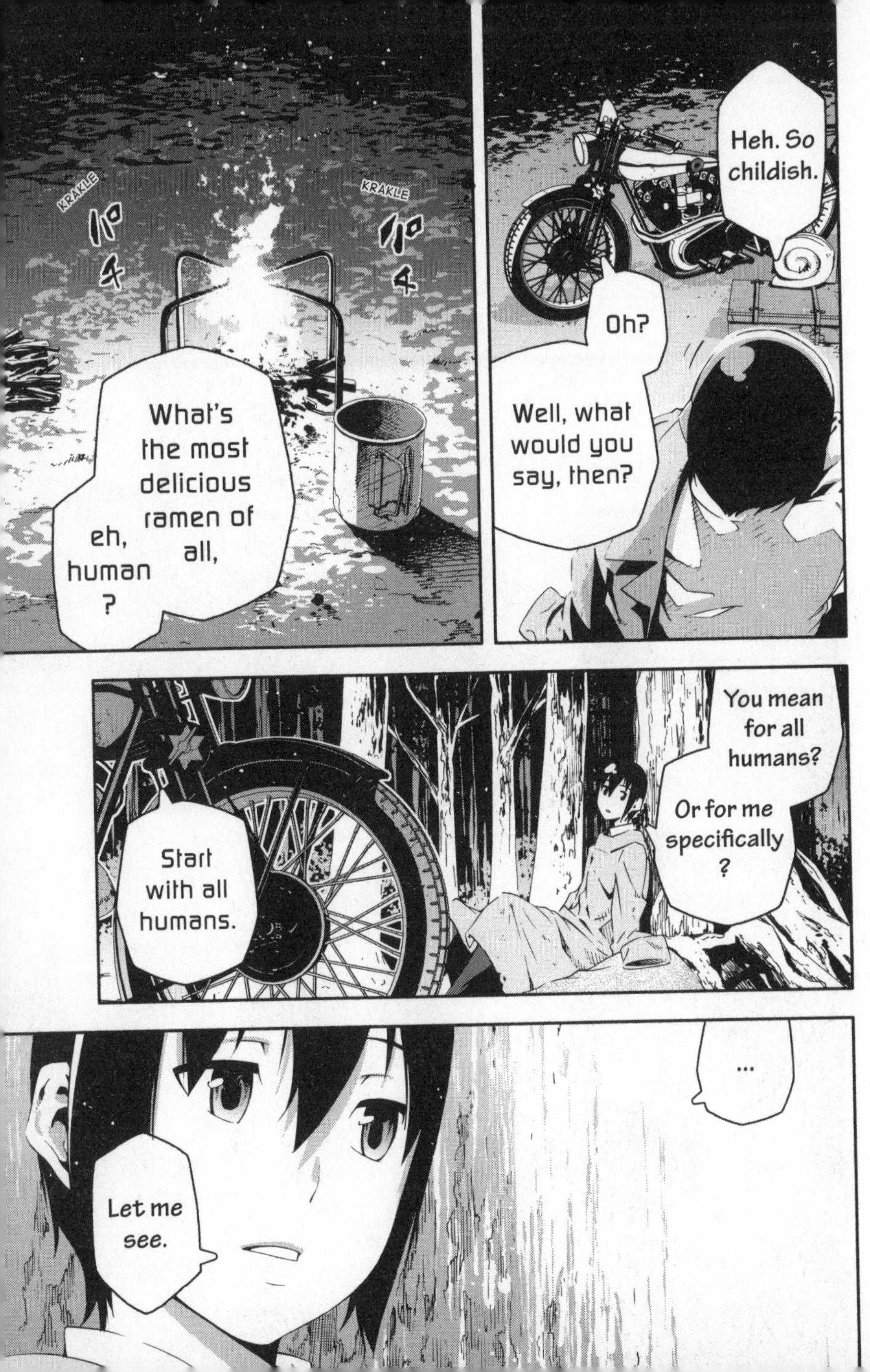
Heh. So childish.
Oh?
Well, what would you say, then?
KRAKLE
パチ
KRAKLE
パチ
What's the most delicious ramen of all, eh, human?
You mean for all humans?
Or for me specifically?
Start with all humans.
...
Let me see.

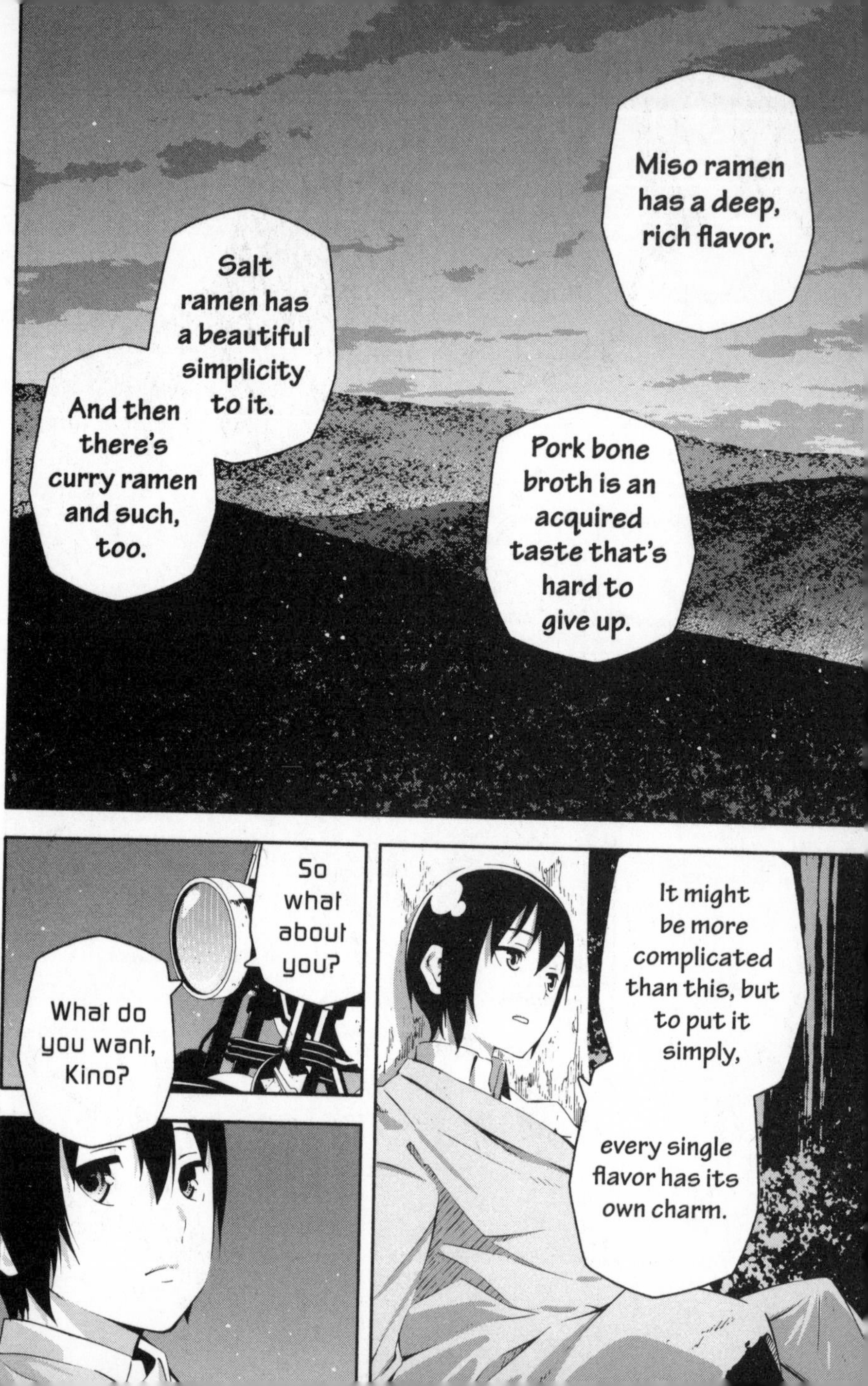
Miso ramen has a deep, rich flavor.
Salt ramen has a beautiful simplicity to it.
Pork bone broth is an acquired taste that's hard to give up.
And then there's curry ramen and such, too.
It might be more complicated than this, but to put it simply,
every single flavor has its own charm.
So what about you?
What do you want, Kino?

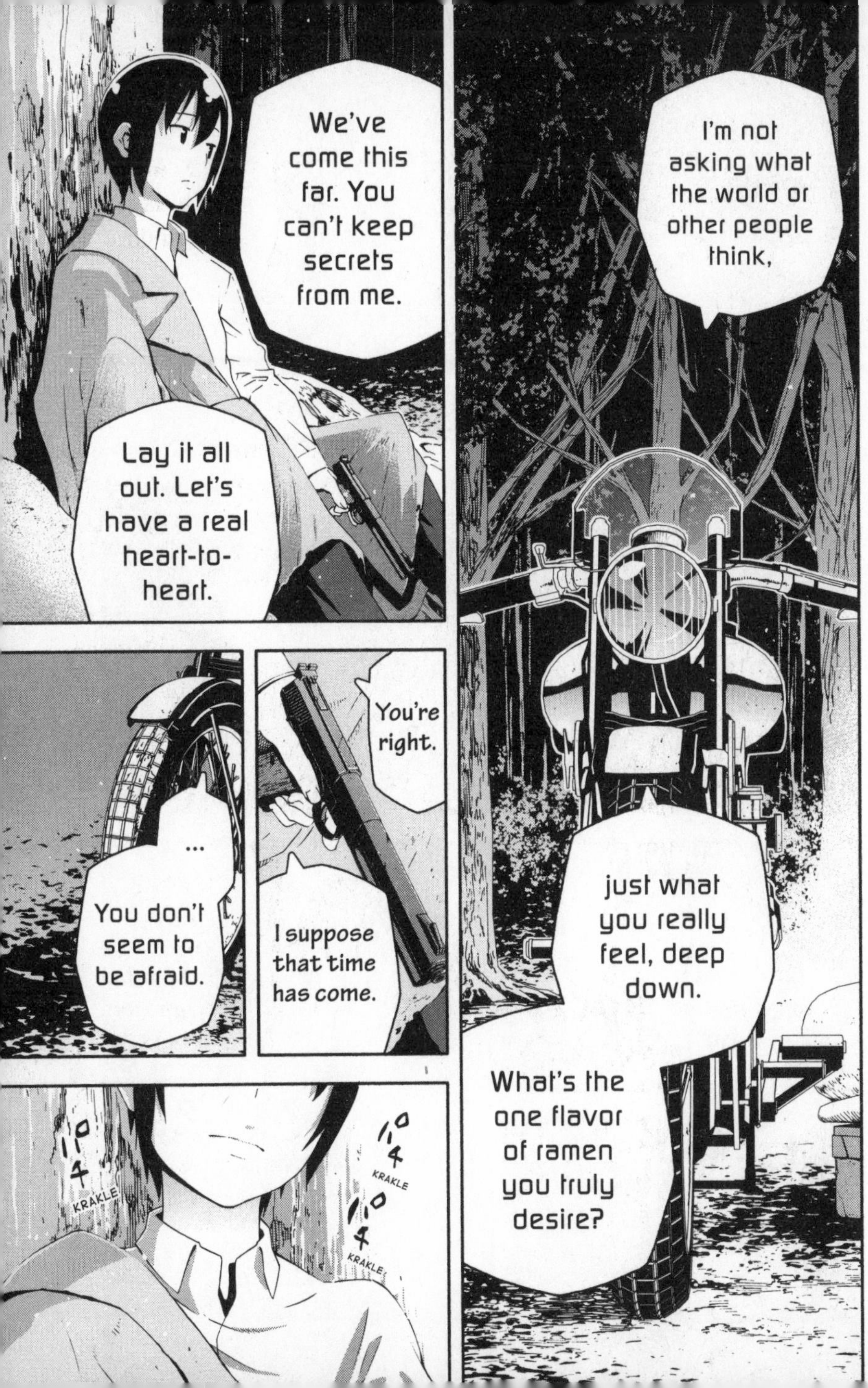
I'm not asking what the world or other people think,
just what you really feel, deep down.
What's the one flavor of ramen you truly desire?
We've come this far. You can't keep secrets from me.
Lay it all out. Let's have a real heart-to-heart.
You're right.
I suppose that time has come.
...
You don't seem to be afraid.
KRAKLE
KRAKLE
KRAKLE

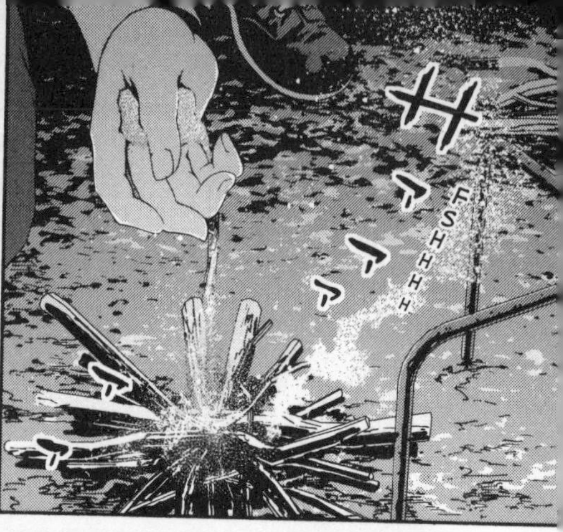
FSHHHH
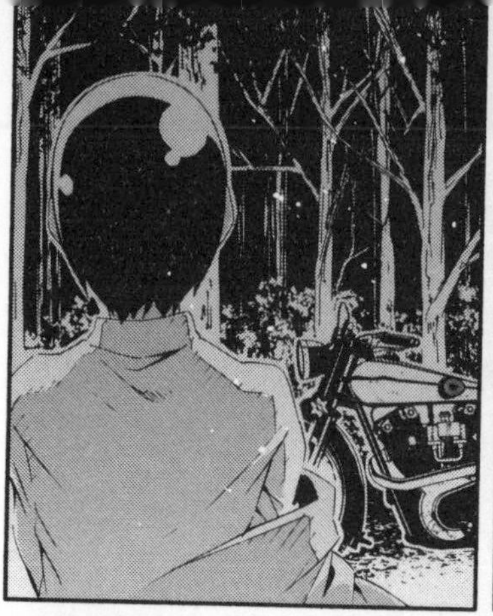
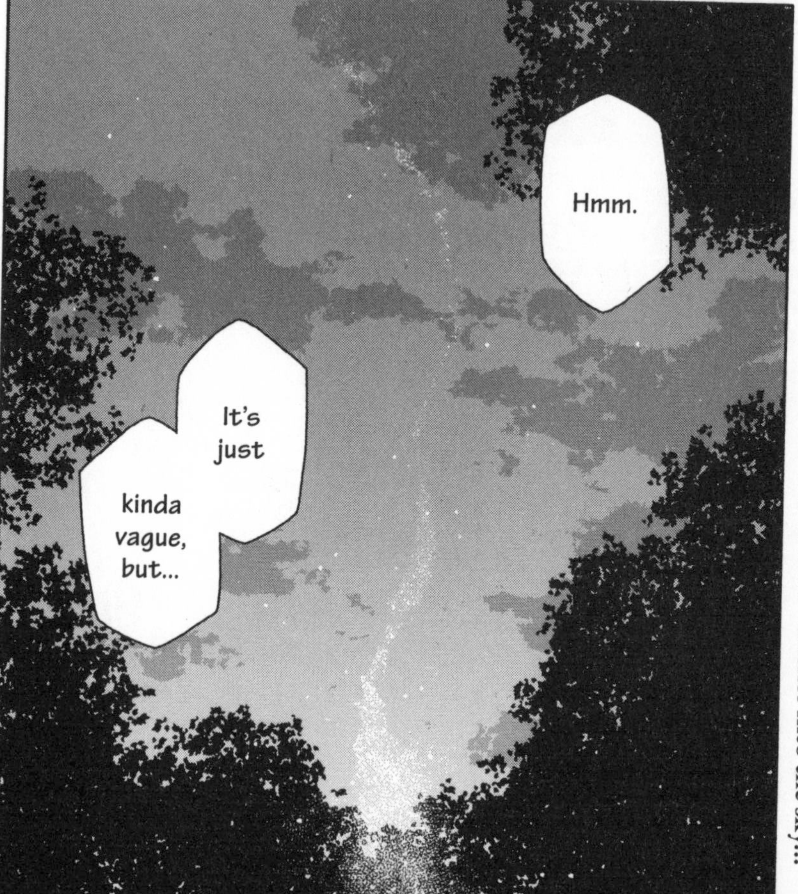
Hmm.
It's just kinda vague, but...
Their favorite flavor vanishes into the sky...

Art Assistant

Taku Umemoto

3D Assistants

yubikitax
Jeri

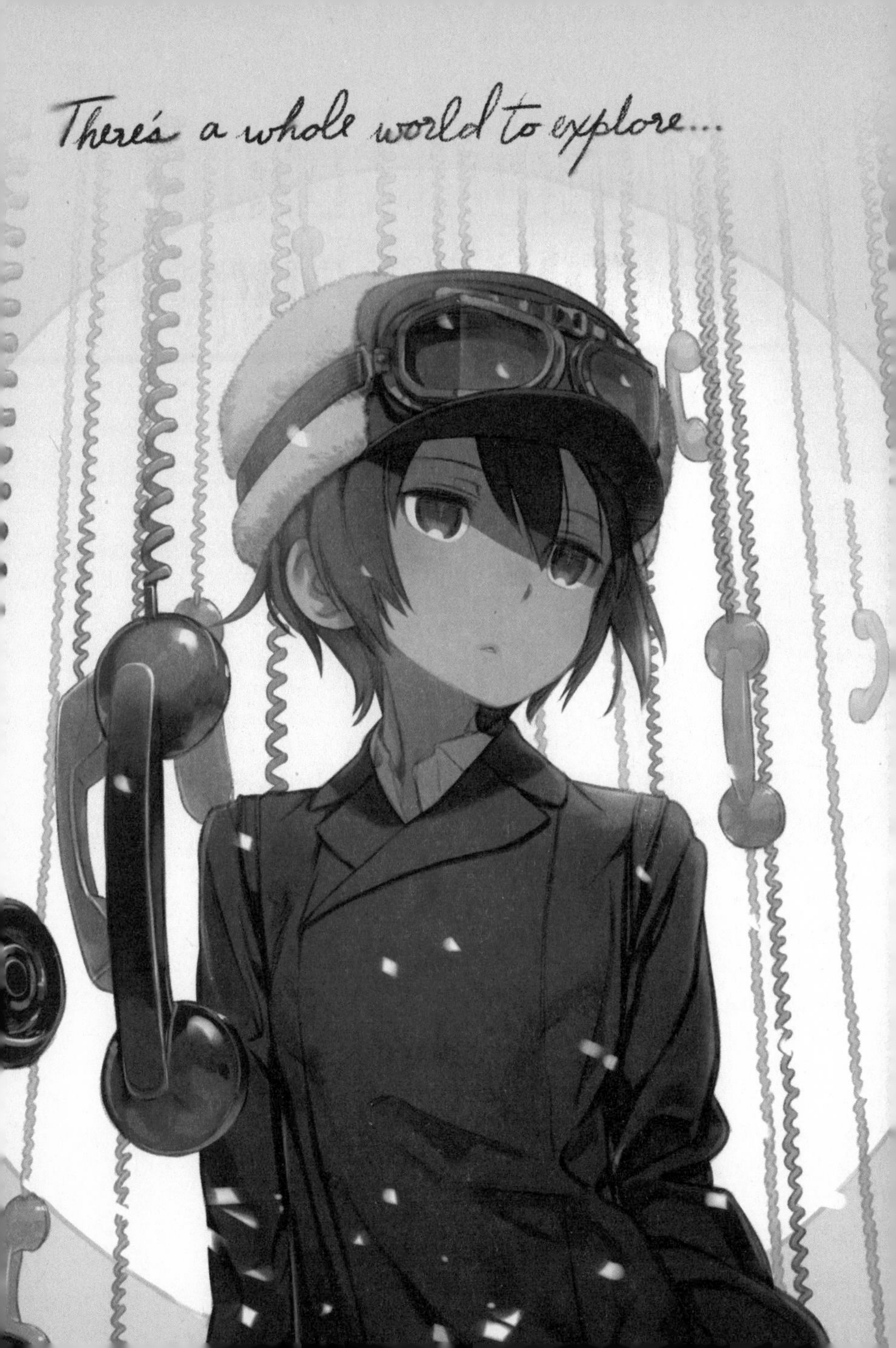
There's a whole world to explore...

GO WITH THE CLOUDS NORTH-BY-NORTHWEST

From the creator of
Ran and the Gray World
AKI IRIE

The story takes place in Iceland, at land's end, 64°N.

Kei Miyama is a 17-year-old with three secrets: he can talk to cars, he can't handle pretty girls, and he works as a private investigator. One case has him searching for a beloved dog, another involves reuniting a woman with a man she fell for at first sight. And then comes a case that strikes close to home—searching for his own little brother.

Tag along as this globe-spanning journey unfolds…

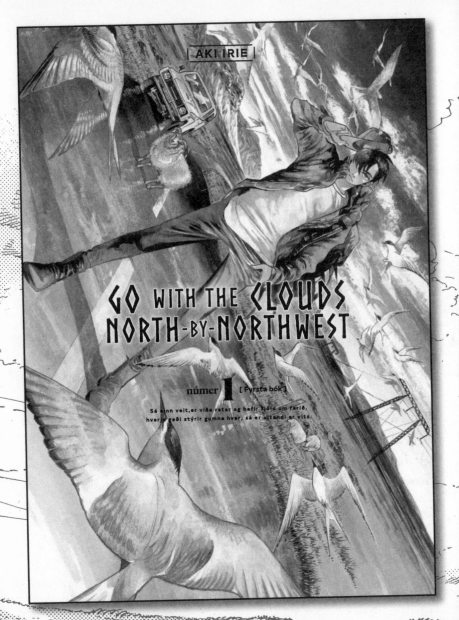

The Basis for the Hit Anime Series!

"After the Rain takes a prickly premise and gives us a story about two people with broken dreams that just might be mendable."
— *Japan Times*

Akira Tachibana was the star of her high school track team, but was sidelined by an ankle injury. One rainy day, she wanders into a family restaurant. The kind manager, Kondo, lets her have coffee on the house. Akira takes a job there to stay close to this presence that gives her a new sense of direction in her life.

The curtain rises on the quiet love story that begins to unfold between Akira, stuck standing on the crossroads of adolescence, and Kondo, at a turning point in his own life...

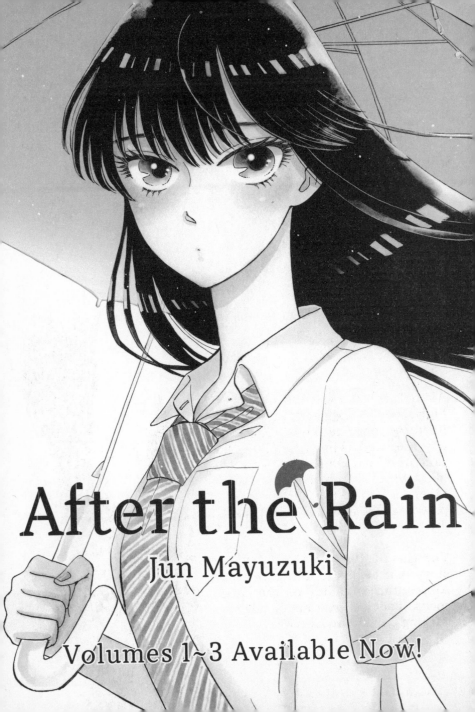

After the Rain

Jun Mayuzuki

Volumes 1~3 Available Now!

The Basis for the Anime Series coming 2019!

To the Abandoned Sacred Beasts

Presented by

MAYBE

During a protracted civil war that pitted the North against the South, the outnumbered Northerners used dark magical arts to create monstrous super-soldiers—Incarnates. Now that the war has ended, those Sacred Beasts must learn how to make their way in a peaceful society, or face death at the hands of a Beast Hunter.

Nancy Schaal Bancroft, the daughter of an Incarnate soldier who met an untimely end at the hands of one such Beast Hunter, turns to hunting the hunter. But once she catches up with her quarry, she discovers hard truths about the lives of the Incarnates...

VOLUMES 1-7 AVAILABLE NOW!

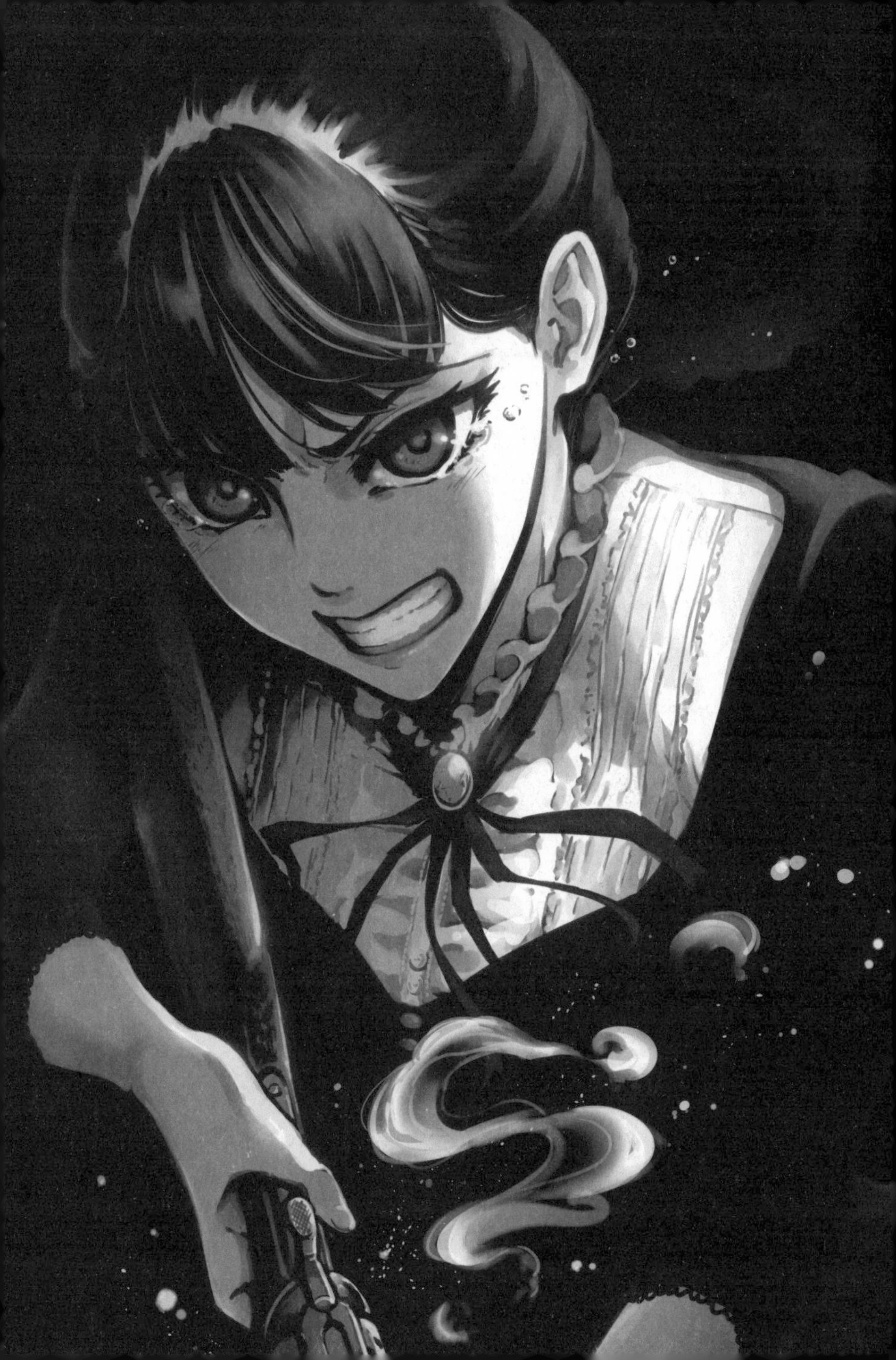

Kino's Journey

The Beautiful World
volume 2

A Vertical Comics Edition

Translation: Jenny McKeon
Production: Grace Lu
            Anthony Quintessenza

First published in Japan in 2017 by Kodansha, Ltd., Tokyo
Publication for this English edition arranged through Kodansha, Ltd., Tokyo
English language version produced by Vertical, Inc.

Translation provided by Vertical Comics, 2019
Published by Vertical Comics, an imprint of Vertical, Inc., New York

Originally published in Japanese as *Kino no Tabi the Beautiful World 2* by Kodansha, Ltd.
Kino no Tabi the Beautiful World 1 first serialized in *Shonen Magazine Edge*,
Kodansha, Ltd., 2017-

This is a work of fiction.

ISBN: 978-1-947194-40-3

Manufactured in Canada

First Edition

Vertical, Inc.
451 Park Avenue South
7th Floor
New York, NY 10016
www.vertical-comics.com

Vertical books are distributed through Penguin-Random House Publisher Services.